S[A]

GERARD
MAJELLA

*His Writings
and Spirituality*

Holy Patron Gerard
please intersede before
the Throne of God

SAINT
GERARD MAJELLA

His Writings and Spirituality

COORDINATING EDITOR
NOEL LONDOÑO B., C.SS.R.

Liguori
LIGUORI, MISSOURI

Imprimi Potest:
Richard Thibodeau, C.Ss.R.
Provincial, Denver Province
The Redemptorists

Published by Liguori Publications
Liguori, Missouri
www.liguori.org
www.catholicbooksonline.com

Originally published as Volume 6 of the series *Espiritalidad Redentorista,
Los escritos y la espiritualidad de San Gerardo Mayela,* by the Committee
on Redemptorist Spirituality, Rome, 1994.

Library of Congress Cataloging-in-Publication Data

Escritos y la espiritualidad de San Gerardo Mayella. English
    Saint Gerard Majella, C.Ss.R. : his writings and spirituality /
coordinating editor, Noel Londoño.
        p. cm.
    Includes bibliographical references.
    ISBN 0-7648-0788-9 (pbk.)
    1. Maiella, Gerardo, Saint, 1726–1755. I. Londoño, Noel, 1949–
II. Title.

BX4700.G47 E8313 2002
282'.092—dc21
[B]   2001038656

Printed in the United States of America
06 05 04 03 02   5 4 3 2 1
First English language edition 2002

CONTENTS

INTRODUCTION

Including Gerard Majella in a series of books on spirituality is almost a contradiction. First of all, because spirituality doesn't well up from books but from the spontaneously lived faith and love. Second, because Gerard was someone in a class all by himself. His experience of Christian and religious life was outside the "normal" framework that we usually lay out. He lived holiness "madly" in complete freedom for the action of the Spirit within him.

All this makes Gerard a saint who is hard to "imitate" in any concrete way. Nevertheless, he is an outstanding example of the fundamental features of the Alphonsus Liguori tradition that has animated generations of Redemptorists: insertion into the salvific plan of God the Father, especially through conformity with the divine will; following Christ the missionary and coming into intimacy with him in the Incarnation, in the paschal mystery, and in its eucharistic celebration; joyfulness and simplicity as special gifts of the Holy Spirit; Marian feeling, service to the community, and closeness to the people.

The various chapters of this book aim to emphasize this paradox about Gerard: he had an exceptional holiness, full of "crazy" gestures, molded in the traditional forms lived by simple people. In some ways Gerard is the most medieval of the Redemptorist saints, but it also must be said that he is the most mystical, the most free, and the most popular.

What follows is a short description of the content of each of the chapters in this book and a brief biography of each chapter's author. (Note: Chapter 1 has been added to the U.S. edition of this work.)

Chapter 1: "Gerard Majella: The Joyful Saint" by Hamish F. G. Swanston. This biographical recounting of Gerard Majella's life was originally a section in Hamish Swanston's book *Saint Alphonsus and His Brothers: A Study of the Lives and Works of Seven Redemptorists,* Liguori, MO: Liguori Publications, 2000, pp 203–245. Hamish F. G. Swanston was born in 1933, ordained in 1960, and has taught at universities in Europe, the United States, and Latin America. On his election at the University of Canterbury in 1977, he became the first Roman Catholic to head a department of theology at a British University since the Reformation. He is the author of a study of the theology of Saint Alphonsus and a biography of Maria Celeste Crostarosa, founder of the Redemptoristines.

Chapter 2: "Gerard Majella: Saint of the People" by Giustino D'Addezio. Father D'Addezio, a Doctor of Theology, is the pastor of Muro Lucano, the town where Gerard was born. On the twenty-fifth anniversary of his ordination, he published a book entitled *Gerardo Maiella, santo del popolo: Itinerario pedagogico spirituale* (Materdomini, 1992). The material from this chapter is excerpted from the first part of that volume, with the translation and adaptation prepared by the editor of this volume. In this spiritual biography the four loves of Gerard stand out: the Eucharist, the Virgin Mary, the Passion of Christ, and the will of God.

Chapter 3: "Saint Gerard and the Popular Piety of His Time" by Angelomichele de Spirito. The roots of Gerard's spirituality are not to be found in the ascetical theories of his age nor in the official documents of the post-Tridentine Church. In this study, the author starts out from the context in which Gerard grew up, and discusses the intimate relationship between Gerard's spirituality and the religious experience of the simple people. The text was presented at the Gerardian Congress on the occasion of the centenary of his beatification. It was published in the Congress's proceedings and in the *Spicilegium Historicum CSSR* 42 (1994), 65–88. The Spanish translation is by Noel Londoño, Province of Bogotá.

Chapter 4: "Penitential Piety of Gerard Majella" by Gabriele De Rosa. The author, a renowned historian of religious sentiment in southern Italy, analyzes the spirituality of Gerard from the penitential point of view and tries to establish the contacts between Gerard's milieu and the asceticism of eastern hermits, an aspect that we are not so accustomed to considering. The first version of this study appeared in 1976. The definitive text was published in G. De Rosa, *Storie di santi* (Rome-Bari, 1990), pp. 23–48) as chapter II, *"San Gerardo Maiella e altri santi populari del Mezzogiorno d'Italia fra Sei e Settecento"* ("Saint Gerard Majella and Other Popular Saints From Southern Italy Between the Seventeenth and Eighteenth Century"). The translation into Spanish for the original edition was by Luís Secondin, Vice-Province of Pilar, Paraguay.

Chapter 5: "Gerard's Letters and Rules for Living." The introduction and notes are by Sabatino Majorano. Gerard was not a literary person nor was he erudite preacher. But he knew how to communicate his spiritual experience through spontaneous dialogue with others. In that sense, his letters are, above all, a conversation in writing. This points the way for the best method of reading his letters: get on Gerard's wavelength, listen to him with simplicity: that is, don't look for the logical flow of the ideas but tune into the profundity of the experience of God.

The translation into Spanish for the original edition is by Angel Berra, Province of Mexico.

Chapter 6: "The Christocentrism of Saint Gerard" by Domenico Capone. The author is very well known in the field of moral and spiritual theology, as well as in the history of Saint Alphonsus. From a book of his, *L'immagine spirituale di S. Gerardo* (Materdomini, 1990), in which he studies the physical and spiritual image of Gerard Majella, we take the second part of his work that analyses the saint's spirituality. With apparently ascetical forms, Gerard covered the path of an elevated mysticism, thereby showing the marvels that God performed in him.

The Spanish translation for the original work is by Luis Pérez, Province of Santiago de Chile.

Chapter 7: "Gerard's Spirituality" by Sabatino Majorano. This is a synthetic reading of the most significant aspects of Gerard's spiritual path, as they emerge from his spiritual writings, integrated with the "points" of Caione and with several testimonies from the trials for beatification and canonization, The text was published in *Spicilegium Historicum* CSSR, 42 (1994) 89–103. The translation into Spanish for the original work is by Narciso Cappelletto, Province of Buenos Aires.

We dedicate this book in a special way to the coadjutor brothers of the Congregation of the Redemptorists, who live the missionary charism in the style of Gerard. But we by no means want to say that Gerard is the saint of the brothers; because he belongs to the people and because his spirituality is a call to all Redemptorists—ordained ministers, coadjutor brothers, sisters, and lay people—to live in fullness and freedom of the children of God. We trust that the labors in preparing all these materials by so many persons will not conclude simply with the publication of these pages, but that they will be an open window among us so that the Holy Spirit may act more effectively.

NOEL LONDOÑO B., C.SS.R.
COORDINATING EDITOR

SAINT
GERARD
MAJELLA
His Writings
and Spirituality

CHAPTER ONE

Gerard Majella:
The Joyful Saint

Hamish F. G. Swanston

GERARD MAJELLA

Gerard, a schoolmaster reported, had been "always cheerful" in class, as an apprentice he had chosen a wrong moment to laugh at the foreman of the tailor's shop, later as the domestic servant of an irascible bishop, he had managed to "keep a good smile on him."[1] He maintained this reputation for merriment through his years in the Congregation: questioned about a rumor that he had been taking a dip in the sea, "Gerard replied with a laugh...."; hearing the music of a village flute-player, "he began to leap and dance"; sitting with the archbishop's secretary, "he laughed a lot at his jokes....."; on someone's beginning to play an air from a modern opera on the recreation room harpsichord, Gerard seized an astonished Father "and danced round the room with him."[2] He was even caught grinning towards the Lord in the Tabernacle as he passed through the chapel.[3] Recording Gerard's salute to Alphonsus as they passed on the corridor, "My Father, you have the face of an angel," Gaspare Caione, Gerard's first biographer, had to add quickly, "and he wasn't being funny."[4]

Gerard wanted others to be jollier. "Stay cheerful," he commands Maria di Gesu when she is not reelected prioress at Ripacandida.[5] Letting Maria Celeste dello Spirito Santo know that he has at last located a copy of the songbook she had been asking for all year, he tells her to "Sing in your cell," that way, he declares, she'll become a great saint.[6] His immediate response to Caione's anxious inquiry about his health is to say "You really must cheer up, my dear Father."[7] He set about jollying laymen, too. Bartolomeo Melchione had been a bright spark about town when a bachelor, but after a year of marriage, "he had become dull and heavy." Gerard cooked him a

3

meal and then spent the evening singing songs with him.[8] Melchione kept up a chorus all the way home to his wife. His friends thought it a miracle. And it must be supposed that his wife forgave Gerard for keeping Melchione out so late. A nice smile turneth away anger.

There were, inevitably, occasions when this easygoingness made life more difficult for another Brother. Tannoia tells a story of Francesco Tartaglione, who had to cook the community supper, sending Gerard to the Naples fish market, and of Gerard's meeting a poor man on the way and handing over all the housekeeping money in exchange for his tray of tinder boxes. Being questioned by the waiting Brother on his return, "Where's our fish?" the cheerful Gerard settled down to tell Francesco how he'd met the man with the tray, how the poor man was hungry, and how he had bought all his stock, and how he was sure "they'll come in handy some day."[9] "This answer," Tannoia records drily, "annoyed Brother Francesco not a little."

Gerard's smiling had gone along with such sudden almsgiving even in his apprentice days. Wondering what he should do with his life, since tailoring did not really interest him, the adolescent Gerard had gone to consult his Capuchin uncle, Eustachio Gabella, at the Santomenna friary: "On seeing how miserably Gerard was dressed, he bought him a greatcoat; but when Gerard, coming out of the friary, met a poor man wrapped in rags, he took compassion on him, and immediately took off the coat and gave it to him." Tannoia records that "his uncle was not best pleased."[10] Gerard took his reproof in good part and went on grinning.

The ex-apprentice, rejected novice, had a try at being an assistant schoolmaster. But his grins betrayed him. Taking him to be quite mad, the boys bound him with ropes and hauled him up and down the street. That schoolmaster reported Gerard to be "always suffering" as well as "always cheerful." But he seemed strangely content to accept the role of village idiot.

There is a tradition of Jesus as madman, as mad in his love for humanity. Reading back from such incidents, therefore,

Tannoia takes Gerard's escapades as evidences of an *imitatio* of Jesus as the madman. "What affected him most as he contemplated the Passion was to see the way our Blessed Lord was reviled as a fool; he therefore resolved to simulate madness so that he could share in His humiliation."[11] Tannoia constructs a narrative in which the village boys are acting like the Roman soldiers who tormented the Lord and Gerard is responding with joy at recognizing his likeness to the derided Christ: "This is little enough to endure for the love of Jesus Christ who made Himself of no reputation for my sake."[12]

Assuredly, the school assistant might have picked up a phrase or two of this "madman" tradition, but it is likelier, more in character, to suppose that Gerard was, in these episodes, simply making an adolescent experiment in self-discovery. "He resolved to simulate madness."[13] Like young Hamlet, he put on "an antic disposition."

Gerard had always been an enthusiastic actor. He had as a little boy, so his sisters Birgitte and Anna Elizabetta giggled to recall, played at "altars," taking, of course, the priest's starring role, "imitating the ceremonies," lots of bowings, genuflections, and breast-beatings, lots of small statues of saints and candle ends and tablecloth copes. His godfather, Alessandro del Piccolo, the goldsmith of Muro, added that Gerard would go back and forth in front of the figurines, imitating the priest's swings of the thurible. No one at the time seems to have thought this altar-making as at all odd. It was just what imaginative little boys did, between playing cops and brigands.

Gerard had placed a statue of the archangel Michael at the center of the "Blessed Spirits" venerated at his altar. He presumed that this courteous spirit would make some appropriate response to his low bow. And Piccolo recalled a nice reciprocity in their relation. Seeing the congregation get up for Communion, the boy, quite naturally, attached himself to the end of the line. When the priest refused to allow Gerard to receive Communion until he had been properly instructed, Gerard was sure that those to whom a good boy prays will come to help him. So it proved. He came down to breakfast one morning to announce that the wondrous archangel had flown to him in the night and brought him Communion just as he'd wanted. That should teach the parish priest a thing or two. "This," says the surely back-to-front Tannoia, "was the origin of the great devotion which this holy Brother entertained all his life for Saint Michael."[14]

There's another reference forward in Gerard's own telling of another childhood anecdote. One day, coming back from a wander round town, he'd brought home a very fine loaf. On his mother's demanding where he had got this bread, Gerard replied easily that a little boy had given it to him. There the matter had been left. But later, when he was a Brother, reminiscing with his sister, he said he now knew what he hadn't realized as a boy, that the child who had given him the bread was Jesus. "Fancy, I thought he was just one of the village boys!" Birgitte laughed aloud at this fine notion. Her brother was giving himself some very pious airs now that he was wearing the habit. "You'd better come back to Muro and see if you can find that boy again!" Gerard, paying no heed at all to the sorts of distinction others might make between childhood imaginings and wondrous vision and every day experience in the house chapel, replied equally cheerfully, "O, I can find him everywhere."[15]

He had more stories yet of his pious boyhood. At Caposele, when the community was sitting round the fire in the recreation room, Brother Gerard told them how he would often stay all night in the unlit church, and how one dawn as he came out of the side door he had been met by a terrible ferocious dog ready to tear him into bloody pieces. A demon straight out of hell it was, for sure. Gerard had a great repertory of these deliciously frightening tales. He told them well—with the true anecdotalist's delight. So the community, of course, shivered and encouraged him to frighten them again. There had been another time, he told them, when a great carving had been hurled down at him as he prayed, a huge wooden figure. He'd barely escaped with his life. Tannoia, trying hard to maintain his character as a reliable historian remarks: "I do not know whether this should be viewed as an accident or not."[16] Less scientific Fathers, on a winter's night, were of a mind to believe that a bad spirit had been aiming at Gerard. And Gerard had to agree with them.

Playacting As "Real Life"

Even the lad who has been chased by a demon and survived, even the lad who can hold a room of adults fascinated with his story of the demon, must earn a living. So, being a pious lad with an unspoilt notion of the clergy, Gerard answered an advertisement for the general dogsbody job at the house of Claudio Albini, 1679–1744, who had been appointed bishop of Lacedonia in 1736. He soon discovered why it was that no servant stayed with the bishop for long. "He was absolutely unpleasable," as Don Pelosi, the agent of the Orsini cardinal of Gravina observed. But, Archdeacon Cantore added, "Gerard was quite the hero, never complaining of his ill-treatment." He was, Caione says again, "always cheerful."[17]

The death of the irascible Albini left Gerard again at a loose end. And having, perhaps, on his visits to uncle Eustachio, enjoyed some talk with Saint Francis and Saint Anthony, whose statues were allowed to be most life-like by all who stood before the Santomenna altar, Gerard wondered if he might fit in the friary community. But the Capuchins declined to receive him. Not after that business with their overcoat. Then, in August 1748, the famed Redemptorist missioner, Don Francesco Antonio Garzilli, 1690–1786, came to preach at Muro, appealing for money for the building of a house at Caposele. Brother Onofrio Ricca, 1727–1792, came with him, to shake out his bedding, cook his supper, and count the collection. Gerard cornered Onofrio, pestering him with questions about the Redemptorists and, delighted with what he was told, soon declared "I will live with you." Onofrio was not impressed. This tailor's apprentice was far too thin for them. "The Congregation is not for you. Among us, hardship is the norm, sleeping on straw, rising to a rigorous day...." And, "with a happy face," Gerard answered, "That's just what I've been looking for."[18] Garzilli was, however, as dismissive as Onofrio. So Gerard, the resilient adolescent, determined to go off as a hermit, told his new plan to his friend Felice Farenga and the pair of them set off for the woods.

Gerard made a rule for their lives in the hermitage, with a fine catalog of austerities and mortifications. He said later, it was another of his recreation-room anecdotes, that they had determined to eat nothing but roots and grasses but after three days their teeth went quite green.[19] So they went back to their mothers' cooking. And to some earlier playactings. Not quite so usual among altar boys. Gerard had seen pictures of the Lord at the flagellation post. "His sisters have told me, that from the time he was nine years old, he used to discipline himself several times a day, especially after Holy Communion, with knotted cords, which he had tied together."[20] But the teenager had grown dissatisfied with this *imitatio*. He needed someone else to play the Roman soldier. "Felice Farenga, who was Gerard's great pal, affirms that he several times tied him to a post at his insistence, and then scourged his bare shoulders with a wet and knotted rope." Gerard was always ready for more floggings. "If his friend wanted to stop he pleaded with him to continue, until at length his back became one wound, blood gushing forth all over the place."[21] This, too, on their mothers' discovering what was going on, was forbidden them.

Gerard found the opportunity for a more approvable acting at the performance of the Muro Passion Play on Good Friday. Nothing elaborate. A reading of the Gospel narrative illustrated by a sequence of tableaux. Gerard, deemed the best actor among the lads, perhaps simply the best actor among those lads the cathedral priest thought respectable enough, was chosen to play Jesus. That priest had a fine sense of the dramatic, as fine as Gerard's own. He staged a stupendous climax. At the Gospel announcement of Jesus' death, the high double doors of the cathedral were thrown open and there was the crucified Lord dying on the huge cross. Relatives of amateur actors are not likely to be their severest critics. But so convincing was Gerard's performance as the bloody, naked, Jesus that when she saw the soldier thrust his lance, and the body shudder, Gerard's mother fainted clean away. "He often used to repeat this story for our amusement in the recreation room."[22] However unfeeling it might be to make such sport of his poor mother, this was too good an anecdote to pass up.

That Passion Play at Muro was performed on Good Friday, April 4, 1749; on Low Sunday the missioners arrived in town. They were led this time by the even more famous Paolo Cafaro, a very small priest with a huge head, so fiery a preacher that he was nicknamed by his fellow missioners, "the Anger of God." The Sunday evening service ended with Cafaro's dramatic exhibition of self-lashing. Just the sort of stuff to fascinate a theatrical boy like Gerard. He stuck like a burr to Cafaro, refusing to be put off by his appearance or by his gruff answers. Gerard's sisters went off to tell their mother.[23] She was as adamant as Don Paolo that her son should give up all thought of running away to be a missioner. Gerard was not the only barnstormer in the family. His mother cast herself as Mary, the sword-pierced Mother of Sorrows: "My son, I conjure you not to cause me this pain by the sword which pierced my heart when I saw you transfixed on the cross."[24] Suiting the action to the words, she struck a splendidly dramatic pose. Tannoia recalled that the Brother made an anecdote out of this, too, gestures and all. It was better than his grimace when he pretended to show them his green teeth. Continuing her part in a melodrama, the day of the missioners' departure, Gerard's mother locked him in his room. But he had seen how romantic heroes in touring company plays effected their getaways. He made his sheets into a rope, tied this to the bed, and slid down. "With one bound he was free." The missioners were already on the road to Rionero but Gerard caught up with them and repeated his plea to be accepted as one of their company. "You haven't strength to be our Brother," Cafaro insisted, "just go home." But Gerard grinned again. Put on the charm. He knew exactly what the romantic hero would say. "Put me to the test." He was ready to prove his worth. So Cafaro sent him on to d'Iliceto, "rather for the sake of getting rid of him than for a wish to receive him."[25]

Gerard never lost his enthusiasm for performing in a Passion. Going down, as a novice at d'Iliceto, to the cave in which Blessed Felice of Cosaro had practiced his severest penances, he organized new representations of the flogging of Jesus. He could find young men in the nearby township who, like Farenga, were willing to take part in these performances. His ardent desires were seconded by a man whom he had converted and in whom he placed great confidence, and by a youth of Lacedonia named Andrea Longarello, who was anxious to become a lay Brother; while Gerard acted the part of the victim they served as the executioners. "This first assistant was Francesco Teta, another one-time tailor much given to depression, whom Gerard had accosted on the road to Sant' Agata and brought home to Father Fiocchi.[26] Andrea remained Gerard's friend and admirer for life. If the Muro priest directing the Passion Play had very well understood the powers of signs and symbols, it had been the intense realism of Gerard's acting which had affected his mother. And the whole crowd in the church square. It was with just such a realism that he directed his play of the Passion in the hermit's cave. "He caused them to tie his hands together and fasten them to a beam, after which he made them strike his shoulders with knotted ropes until blood poured forth in all directions and his body was a mass of wounds."[27]

Gerard had by this time collected more props. "After the flogging, he placed a crown of sharp thorns on his head and persuaded them to beat them into his head with a hammer." Then one of the large commemorative crosses placed against the church wall at the close of a mission was brought into play. Reading the Baroque devotions of L'Anno doloroso, 1690, by Antonio da Olivadi, Gerard had been discovering all sort of new details of the Passion and Death of Jesus. "He had read that the hands and feet of Jesus did not reach the augur holes which had been made for the nails, so the executioners had to draw them to the holes by main force." Gerard determined to share this suffering also. "He had his limbs stretched on the cross until his bones were dislocated." But this limb-stretching was the end of such plays. "The Anger of God" had been provoked. "Brother Gerard went on with these tortures for a great part of the time he was at d'Iliceto and only left them off in obedience to the order of Father Cafaro."[28]

There is a tradition that Cafaro, or some other Father on the Rionera mission, had sent home a message that the community was to expect "a useless Brother." It was not unknown for a Father to use that language about a Brother, any Brother. Or, indeed, about a Father. In a very bad moment, Alphonsus described the great de Paola as "a useless subject."[29] However, it was not another but Gerard himself who made this judgment, on his deathbed, "I am a useless subject for the Congregation."[30] Observing him about the house, Cafaro had in fact been very ready to allow that the thin lad was proving a good Brother. He was passing that test he had asked to take. Cafaro's estimate was quite different from that of the maniacally self-important Don Matteo Criscuoli, b. 1718, professed 1747, dismissed 1755, who was left in charge when Cafaro went off to preach a mission. In this man's eyes, Gerard could do no right. He was always down on him. Imposing severe penances. Forcing him to eat on his knees. Denying him Communion. Many times requiring Gerard to trace forty or fifty or sixty crosses with his tongue on the floor until his tongue bled so profusely that the pavement was stained red. The other Brothers were appalled. So was a young student in the house, Francesco Maria Tannoia, but he was also, he said later, filled with wonder at Gerard's constancy in these trials. It was as early as this, he remembered, that "we began to say "Brother Gerard is a great saint."[31]

Getting a Story Straight

The Congregation's memory of this saint shows that no one of them knew quite how to place Gerard. They were unable to get their memories into agreed shape. There's no settled tradition of the stories they wanted to tell of Gerard's hearing the unuttered commands of a rector, of his leading a troupe of students on pilgrimage, of his leading a company of village louts into the church, of his encountering a gang of laborers at a swollen river's bank, of his being accused of gross misconduct with a girl.[32] There are at least two versions of all these and more stories. Gerard had been unpigeonholeable since birth, or at least since two different dates of his baptism were reported by the parish priest of Muro.[33]

In one pair of stories, Gerard set out to ride from Melfi to Lacedonia, late at night, and in the dark lost his way in the wood of Olfante. Rains fell. Thick fog surrounded him. There was real danger of his horse's missing his footing and both of them being flung to their deaths down a ravine. Then a footpad comes out of the dark. "Behold, my hour is come," he snarls above the noise of wind and rain, "You are in my power." He laughs horribly. Devilishly. But Gerard can handle him. "I command you in the name of the most adorable Trinity to take my horse's bridle and lead me safely to Lacedonia." The brigand bent his head submissively, took the bridle, and led him right to the door of Don Constantino Capucci. This good man, being roused from his bed, for it was now ten o'clock at night, was very surprised to find Gerard tapping at his door. Thus far the story as Capucci repeated Gerard's tale to Tannoia. But, though a good story, it is not quite good enough.

Constructing a context for his revised version, Tannoia would have it that Gerard sat down to a late supper with Capucci and explained how he came to be at his door so late. He can now re-order the narrative as the Redemptorists, Don Carmine Fiocchi, 1721–1776, the gossipy rector of d'Iliceto, for instance, or Don Francesco Giovenale, 1719–1782, liked to tell it. Gerard recounts his horrid experience of rain and dark and ravine. "Then a man," he says, but at once corrects himself, "or rather a demon," came out of the dark. "Behold the hour and the man," he shouts, "Now I am your master. Hope for nothing. You have disobeyed your Superiors and God will not forgive you." The demon now seems not only to be "in human form" but in the precise form of a Redemptorist rector as he points to disobedience as the way a subject slips into the power of a demon. Gerard says nicely, "I was a little surprised by what he said." He knows full well that he is not a disobedient subject. The demon, therefore, is lying. He can have no power over Gerard. "Fiend that thou art, I command thee in the name of the most holy Trinity to take the bridle of my horse and to lead me straight to Lacedonia without doing me any hurt." And so, in enforced obedience to the obedient Brother, the demon did. This is now a story entirely fit for Redemptorists to hear and retell. After all, as Tannoia says, "the faithful servant was not like a light hidden under a bushel, but God placed him on a candlestick that men might see his works, and that souls might thus be led to glorify their heavenly Father."[34]

Tannoia, poor honest beekeeper, was always plodding after the sprightly Gerard. He well discerned that this Brother could not be kept within the bounds of what Fathers thought appropriate. Gerard, he knew, was almost, at times, indistinguishable from a Reverend Brother. There was that little pile of books in the tailor's shop, for instance. Scholarly books. Cafaro was accustomed to give little elementary talks to the Brothers on the mysteries of Christian faith. He found that Gerard was following up what he had been hearing with real excitement. "When Gerard was in our house, during that rest hour which the Rule allots to each subject, he ordinarily used the time not for sleep but for reading."[35] He became as lively a theologian as any of the students. More than most of them. More than most of the parochial clergy around. They acknowledged this willingly. All over the area. Whenever Gerard went with the missioners. At Naples, learned gentlemen came to hear him expound the doctrine of the Church, most especially the doctrine of the most holy Trinity.[36] The Canons of Corato got him to speak to them of "the mysteries of God."[37] Bishop Muojo of Muro, when Gerard went back to his hometown, was much impressed by "the precision of his disquisitions on theological topics."[38] So were bishops Basta of Melfi[39] and Amato of

Lacedonia.[40] Don Giuseppe de Lucia remembered how, on his
entering a conversation with Gerard, he expounded the doctrine of the Incarnation as perfectly as Saint Augustine or Saint
Thomas could have done.[41] Some, of course, were not so pleased
that a lay Brother should be received as a theologian. Not that
it did them much good to complain. Celestino de Robertis
thought it great fun to spread the story of the Naples priest
who entered into controversy with their uneducated Brother
about the Most Holy Trinity.[42] The opinionated cleric had to
make a hasty retreat. Paolo Cafaro's resigned comment must
have come to mind again: "Wherever Gerard goes everything .
is turned topsy-turvy."[43]

As Tannoia, the ex-novice master recognized, the wonder
of Gerard was not that he had learned so much. Given a sab-
batical year, Tannoia might himself have learned as much. No,
the wonder was rather his being so splendid a teacher. Don
Donato Antonio Spicci, one of Gerard's hometown Muro
priests, coming one day into the tailor's shop at d'Iliceto, saw
a copy of the *Life of Maria Crocifissa Tomasi*, 1645–1699, on
the table, open at her account of the inward loneliness of Christ
on the cross and of the reciprocating loneliness of the Christian.[44] The priest's face showed the superior surprise he felt at
a Brother's reading so sophisticated a book. So, since Don
Donato Antonio was ready enough to take up the book and
flip through the pages, Gerard asked for his comments on the
passage. Not much impressed by the priest's pious waffle,
Gerard allowed himself another little laugh, "You a theologian! And you don't get the sense!" So he put him to a seem-
ingly simpler test, requiring the priest to comment on the first
verse of the fourth gospel, "*In principio erat Verbum....*" Finding that he now kept total silence, Gerard could not stop himself going a step further with his teasing, "Come on, it is not in
French or Hebrew, so anyone should be able to understand
it." He told him to study the passage for a while and then tell
him what he thought. So the priest sat down to read again
what he read each morning at the end of his Mass. But after
reading, and rereading, and considering, he had nothing to

say. "You've read it?" asked Gerard looking up from his sewing, "Yes," said Don Donato Antonio, by this time having given up all sacerdotal swagger. "Well, let's hear what you think it means." The house physician, Doctor Nicola Santorelli, had stopped by the workroom and, seeing how the priest reddened in his confusion, could not prevent himself laughing aloud at his discomfiture. This made him redden more brightly. "Now then, Donato, don't blush so," said Gerard with a grin, putting them on equal Christian name informality, "Come here." Then, making the sign of the cross on his forehead, he told him to give exegesis another try. And the priest began to interpret so confidently and well "that it seemed his words had come from Paradise," so, thoroughly pleased, he trotted off to tell Caione how very well he now understood Saint John's meaning.[45] Even Doctor Santorelli began to feel that he could do a little theological reading, too. "His words," he owed, "rendered the most abstruse doctrines intelligible and those which seemed the most obscure became clear and plain as he talked."[46]

It was a puzzle to most of these educated persons, priests and laymen, as Doctor Santorelli said, how such things could possibly be understood by "a poor lay Brother." It is a puzzle now that none of them seem to have noticed how natively intelligent Gerard was. Even his exercise of a skilled worker's intelligence had to be set down to some miraculous power. Don Donato Antonio, coming back to the tailor's shop, discovered Gerard, having put aside his book, pouring over a paper pattern intent on cutting the cloth so that he would get, as the rector had ordered, two habits out of it. "Anyone could see," Donato Antonio said later, "that it just couldn't be done." There wasn't enough cloth in the bolt. But Gerard, pausing only to remark that a man must do what obedience says he must do, turned the paper pattern about, took out his scissors, and cut. When he'd done, there were the two habits ready to be sewn. But everyone else in the shop was simply convinced that there was more cloth in the pieces on the shop floor than in the original bolt. It was all a great mystery.[47]

They were, these priests and doctors, able to deal much
more easily with Gerard's quickness in discovering what was
going on in another's heart.

"He laid open the deepest wounds of their souls to some,
and set before others the duties of their station, and their infi-
delities in the performance of them."[48] It may seem more remarkable now that, so far from these strangers' resenting such
invasions of their minds and hearts, "the fame of the spiritual
endowments with which God had favored Gerard, and the
sway he exercised over the hearts of men, caused him to be
sought after on all sides."[49] They sought him at Melfi, where
he quietly exposed a hypocrite mystic, at Cedogna where he
stopped a townsman in the street to talk about his secret vice,
and at Naples where a shopkeeper came back from chatting
with the Brother at the door to tell his other customer that
Gerard had spoken of something which he had supposed known
"only to God and me."[50]

His contemporaries were as ready to credit Gerard with as
fine a knowledge of their physical condition as of their hearts'
secrets. There was this Alessandro, a middle-aged widower,
who had recently married again. He brought his new wife to
Caposele. There they met Gerard and fell to explaining their
hopes for a child. "Your wife should be happy and of good
heart," said the grinning Brother, always the encourager, "After all you've suffered, she is forty days pregnant," and, he
added to complete their joy, "It will be a boy." All came true.
Just exactly as Gerard prophesied. Alessandro, of course, was
already calling the child in the womb by this kind Brother's
name. And every time he called "Gerard, Gerard," he could
feel the baby kick in response.[51] So the bachelor Gerard slipped
into a reputation for knowing about pregnant mothers. And
their unborn children. And their anxious husbands.

Gerard's gracious fame could not but be spreading.[52] "The
populace followed him."[53] So did others. On Doctor Giuseppe
Salvadore of Liveto's coming to visit with Abbot Prosper
d'Aquila from Sant' Andrea, Gerard, to avoid any boring pious talk, turned the attention of these grandees towards the

abbot's servant. He asked the young peasant to play him something on the harpsichord. The villager said he knew nothing of music. He wished to be excused. "The Abbot and the doctor meanwhile amused themselves at his embarrassment." But Gerard again asked the lad to play for him. And so, perhaps he had been practicing in secret on the abbot's expensive instrument, he sat down at the keyboard and played for them. Gerard could evidently establish an immediate sympathy with such a young man. The two men's sons were allies in an escapade. Abbot and doctor were left to think whatever they might.[54] There's a similar camaraderie revealed in the story of Gerard's meeting another youngster carrying a vast cord of wood, far too heavy for him, and Gerard's heaving up one end and bearing the burden with him all the way to d'Iliceto.[55] That camaraderie was felt in the house, too. The student, Domenico Blasucci, was commonly to be found at the door of the tailor's shop, knowing that when Gerard arrived they would be swapping a few cheery words. Domenico was a fellow Muro townsman, but there was more than local patriotism bringing the two young men together. There was real affection. So Domenico often thought of a reason for passing that way through the house. Like the time he found a needle in his cupboard and recognized at once that poverty demand he return it to the house tailor that very minute.[56]

Perhaps such easy friendliness with a fellow youngster is not so remarkable. But as evidently, Gerard was capable of working his way into friendship with a late-middle-aged Canon. Camillo Bozio of Atella was brought to admit, after a moment of professional outrage that a Brother should be talking theology in his sacristy, that this Brother was not only a competent commentator on Scripture, but a fine companion on a lengthy walk. There was a cheerful piety about his talk. Quite unlike the stuff he had to endure at meetings of the diocesan Chapter. He long remembered the time he and his new friend came upon a country church and how, going in, Gerard had sat himself down at the organ to play an impromptu hymn:

O happy flowers, night and day
Near my Jesus you can stay

Bozio remembered, too, the fun they'd have when he tried to join in.[57] He just couldn't keep up with the jaunty rhythms Gerard was giving the hymn tune. He hadn't Gerard's warmth for such devotions. "My voice was too cold."

Bozio turned out to be a likable Canon. But Gerard was managing to make friends even with the "Anger of God." He discerned the essential fineness of the man. Cafaro was a courteous Christian, unable to sit quiet when he noticed, as he too often had to notice, an incivility in the house. He let Alphonsus know that the d'Iliceto bursar, Father Lorenzo d'Antonio, 1711–1769, was "too down on the Brothers." He let Brother Gabriele Puzzo, 1722–1750, know that he should not be putting himself "above the others," and exemplified his egalitarian appreciation of the Redemptorist vocation in signing himself to this lay Brother as to each Father, "Your Servant and Brother."[58] On Falcoia's death, Alphonsus had chosen Cafaro to be his spiritual director. Gerard had made the same choice.

There came to be such a sympathy of heart and mind between them that when Rector Cafaro died at Materdomini, in the summer of 1753, Gerard remarked assuredly in the recreation room, "Don Paolo is a great saint. He enjoys the sight of God in heaven." Cafaro had been the ideal Redemptorist. He had been the true imitator of Paul in all things. "And his throne of glory is not far from Saint Paul's, on account of the thorn in the flesh from which he suffered." Apostle and Redemptorist would be talking of their recoveries together. Like patients released from hospital. Tannoia's gossipy interest is hooked by this reference to some secret thorn. And Alphonsus was intrigued that Gerard knew so much. The rector major had supposed himself the only one of them privy to Cafaro's special pain.[59]

Perhaps the true wonder was how little interest any of the others in the community had taken in their rector. Not thinking it their business to ask what made him so angry in the pulpit. It may be that Gerard, in his ordinary companionableness, recognized another sufferer. For he was at various times himself the victim of terrible bouts of depression. There is a famous instance of such a time in September 1751. Gerard, trudging down the d'Iliceto corridor, was overheard muttering "I can bear it no longer." These were, the Brother who overheard him insisted, Gerard's very words. "His heart was so dried up in him that he felt almost driven to despair." His friend Domenico was coming the other way down the corridor. Seeing the usually cheerful Gerard in such depression, Domenico, quite heedless of the Rule, stopped to talk, "Brother Gerard, what's up?" And he, with a bitter sigh said again quite aloud for anyone to hear, "I cannot bear it any more." Domenico knew just what Gerard needed. The student gave the Brother a hug, making, as the nervous chroniclers aver, the sign of the cross on his breast. So Gerard was freed from his dumps. He returned to a wanted cheerfulness. And to those accustomed occupations of a Brother.[60]

Taking Risks, Getting Accused

Gerard made a note to remind himself of what that little demonstration of brotherly sympathy had meant to him and what it might mean to another. He wouldn't every time risk an impetuous hug, but he'd do his friendliest best for anyone in the house suffering a like distress, "anyone who is where it has pleased the divine will to place them and they cannot bear it any longer."[61] He'd put them in his prayers. He'd give them a grin when they passed in the corridor.

As Gerard was popularly esteemed to have powers for the quieting of an uneasy spirit, so he was celebrated as the carrier of others' physical burdens. That incident with the cord of wood is an instance. There's another story of his getting a gang of log rollers to swing into action with him, manage the unmanageable tree trunk together, and raise the roof beam high.[62] Another of his meeting a poor old woman on the steep path up to Sant' Agata. She had a load of washing on her head.

Though he was by now gentleman enough to go red with shame, he took the bundle and carried the washing right through town into the public square. There are many Christian exemplars for such a carrying of another's burden on a steep hill path, from Simon of Cyrene onwards. But, in relating this story, Tannoia properly recalled stories of the gentleman Vito and the Amalfi porters. "In this, he imitated Brother Curzio, with whose manner of life he was well acquainted."[63] Gerard, as he stooped to lift the laundry basket, like Gioacchino when he carried the tray of loaves, was accepting a further demand of that code of brotherly honor which Vito had established among them.

In the more popular forms of knightly romance, that old woman would have revealed herself as a powerful fairy able to translate the questing hero on the instant to the palace of his lady. But those who followed Vito could expect no such short cuts. And men of his honor would have to be very careful in dealing with any lady. Gaudiello's experience with the infatuated Neapolitan dame should be a warning to them all. Yet the smiling Gerard was a little careless of appearances in such matters. He was always easy in his relations with women. They could see that this Brother was not a power-seeker. Simply a sharer of what he had been given. They could speak as equals, even when they were asking for direction. He was "continually writing letters to troubled souls" and "giving marvelous support" to the weary, showing himself to be in command of "a unique teaching in the school of prayer."[64] Especially did Gerard delight in the Teresian nuns of Ripacandida and their young prioress, Mary of Jesus. "When they conversed together on spiritual topics," Tannoia says, "they were as two burning flames mutually enkindling each other."[65] For a time not a week passed without his writing to the nuns and their writing to him. So inflamed were they that on one of his visits when they were contemplating the wondrous love of Christ for them, Gerard had to take such a grip on the grill between them to moderate his transport of desire that it bent within his grasp, "as if it had been melted wax."[66] It was shortly after this, in

1752, that the worried bishop of Melfi stopped all Gerard's communications with these nuns, both visits and correspondence. Gerard wrote all smiles to the bishop, reassuring him that they were all entirely ready to do whatever he wanted of them. "Your Most Reverence must be cheerful."[67] He seems not have been sensible of the danger at which the bishop had been hinting.

It sometimes appears that it was more than ordinarily difficult for Gerard to appreciate any danger of the kind. He was not ignorant of the nastier aspects of small-town gossip. The Muro population had included a few calumniators. He certainly knew that he should not go about alone. Once, at Oliveto, Gerard was told that Don Fiore would not be traveling with him on account of some sickness. Gerard sent him the message that he must recover at once. And he worked the necessary miracle to get him well enough to travel.[68] But Gerard could not be forever taking such precautions. Not when there was good to be done. Doctor Gaetano Federico of Castelgrande recalled that Gerard, being woken at two in the night by Sibyl Sebastiano, agreed to say a prayer with her daughter, Caterina Mucciaccio, who was writhing in the doctor's doorway. All of a sudden the demon molesting her cried out in defeat. "Grr, the wretch wins!" The Brother, thus encouraged, took off the cord around his waist and strung it about the girl, all the time whispering to her.[69] At least he had the sense that time to tell the doctor not to leave them alone. Another time at Codogna, when he was staying with Don Constantino Capucci and his family, he did not take even that elementary precaution. Donna Emmanuella in the kitchen was not at all happy that Gerard should be talking with their two daughters and the young maid in the room above. "Saints have always trembled when they were in dangerous situations, but this man is conversing with my daughters and my maid without any fear or restraint whatever." On Gerard's coming down into the kitchen with his usual grin, Donna Emmanuella didn't care for his smiling and asked him just what he found so funny. "I have to thank you," Gerard replied, "for having remembered my weakness, I wish all mothers were as thoughtful." It was awkward for her to talk of such things with him. She had no liking for the embarrassing turn this conversation was taking. "Do you not remember," Gerard asked, "what you were saying to yourself only a minute ago?"[70] He knew this mother had been muttering sense.

But even if he remembered Donna Emmanuella's scolding, Gerard was not able to preserve himself from an even riskier entanglement with another Lacedonia family, friends, or at least acquaintances, of Don Constantino and his wife. The magistrate Candido Caggiano had three daughters and a son. The boy being already a subdeacon and two of his sisters, Saveria and Veronica, being nuns, it seemed to the youngest Nerea, a girl of twenty years, that she should enter a convent, too. This provided a financial problem for her parents. Three doweries in so short a time would threaten even a comfortably off family. So Gerard, as he had so often done for girls in such circumstances, collected the necessary two hundred ducats from his richer patrons.[71] But three weeks after she had been received at Foggia, it was apparent to Mother Celeste Crostorosa that Nerea did not have a vocation for their convent and she was sent home. No girl at that time could easily face her townsfolk as "a failed nun." And three weeks was quite long enough to give her such a reputation. Nerea was full of resentment against Gerard who was so clearly responsible for getting her into this mess. She felt outraged. She flung accusations about.

It is not entirely clear what Nerea alleged. It may be that she told the parish priest, Don Benigno Bonaventura, that Gerard had molested her. It was certainly he who forwarded the accusation to Alphonsus. But it is likelier that she told her family with sensible self-preserving care against parental fury, that Gerard had been playing around with another girl. There's a version of this nasty little tale which suggests that Nerea accused him of sinning with the fourteen-year-old Nicoletta Capucci, one of those girls with whom Gerard had been laughing in the upper room while her mother prepared supper. Perhaps Nerea had wanted to be sharing that seductive laughter. Perhaps she even believed there might be something to her accusation. After all, Donna Emmanuella had been made nervous by Gerard's behavior in the house. There was another report that Nerea had allowed herself to be seduced by her confessor, and that, on her becoming pregnant, this priest had been the first to suggest that they put the blame on Gerard.[72]

Celeste, knowing nothing of what was going on, celebrated Holy Week 1754 with unperturbed devotion. Gerard was there, too. He gave her a crucifix with a striking quotation from the liturgy they had sung together that week. "O wood more wondrous than every other wood, being found worthy to carry the Son of God."[73] But he said nothing of what the ex-postulant was doing. They were not to meet again.

Nerea was making an accusation to which every missioner, wandering from village to village, house to house, sleeping in strange beds, eating at strange tables, felt himself exposed. This accusation had been made against Alphonsus himself at Villa dei Schiavi in 1737. And by the local clergy. They resented the missioners getting money from their parishioners for Mass stipends. "They went so far as to say that the missioners intrigued with a woman whom they identified, alleging that she was received into the missioners' house by night; and this wretched creature lent herself to the accusation, defaming Alphonsus even more than the others."[74] Going to the local baron for protection of his name, Alphonsus had been met with unlooked-for reproaches. "What have we here, one of those filthy hermits?" But he had been vindicated very fast. And had written into the 1747 Constitutions that none of the Fathers should go parish visiting unless accompanied by a Brother or some local priest.[75] The Fathers had not supposed perhaps that a Brother could have any reputation to lose. Or that anyone would bother to accuse a Brother.

Now, it seemed to everyone who had been greeted by Gerard's easy smile when they passed in those draughty corridors of d'Iliceto that the charge had some credibility. Gerard was a really attractive young man. They had been recognizing this when they were sending him out to charm money from the local gentry and their ladies. "Women wanted to give him their earrings and men would have him take their best waist-coat buttons."[76] But he was, it had to be admitted, very high spirited. Too high spirited for his own good, perhaps. Dancing in the recreation room, indeed.

When Villani arrived at d'Iliceto, sent by Alphonsus to investigate, no one in the community was prepared to say that such a thing as Nerea alleged was downright impossible. Gerard was, therefore, sent, already in disgrace, judged quite capable of getting into such a scrape, to be sentenced by Alphonsus at Pagani. This was, likely, the first time they'd met. And, "since men of eminent sanctity have fallen under similar circumstances,"[77] since he himself was always quick to discern an occasion of sexual sin, since the d'Iliceto community had not given a character reference for their Brother, Alphonsus felt inclined to believe the accusation. He set the enormity of it before Gerard. Later, it seemed to Alphonsus that he had arranged this interview with Gerard so that the accused could provide a full explanation, a self-defense. At the time, it must have felt to Gerard that Alphonsus was simply following the line marked out by the d'Iliceto Fathers. So Gerard said nothing against his accusers. It was, he knew from Antonio Torres, impossible to remember the calumnies and the blasphemies thrown against Jesus and then to seek to vindicate one's character.[78] The significance of the carved crucifix he gave to Celeste was plain to Gerard. "For your sake the Savior died on a cross, saturated with opprobrium."

Alphonsus had customarily talked and written of "the theater of the Passion" and now, in this most intense of all the dramas in which Gerard was representing Jesus, Alphonsus assigned himself the part of Pilate. Not having the evidence to warrant dismissing Gerard but feeling that he must fulfill the expectations of all who were watching them, inside and outside the Congregation, Alphonsus acted in quick defense of the Congregation and its reputation. He could not think of Gerard's reputation at such a time. Later, he might have come to think that it was only by the justification of an innocent member of the Congregation that there could be any effective justification of the Congregation. But for now, Alphonsus forbade Gerard's receiving Holy Communion. He was not to have any communication with anyone outside the Congregation. He was to take himself off to Ciorani.

Gerard, secure in his innocence, secure in the just God's working his purpose out, knew that in this silent *imitatio* of the unjustly accused Christ he was behaving just as Vito would have the Brother behave. A man of honor does not defend himself against vulgar abuse.

It was saddeningly evident to Gerard that Alphonsus had put himself into a most awkward position. As the bishop of Melfi had discovered during the affair of the Ripacandida nuns, Gerard's consciousness of his own innocence allowed him to think only of the peace of mind of his superior. He felt he should be comforting the rector major ahead of the dark time. Alphonsus seems obscurely to have felt some mysterious reversal in their situation. He did not know what to do with this Brother who said nothing for himself but who, meeting him in the corridor declared, as if he were determined to sustain Alphonsus's sense of his own integrity against the shock that must come, "Father, you have the face of an angel."[79] And Gerard's smiling ways were having their effect again. Guilt does not look so. If Alphonsus were not sometimes disturbed by Gerard's serene care for him, others in the Ciorani community were becoming very restless about their part in this affair. Most especially about the ban on his receiving Communion. They wanted it over. One of them suggested that at least Gerard could serve his Mass. "Don't tempt me," said Gerard, "I should snatch the host out of your hands." Caione remembered an incident on the stairway. One of the Fathers suggested going to the rector major and asking that the ban on Communion be lifted. Gerard hesitated a moment before saying, "No. No." Then giving a hard blow with his hand to the balustrade to steady himself. "We must continue under the pressure of the will of my dear God."[80]

Meanwhile, not having obtained a confession from the Brother, nor any evidence of his guilt or innocence, Alphonsus was getting very frustrated. Don Saverio Rossi, the rector of Ciorani, was now required to make more regular reports on this Brother's behavior. Tannoia himself remembered being set by Alphonsus to be an unofficial spy, "watch him as narrowly as possible."[81] But it was not by such snooping that the truth was discovered. It is, in fact, not at all clear how the truth was discovered. It may be that the seductive priest himself wrote a letter to Alphonsus. Caione says that the man was now on his deathbed, and that his confessor required that he disclose his part in the affair. Or maybe it was Nerea who wrote. Perhaps she could not bear the weight of her own conscience. Or maybe it was her confessor who imposed this recantation. Or again, she may have at last told her family the truth. Her appalled parents, the magistrate and his wife, may have written to Alphonsus. Or their son, the subdeacon.[82] There was, Tannoia knew, more than one letter to the correspondence. He did not want to linger on these. He was anxious to get his *Life* of Gerard back on course. But there was still that second interview with Alphonsus to be mentioned.

Making a Claim to the Rule

Alphonsus felt now, as any good superior, any good man, would feel, very uncomfortable with himself and his government of his subjects. By this time, he had listened to Margotta's account of Gerard's goodness. And to the satisfactory reports of Rossi and Tannoia that they had nothing to report. There was no more doubt about this Brother's obedience than about his chastity. Alphonsus must clear things up. This time, he felt it better not to order Gerard to travel to him. Roles were, to his mind, already somewhat reversed. He came across from Pagani to Ciorani. But that was condescension enough. He would see the Brother across a desk. And Gerard, seeing his difficulties, was anxious to help him. He was certainly not going to explain how well Alphonsus had played Pilate in their scene together. But he was hoping to make his sense of a good Redemptorist Brother absolutely clear to the rector major. So, to Alphonsus's urgent question "Why did you not defend yourself?" Gerard answered, as only Alphonsus could have told Tannoia (unless some Father were at the keyhole), "How could I, since the Rule commands us not to make excuses, but to bear every mortification in silence."[83]

This scene has been a favorite with Redemptorist illustrators. Paintings of Gerard pointing to an open copy of the Rule on Alphonsus's desk are on every house wall. Its significance has not, however, always been thoroughly appreciated. Developing a sentence from the old *Regole Grandi,* it had been suggested in Rule VIII of the 1744 Bovino text that the Fathers, "these beloved disciples of the Divine Majesty," might, in their search for meekness of heart, "attempt the humblest and most menial tasks in the community" and the example had been given of "sometimes working in the garden." In this same Rule VIII, it is ordered that these same disciples who are to do occasional gardening as a mortifying exercise shall never "excuse or defend themselves" to a superior, "even if accused or calumniated falsely."[84] This Rule is itself developed further in the Eighth Constitution of the Conza text, the first official Rule of the Congregation, in force from 1747 until the promulgation of the Pontifical Rule in 1749. "They shall try as much as is in them, not to excuse or defend themselves," even though they be calumniated. In this, they will be imitating the saint of saints. "The Lord never defended himself or excused himself, no matter how greatly calumniated or accused, except in those things which concerned the glory of His heavenly Father." Again in their seeking after humility, it is recommended that they sometimes work in the garden, even wash dishes, wait at table. Seeking after humility is to be an hieratic activity. Decently graded. "The Superior, to edify his subjects, may serve at table on Friday."[85] As plainly, Chapter I of Part II of the 1749 Pontifical Rule, organizing the relations of Fathers in a house, declares "they shall not excuse themselves or defend themselves" when rebuked by a rector.[86] Silence under accusation, like gardening and waiting at table, is being presented as an extraordinary perfecting discipline in the spiritual lives of Fathers. Neither this Rule, which lies open in those paintings, nor any of the earlier texts is making reference to the conduct of Brothers.

The Pontifical Rule had been obtained by a Father and Brother praying together, working together, suffering together in Rome. That much had been gracefully recognized by Villani when he brought Francesco with him to take leave of Pope Benedict. As the first to know themselves to be members of the new Congregation of the Most Holy Redeemer, Father and Brother had gone on a grateful pilgrimage to Loreto together. But the Fathers had not, as they read, translated the Rule into the language of shared vocation. Nor, of course, had the Brothers. There is a shock for all of them in that pictured scene of Alphonsus and Gerard with the Rule open between them. They had taken Brothers' endurance of blames for granted, as they had taken their garden and refectory and latrine services. Brothers were naturally treated as those at the base of every hieratic organization were treated—as rightless domestic servants were treated. Gerard is asserting the startling new notion that the Rule applies to Brothers as to Fathers. He has exercised his right to perfecting silence precisely as a Redemptorist living within the Rule. Like a Father.

Alphonsus was, of course, intelligent enough to catch Gerard's meaning. At the development Gerard was proposing for his self-understanding within the Congregation. There was in this claim much to unsettle Alphonsus. Much that he would instinctively resist, at least when the same claim to live under the Rule like Fathers was made by other Brothers.

Meanwhile, Gerard, in energetic harmony with the rector major, is repeating his version of Alphonsus's own exhortatory sequence: "How necessary it is to become a saint," "I have been given this opportunity to become a saint," "What, then, must I do to become a saint?" Answering that question, he recognizes that he is not being asked to do very much individually. They are all called to be saints together in the Congregation. "I have what I need to be a saint because others are paying the price."[87]

The rector major may have found Gerard, after their second interview, an awkward reminder of a moment when the Congregation had proved to be a less than transparent figure of the communion of saints. So Francesco Margotta had quite easily persuaded Alphonsus that Gerard should go back with him to the Naples station for a while. Be out of the rector major's sight for a bit.[88] It was during this next stay in the city that Gerard's sense of their all being Redemptorists together in one mission community, Brothers with Fathers becoming saints within the protective Rule, working with the citizens for the realization of the Kingdom of God, achieved its largest expression.

Long ago, taking a gaggle of students on an expedition, Gerard had slipped into a Father's mode, talking of "my family."[89] Rather like Alphonsus himself. No one of those youngsters had thought this odd. At least no one of them is recorded as thinking his paternal use, expressing a paternal care, as odd. Now, he was dressing as well as talking and generally behaving in the ways that Fathers dressed, talked, generally behaved in the city. The Congregation's reputation was generally enhanced by his playing the Father's part. "My Father," the poor madmen at the asylum would say after one of the Brother's catechetical instructions, "we wish you would stay with us and never leave us again; you must not go away, no one tells us such beautiful things as you do."[90] Gerard's pastoral care was exercised for several priests of the city, too. "Monsignore Amato himself, the flower of bishops in that time, was never weary of listening to him."[91] He was, like the deacons Stephen and Philip, announcing the Gospel. In ways that Tannoia recognized as almost priestly. There was "an innumerable multitude of people who might almost be called his penitents."[92] Gerard was chatting pastorally at the doors of librarians, printers, and "other tradespeople of our acquaintance."[93] Naples, like Melfi, becomes a "theater" in which Gerard made his appearance.[94] He'd take any chance for a spot of comic acting. On one famous occasion he opened the door to find a servant of the Duchess of Maddaloni there with a message that his mistress wished to meet the famous Brother. Gerard knew how some crotchety, nose-out-of-joint Father might reply. He did his imitation. "I cannot make out why such a fuss is made over this Brother. He's half a simpleton. They are strangely deceived about him in Naples, I see. Tell this to Her Grace, if you please."

Gerard could never give up joking. Or acting. But he had learned to be more careful in one important concern. Coming out of Santo Spirito church, he was stopped by a lady who said winningly, "Brother Gerard, I hope that you will do me the favor of coming to my house: I have a son who is ill and suffering greatly." Even the sick lad's pain did not confuse Gerard's clearer sense of the old danger. "Madam, what use could my visit be? However, I promise to recommend him to our Blessed Lady." This was not the only occasion during this stay in Naples when Gerard's attractiveness was recognized by a lady. But Tannoia simply notes that "he used always to make similar answers at such times."[95]

Whether or not these events happened in quite the way Tannoia describes, Francesco Margotta thought that far too many stories were going the round of Naples. Gerard was living a life altogether too exciting for a young man. Part of the difficulty was that, in his kindly haste to get Gerard away from the scene of that punishment time, Margotta had not stopped to think what work Gerard would be doing in Naples. There was no set job for him. He was simply going about doing good. And making friends. Among these, Alphonsus's favorite Naples Jesuit, Don Francesco Pepe, who gave Gerard coadjutor authority to distribute several thousand plenary indulgences to whomsoever he deemed would perform the required pious acts in a proper spirit. This was perhaps Pepe's kind return for Gerard's sending a couple of poor girls to try their vocations as lay Sisters in the city convent that Pepe had founded.[96] Alphonsus would have been entirely approving of such a hustling of girls into religious life. Out of the danger of marriage. Even after the Nerea incident. He was not pleased, however, that Margotta was teaching Gerard to beg for his midday meal with the other starving folk at the door of the San Girolamo

monastery.[97] And neither Margotta nor Alphonsus cared for
the reputation that Gerard was, quite deservedly, acquiring as
a wonder-worker on the city streets. He was prompting madmen at the hospital, grocers at their shop doors, prostitutes at
the alley corner, and passersby, however too much in a hurry
to buy a tinderbox, to pause for a moment and consider whether
they might not be living in a communion where miracles could
happen. It was, evidently, still true that "wherever Gerard goes
everything is turned upside down." So Margotta wrote to
Alphonsus suggesting that he recall Gerard to Materdomini.

Alphonsus took up the suggestion. No sense letting a
Brother get a reputation in what was the Fathers' line of work.
He remembered that there was some fuss at Materdomini about
the cooking, another case of a Brother's looking indispensable.

> Since Brother Gerard is back again, let him be Bursar,
> especially since, as I recall, Brother Gennaro is deaf,
> and, moreover, has been put to working on the build-
> ing site.[98]

At Materdomini, the Father died, the student died,[99] most
of the community had a bout of sickness. Gerard, too, became
ill. But not from the cooking. Or the bad air of the place. Or
from some personal weakness. He was discovering the price
he should be paying for the good of another.

The Price of Another's Good

"God had afflicted Father Margotta for some months with
such an interior desolation and aridity that he was in a most
pitiable state."[100] No pilgrimage Margotta made to the various
Neapolitan shrines relieved his depression. Gerard had warned
him as much. But the poor man would persist. The conventional remedies were failing the conventional man. Margotta
was the more distraught. Gerard could not leave him to his
suffering. One day, Doctor Santorelli found Gerard at his
bursar's table obviously engaged with a business which both

pleased and saddened him. "I am writing to Father Margotta to tell him that his trial is over, and to congratulate him." Soon a letter arrived from Naples to tell the community that Margotta's sufferings had ceased. Gerard was paying the price for Margotta's recovery. "He lost his wonted cheerfulness on the day he sent his letter to Naples, he became quite pale and cast down." Caione, struck by this unaccountable alteration, ordered Gerard to declare the cause. "I could not bear to see Father Margotta suffer any longer, so I prayed to God to let me suffer in his stead."

Gerard recovered from that sympathetic illness. But he had the firm notion that the recurrent bouts of sickness from which he was emerging weaker each time would lead to his death. In January 1755, he told Brother Gennaro that he was certain he would die soon, and die alone.[101] Early in March, he asked Doctor Santorelli, "Do you realize that I am to die this year of consumption?"[102] He recalled those indulgences that he had been given by Father Pepe, and wrote off to Celeste Crostarosa, on March 8, assuring her that she and all her nuns and all those who followed them into the Foggia convent should enjoy these indulgences in perpetuity. The Jesuit had taken some care to hand over just those indulgences that would give Gerard most satisfaction to distribute. He had them for the feast of the Blessed Trinity, and for all feasts of Christ, all feasts of Mamma Mary, feasts of Saints Michael the Archangel, Gioacchino and Anne, Joseph, Elizabeth, and John the Baptist.[103] They must be careful to keep his authorizing letter safe, in perpetuity. It strikes him that he is in such a case that he should now be making a holy bargain with them: "I set it down that whoever is prioress of the convent when I die shall see to it that all the Sisters apply, for the next eight days, what indulgences they can for my soul, and I in return agree to pray to the Lord God for them."[104]

Between bouts of sickness, he was still at work. Still using his charms on possible benefactors for the Congregation. Still assisting missioners. In the spring and early summer of 1755, the last year of his life, Gerard went the round of villages in the valley of Sele: San Andrea di Conza, Serino, Calitri, Senerchia, Oliveto Citra, Contursi, Auletta, Vietri di Potenza, San Gregorio, Buccino.[105] It was while he was collecting money at San Gregorio in July that he began to vomit blood at night. Hearing this from the archpriest Salvadore at Oliveto Citra, the rector wrote to inquire their Brother's own sense of his condition. Gerard wrote home at the start of August, "If you wish me to return, I will do so at once, on the other hand, if you wish me to go on with the collection, I will do so; just send me an order and all will be well."[106] Caione decided that he should stay at the archpriest's house until he was ready to continue begging. But, by the end of August, it was evident to Gerard that he was not regaining strength, rather his fever was coming more often, and with increasing force. He must return home. At Materdomini, he fell into dysentery, violent perspiration, delirium, frequently passing into total unconsciousness, and spitting more than a pint of blood each day.

Filippo Gallela, a young apprentice joiner, another of those country lads with whom Gerard so readily established a grinful easiness, walked the twenty or more miles of mountains from Muro to Materdomini, thinking only to be in the house with him. That would be happiness enough. But Gerard had his visitor called up to the infirmary, assuring him with a smile that he would delay his death a few days. There was a short period of remission, during which, by a curious reversal of expectation, on September 14, it was the holy prioress who died at Foggia. Gerard, on being told, at once confirmed that Celeste was "now enjoying the beatific vision."[107] He knew her well enough, he knew the goodness of God well enough, to be able to say that. Then Gerard's health fast deteriorated. The younger Brothers in the house, Andrea D'Anticona, 1733–1822, Saverio D'Auria,1734?–1802, and the novice Brother Carmine Santaniello, 1737?–1807, who had just joined the Congregation, took turns with the elder Stefano Sperduto, 1725–1805, in a twenty-four hour watch.

In the evening of October 15, Brother Stefano sat by him and, seeing him so obviously near death, asked quietly, "We have always loved one another; will you remember me when you enter into the presence of God?" One Brother to another, Gerard replied, "How could I ever forget you?"[108] Later, he said he was thirsty. Brother Stefano went out to fetch a cup of water. The kitchen was, as usual, locked at night, so it took some time to get the key, the cup, the water. By the time he returned, Gerard was facing the wall, unconscious. He was dying alone. Like Vito, and, as Maria Crocifissa had taught him, like Christ.

After the news was known, Caione reported to Alphonsus, "a multitude of people," "a great gathering of folk," crowded to the church, manifesting "a universal esteem," "a universal sorrow," as they snatched for relics.[109] "The people," Tannoia remembered, not unsympathetically, "began to cut off his hair and tear pieces from his cassock."[110] They wanted to hang onto him. So did the Fathers. Don Francesco Buonamano, 1706–1777, the rector, was so enthusiastic for dipping napkins in the dead Brother's blood that he had a vein opened in Gerard's arm not once but twice, immediately after his death and then again while the bier was standing in the church. Andrea Strina, 1726–1797, held the basin to catch the gush of blood. But the Fathers found themselves being thrust aside. "It was necessary to post guards to protect the body."[111] There could however be no resisting the people. Gerard was already their saint.

The Fathers made another effort to secure Gerard for themselves. On the discovery that the local painter was out of town, they had two death masks made. On the man's hurried return to retrieve his share of the memento market, Caione had a posthumous likeness taken as the body lay on the bier. Don Benedetto Grazioli of Atella paid for a large number of death-cards to be printed from this portrait. The Fathers sent one of the masks to Alphonsus. Don Benedetto forwarded a couple of the cards.[112]

In a further effort to keep Gerard as their own, to retain their control of their Brother's posthumous celebrity, Redemptorists began to put their memories of Gerard down on paper. Giovenale's jottings were posted to Alphonsus towards the end of 1755. Mauro Buono Murante, 1735–1761, the fifteen-year-old for whom Alphonsus had in 1752, on a moment's extraordinary enthusiasm, founded a one-pupil school at Ciorani, was also required to set down what he recalled of missioner Gerard's visits to his hometown.[113] "Do not forget," Alphonsus wrote, "to bring me the accounts you will have been able to collect about the Brother Gerard."[114] By then Caione had composed a decent little obituary essay, demonstrating his talent for ordering bits of evidence, so Alphonsus sent him Giovenale's *memoire* with a fussing set of instructions on how he should combine the different pieces of evidence that the Fathers would send him. "I send you herewith the notes taken by Father Giovenale on the life of Brother Gerard. Preserve and take a copy of them as well as you can, as I have asked you to do. See also about the time that you devote to this matter. It would be well for you to spend about a quarter of an hour every day on the work, and thus you will gradually get the work done. I send you also your own manuscript. It will serve to remind you of a great many things."[115]

Caione worked to a model. After introductory stories of the strange adventures of the child, of his untaught wisdom by which he put to shame theologically expert scholars, of his leaving his mother to follow his divine vocation, he shapes his central narrative after the Lukan pattern of Jesus' setting his face towards Jerusalem, the Mount of Olives, and beyond. Caione sets Gerard on a journey through Senarchia, Auletta, Vietri di Potenza, San Gregorio, until he comes to Oliveto. On his way, like Jesus, he works a range of miracles, multiplying loaves, raising an epileptic child, casting out demons, subduing winds and waves, confronting the women and men he meets with their hidden sins.[116]

Gerard's journey, on this telling, is most like Jesus' journey at its close. Tannoia may have been making conventional use of the spiritual directors' language when he wrote that, in the service of irascible Bishop Albini, Gerard "did not drag his cross but carried it joyfully."[117] But Caione had recognized that Gerard had himself made his dying a crucifixion. "Uniting his sufferings with those of his Redeemer."[118] Keenly sensitive to what was happening in this dying, he preserved every fragment of the Brother's conversation which hinted at compassionate identification with Jesus. "I write to you from the cross," Gerard had assured Maria of Jesus, "suffering my agony." "I am hidden in the sacred wounds of Jesus," Gerard had told Gerardo Gisone, 1720–1765, "and his wounds are in me."[119] Along with this inward psychological reciprocity, there were sickroom circumstances which seemed to be furthering his desire for identity with the Crucified. "They have all abandoned me."[120] This was not said regretfully. Gerard was content to be abandoned as Jesus had been abandoned. He was content to be sharing each experience. It was quite happily that he confided to Gisone, "I suffer continually all the pains, all the sorrows that Jesus Christ suffered during his Passion."[121] Others were ready to recognize this identity. It had been clear to Brother Carminiello that at his cry "My God, my God, where are you?" Gerard endured a desolation which was just the desolation of the dying Jesus. Carminiello had thereupon responded like the good thief on Calvary. "Remember me when you enter the presence of God." Brother Saverio, too, understood Gerard's asking for water as an echo of Jesus' cry, "I thirst."[122]

There may seem something "staged" in the ways that Gerard's carers and Gerard himself attended to such likenings. It was always difficult for others, difficult for Gerard himself, to tell the difference between his playacting and his truth. Probably there was not much difference. The pains of those dramatic whippings, arm-stretchings, were real enough. And it seemed to those with him in the infirmary that, more truly than at the moment of the Muro Passion Play, which had so disturbed his mother, Gerard was "thrust through by the lance," truly fulfilling the pattern of Jesus' death.[123] If there ever were much value in a distinction of "following" from "imitating" Christ, Caione thought it quite irrelevant to his presentation of the mystery of Gerard's death.

It is striking that Caione, who had had an opportunity to know Gerard well during the last months of his life, should think it right to put his life story into that Gospel shape. That he should authorize a wholly Christic version of Gerard's dying. And record without any demur, Gerard's identifying self-awareness: "I have figured out that this bed is the will of God for me: I am nailed to this bed as he himself was nailed."[124] It is as striking, and touching, that Caione should close his narrative of this imitation of Christ with a personal prayer expressing just Gerard's sense of Father and Brother living together within a Rule towards the companionable Kingdom:

> My dearest Brother, pray God, whom you love most ardently, for me, a poor sinner. Make my heart burn with love of Christ God, so that I may be in your company.[125]

"Gloria Patri..."

While Caione, more sensitive in this at least than Giuseppe Landi, 1725–1797, certainly more sensitive than Tannoia, who was also obediently setting down his recollections of Gerard, could well recognize the likeness of the suffering Christ in this Brother, Gerard himself had been a yet more imaginative contemplator of the mystery of the Cross and our sharing in this mystery. He had appreciated the Trinitarian value of his sufferings.

Of a sudden, sometimes, others were made privy to Gerard's expertness in theology. "One day when I was at Naples," Celestino de Robertis chucklingly recalled, a priest began asking Brother Gerard all his old seminary questions about "the difficult mysteries," such as "the generation of the Word," "His co-eternity with the Father," "the Procession of the Holy Spirit from the Father and the Son." De Robertis was proudly astonished to hear his Brother deal with each *quaestio*. "He expressed himself with ease and clarity on matters which the best theologians treat with caution."[126] Gerard had been meditating intelligently on what he had learned in his unsystematic reading, especially what he had gathered of Augustinian and

Thomist comment on the fourth gospel. He had been placing what he had further understood through these meditations within that Trinitarian tradition of a Christian's relation to Christ which is most vitally expressed in the writings of Saint Teresa of Ávila, 1515–1582, and, his personal find, Maria Crocifissa dei Tomasi, 1645–1699.

Alphonsus, in his meditations, had so identified with Jesus, the heir, that it became difficult for him to contemplate the Crucifixion as anything but a manifestation of the inexorable outward demand of the Father's justice. Gerard, unencumbered by any anxieties concerned with fatherhood and authority, was free to appreciate the cross as a presentation of loving. Of loving with the Trinity. Of love overflowing. The Father's love sustains the Son in his awful expression of their love for us.

He could hear, too, with the Evangelist, that at the climactic instant love at the cross, Jesus handed over the divine Spirit to the Christian. "The grace of the Holy Spirit," he could write to Gaetano Santorelli during the terrible Eastertide of 1754, is "always within the spirit."[127] Sharing the Spirit, the Christian will be alive with Jesus to do the will of the Father.

Gerard's language, as he makes his grand effort to articulate his sense of the divine will within his living, becomes so intense that only one of the transcribers of his Rule of Life was prepared to copy out his climactic apostrophe:

> To do what God wills it is necessary only that I should will, yes I, I, I, should will only God, and it is by God's will that I will God, that I will only what God wills.[128]

That "I, I, I" proclaims that nothing of himself is lost, nothing of his will, in willing only what God wills. Those repeated affirmations are of a self who is finding himself, and finding himself free to will, as he wills what God wills.[129]

What God wills is total loving. "The Holy Spirit will enable you," Gerard told a lay companion, "to know how much more you should suffer for the love of him who suffered so much for our love."[130] Love is sustaining. Total love is totally sustaining. So it is that when, under the loving will of the Father, that compassionate suffering with his Son seems too great to bear, "the grace and consolation of our Holy Spirit," will keep us loving.[131] At this apprehension of "our Holy Spirit" Gerard no longer felt like a madman in his loving.[132] No longer felt that he could not endure life in the house a moment longer. He could make sense of himself. He could endure. For, through "our Holy Spirit," he could see how it was that Jesus should endure each loving demand of the Father. Gerard could see the Father upholding his crucified Son in his arms under the loving hover of the Spirit. He could appreciate the Cross as the showing forth of the love of the Triune Godhead:

> Whenever I see the Cross, I am determined to make this little devotion of always saying a *Gloria Patri*.[133]

As it is with the Crucified, it is with Gerard. He is experiencing that love. He had come through reading, meditating, waiting, into an appreciation of Christians' enjoying together the inwardest life of the Trinity. "You cannot imagine," he told Isabella Salvadore, in his very last letter, "how much I love you in God."[134] In the wonder of Trinitarian life, Gerard is at last discerning the way, both self-aware and aware of the girl's feelings, to speak of love. There is not going to be anything so juvenilely romantic as the grill's melting between them; this love,"I must repeat," and there is a quickening of pace as Gerard attempts to prevent any repetition of the Nerea misunderstanding, "is a love divinized in God." That, he tells the archpriest's niece, must be their shared truth.

She and he and all those blessed spirits who have stood by him since his altar-playing days and all of us may be of good heart, joining in that grand shout, "Blessed be our Most Holy Trinity."[135]

CHAPTER TWO

Gerard Majella: Saint of the People

Giustino D'Addezio

CHRONOLOGY OF GERARD'S LIFE

April 6, 1726	Birth in Muro Lucano, southern Italy
June 5, 1740	Receives the sacrament of confirmation
April 13, 1749	Redemptorist mission in Muro begins
May 17, 1749	Arrives at Deliceto as an aspirant
April 10, 1752	Death of Gerard's mother
July 16, 1752	Makes first vows
May 1754	False charges by Nerea Caggiano
July 1754	His innocence proven, he is sent to Naples
November 1, 1754	Assigned to the shrine of Materdomini
October 16, 1755	Dies at dawn in his room at Materdomini
January 29, 1893	Beatified by Pope Leo XIII
December 11, 1904	Canonized by Pope Saint Pius X

"I'M OFF TO BECOME A SAINT"

Gerard Majella was born in Muro Lucano on April 6, 1726, the son of Domenico Majella and Benedicta Galela. He was baptized in the church of the Most Holy Trinity by Father Felix Coccicone. He made his confirmation on June 5, 1740, in the church of the Virgin of the Carmine.

When his father died, he was placed as an apprentice with a tailor named Pannuto, from where he passed into the service of Monsignore Claudio Albini, the bishop of Lacedonia, who had confirmed him. But Gerard wasn't satisfied; he felt the call to a total dedication to the service of God. When he asked for admission to the Capuchin monastery, he was turned down because of his frail constitution. But Gerard didn't give up. He waited for God's good time. It came at Eastertide in 1749, when the Redemptorists arrived in Muro to give a mission.

Gerard was twenty-three years old now. He followed all the sermons with vivid interest, and felt even more strongly the desire to join that congregation as a coadjutor brother. But he was turned down once again. Meanwhile his mother, Benedicta, had been watching the whole thing; she intuitively realized the strong determination in her son's heart. And so, on the final day of the mission, she locked him in the house and went to the church to attend the service bidding farewell to the missionaries. When she got back, she found the window open, the sheets knotted together, and a message: "I'm off to become a saint."

Gerard left with the Redemptorist missionaries. Father Paolo, who led the mission and who insisted that Gerard was too weak to face the hardships of a life of austerity found himself constrained to accept Gerard on a trial basis. He was sent to Deliceto, to the Sanctuary of Our Lady of Consolation; Gerard was happy. It was May 17, 1749. Three years later, on the feast of the Most Holy Redeemer, he took his religious vows.

And from then on, until his death, Gerard entered into a period of missionary experiences in the provinces of Foggia and Potenza, much to the profit of everyone who met him. He was also assigned to collect funds for the missions; and his travels were changed into new itinerant missions. It turned out that he was a connoisseur of souls, an advisor to priests, good at persuading people who were alienated from God, and concerned with vocations to the religious life. He became the friend and spiritual guide of the Carmelite nuns of Ripacandida, of the Benedictine nuns of Corato and Atella, and of the Redemptoristine sisters of Foggia and their foundress, Mother Maria Celeste Crostarosa.

The great achievements of this period were accompanied by a series of harsh trials, exhausting marches with the mis-

sionaries, physical collapse, aridity and darkness in his interior life, an infamous calumny that blocked off all contact with
outsiders and even prevented him from receiving the Eucharist.

In August 1755, Gerard returned to Materdomini, the
Marian sanctuary he loved so much. His tuberculosis worsened, and two months later, his earthly life ended in the loneliness of his room at dawn on October 16.

His simple and short life (twenty-nine years, six of which
were spent in religious life), interwoven with extraordinary
deeds, is a clear expression of the love of God and of Gerard's
docility to the action of the Holy Spirit.

"LET'S GO VISIT OUR FRIEND IN PRISON"

P rayer burst out spontaneously in the heart of the boy
Gerard. He was barely five years old, yet he went by himself to the sanctuary of the Virgin of Capodigiano. He very
much liked the beautiful Lady who held a child in her left arm.
To his enchantment and surprise, he saw the infant approach
him and invite him to play, placing in his hand a loaf of deli-
cious-smelling white bread, as the Lady smiled in pleasure.
This episode from his childhood marked the beginning of his
spiritual ascent. That bread was the mysterious announcement
of another kind of bread, the Eucharist, which would always
be the nourishment of his burning love for Jesus Christ. The
years passed, and many events carried Gerard far away from
there. He had already learned that "the boy who gave me
the bread was Jesus himself...whom I now meet everywhere I
go."

Back home Gerard started insisting that he wanted to make
his first communion and receive Jesus in his heart. "Son," his
mother told him, "first you have to grow and get big." One
feast day the boy, convinced that by now he *was* big, mixed in
with the adults and approached the communion rail. But the
priest, when he saw how small and fragile the boy was, rudely

told him to go away. And Gerard, in tears, had to remove himself from his beloved Jesus. His weeping lasted all day. That night when he was already fast asleep, Saint Michael the Archangel woke him up, took a white host from a ciborium, placed it on his tongue, and disappeared. Was it a dream? The next morning Gerard himself told the story to his mother, his sisters, and Signora Catalina Zaccardo: "Yesterday Father didn't want to give Jesus to me, but tonight Saint Michael the Archangel gave him to me." Years later Gerard would confirm this fact to his spiritual director and to a jeweler, Alessandro del Piccolo.

At the age of ten he officially made his first communion. His intention was to receive Jesus frequently and to prepare himself for communion with sacrifices and penances that love inspired him to do. After receiving the Eucharist, he remained motionless, in ecstasy, as if time had stopped.

Gerard would invent new games for his little friends: "Let's go visit our friend in prison," he would tell them. Everybody cheered and followed him, drawn by the force that poured out of this lad who was in love with the Eucharist.

As a religious, his love for Jesus "the prisoner" swelled to gigantic proportions. He could remain longer at the feet of Jesus in the Blessed Sacrament, even all night. It was easier because now both of them were beneath the same roof. Jesus himself had to chide him affectionately: "You crazy little fellow, what are you doing?" And Gerard answered: "Aren't you crazier, because you stay locked up in the tabernacle? If I'm crazy, it's with love for you."

Gerard's simplicity enchanted his friend Jesus, who amused himself by attracting him, even at times of busy activity in the Redemportist community. As a result Father Cafaro called Gerard to attention on account of his "strange behavior," humiliating him harshly. Gerard accepted his superior's complaint with deep humility. Later, as he passed by the church, he heard Jesus calling him from the sanctuary, and he had to tell him: "Lord, let me go on, please. I've got a lot to do; otherwise Father Superior is going to give me a talking-to again."

The year 1754 was a time of great interior trials. Gerard was without advice from his friend Jesus, and alone in the bitterness of his own insignificance. A young woman from Lacedonia, Nerea Caggiano, had entered religious life, thanks to the help of Brother Gerard. At first she seemed content, but she wavered and then decided to return to her family. She felt humiliated, and in order to dump her guilt upon somebody else, she invented a conspiratorial love story between Gerard and a girl who was the daughter of a friend from Lacedonia. Nerea spoke with her confessor and together they wrote to Gerard's major superior, Father Alphonsus Liguori.

Gerard was immediately summoned to Pagani to face his superior. Confronted with the calumny he found no response except silence. The superior could have expelled him immediately, given the seriousness of the charge. But he limited himself to forbidding all contact with people and depriving Gerard of holy Communion. That was worse than the calumny itself. What would he do now without his Jesus? He responded to the sentence with a bow, and retired to the silence of his cross. "The Lord does not wish to come to me because I am unworthy. He wished to punish my lack of love."

There is no lack of anecdotes from this period. One day a priest invited him to serve Mass. "Don't tempt me," Gerard murmured, "because I would grab the host out of your hand." And when someone asked him how he was holding up without holy Communion, he replied: "I manage with the immensity of my beloved God." It was as if to say, if he does not wish to come in the sacrament, I will meet him in the beauty of all creatures.

Meanwhile in Lacedonia young Nerea, who hadn't measured the gravity of her words, fell prey to remorse. She returned to her confessor and told him the whole truth. Her previous statement had to be rectified immediately. When this clarification arrived in the superior's hands, he called in Brother Gerard and asked him why he had not answered the charges against him. With complete tranquillity he answered: "How could I do that when the Rule demands that we don't excuse ourselves and are to suffer in silence?"

"I HAVE WEDDED MARY, MOST HOLY"

Gerard, why don't you get married?" Gerard's neighbors
kept asking him, seeing him carefree, more interested in
going to church than in finishing the orders from the tailor's
shop. But he answered: "I got married to Most Holy Mary."
Few people understood what he was talking about, although
many recalled what happened that third Sunday in May when
the feast of the Immaculate Conception was celebrated in the
cathedral: The crowd was enormous; Gerard was in the first
row, absorbed in the contemplation of the Virgin. Suddenly
they saw him step forward, remove a ring, and put it on the
finger of the statue, saying, "I have wedded the Virgin." The
whole thing seemed a momentary episode, but Gerard had
gotten engaged forever with the Mother of God.

Ever since childhood Gerard had been a fervent devotee of
the Virgin. In front of her image he spent hours in prayer, especially on the Marian feast days. On those days Gerard appeared to be drunk with gladness. He leapt and sang through
the streets, paying no heed to the mocking laughter of people.
Years later, during community recreation, he said mockingly
to Father Strina, "You don't like the Child Jesus." To which
the priest replied, "And you don't love the Virgin"—which
was something he should have left unsaid, because Gerard
seized the priest by the arm and began to leap and jump up
and down, dragging him along as if he were a feather.

At the age of twenty-three, upon entering the Congregation of the Most Holy Redeemer, he was sent to Deliceto, the
shrine of Our Lady of Consolation. His joy was so great that
he paid no attention to the remark by the superior: "And what
are we going to do with this postulant?" The letter of recommendation that Gerard had brought with him said that the can-
didate was very sickly, was of no use for hard work, and would
just be another mouth to feed. Gerard was walking on air. Then
he hastened to prostrate himself at the foot of the altar of the
Virgin to pour out all the tender feelings in his heart.

One day Father Cafaro told him to accompany two young aspirants to Ciorani. It was a long trip and so, when they were halfway there, they spent the night in the hospice of Ponterola. Gerard requested food for the three of them, worried that the two young men needed rest, and that homesickness for their families might make them sad. The dinner was served by the daughter of the owner, an olive-skinned girl who was used to dealing with vulgar travelers and was now attracted by Gerard's courteous manner. The next morning, as he was paying the bill, she devised a way to confess to Gerard that she had fallen in love with him at first sight. "Oh, too bad," he replied, "but I am married to a bride who is even more beautiful than you." And before the girl could react to that, he added, "I have wedded the Virgin." And thus he continued his journey to Ciorani.

Mary was his true love, his advocate, the princess of the castle, the reflection of the beauty of God. And through her he looked at other women. Writing to the Carmelite nuns at Ripacandida, he did not hesitate to say: "All of you represent and remind me of the Mother of God."

In the sanctuary of Mary the Queen, near Foggia, he felt weak with a sweet loving delirium for his "lady" and fell to the ground as if dead. The students who were accompanying him on the trip were frightened and asked, "Are you sick?" "No," said Gerard, "It's an illness I've been suffering from for a long time." Love, after all, is the only incurable illness.

"To Suffer, Abandoned by God"

Gerard's habitual expression, "I'm going to pay a visit to Jesus in prison" conceals, in its simplicity, the conviction that in the white host was hidden the crucified Christ, a victim of love for human beings. For Gerard, as for Saint Alphonsus, it was Jesus in the tabernacle who goes up to Calvary and, at the same time, the Jesus on Calvary who—after the Resurrection—makes himself present in the Eucharist in order to indicate the continuity of his self-donation. Thus the Eucharist,

the memorial of the Passion, speaks of sacrifice and of crucified love.

Day by day he felt swelling inside himself the attraction to
the cross, which he sought out with the craftiness of a lover
and received with patience from the sometimes brutal hands
of men. As a young man, full of enthusiasm, he wanted to
identify himself completely with Jesus, "divine, wounded with
love," and he asked his companions to whip him and slap him.
They made a game of it; but Gerard took it seriously, because
his heroic will pushed him to become engrossed in the bloody
sacrifice of Christ.

But now, as a religious, he wasn't content with external
sufferings. As Lent approached, he drew up a complete program of sacrifices, accentuated with phrases such as "Jesus
dies for us, and I wish to die for him." And he let himself be
swept along by his "madness," seeking every possible way to
identify with the Crucified.

He wished to experience the interior passion, and Jesus
didn't keep him waiting. While his physical condition was de-
teriorating, his spirit was refining itself for the night of the
cross. One clear sign of his interior state is the letters sent to
Mother Maria of Jesus throughout 1754. In one of them he
says:

> I have gone down in such a way that I think I no longer
> have a way out. And I think that my troubles have to
> be eternal. But I would not be worried if they were
> eternal. As long as I loved God and gave him pleasure
> in all things, that would be enough. This is my suffer-
> ing: I believe that I'm suffering, abandoned by God.
> Mother, if you don't help me, I will have more prob-
> lems. Because I find myself totally downcast and in a
> sea of confusion, almost near desperation. I think that
> for me God does not exist and that his infinite mercy
> has run dry for me. The only thing that remains over
> me is his justice! Look and see in what a miserable
> state I find myself.

Gerard was intimately united to the sufferings of Christ on the cross. He took upon himself the sins of all those whom he met on his missionary journeys and whom he managed to convert. Thus his life was ebbing away on the Calvary of his own bed, where tuberculosis consumed the poor body, already exhausted. On October 15, 1755, the feast of Saint Teresa of Ávila, he told Dr. Santorelli with a certain grace: "It seems a joke, dear doctor, that I'm dying of tuberculosis...because I asked the Lord to let me die abandoned as he was. I know that in the Congregation every charity is expended on the sick, but when someone is contagious, people take a lot of precautions."

"HERE THE WILL OF GOD IS DONE"

On the door of his room Brother Gerard placed a sign with this phrase, "Here the will of God is done, as he wishes and as long as he wishes." It was around the end of August, a few weeks before his death. Father Caione, seeing that the end was approaching, exhorted him to conform himself to God's will. Gerard answered with a smile: "Yes, Father, I imagine that I am united to the will of God and that I am confined to this bed as if I had been nailed to the very will of God. Still more, I imagine that God's will and I are one single thing."

Jesus Christ came into the world to carry out the will of the Father and reestablish relations between God and human beings, and he taught this obedience through his sacrificial self-surrender (Heb 5:8; 10:10). In this school Gerard discovered the meaning of life, what he called "my truth," that is, love of the divine will. This was a school of total self-donation, of greater sacrifice, of complete service.

His companions in the community called him "Let-me-do-it," because whenever there was an uncomfortable job or an extra assignment to do, Gerard was the first to volunteer. For many years now the Holy Spirit had been active in his life so as to shape him into a true follower of Christ, obedient to the Father. That was why he said in his personal resolutions:

"Some strive to do this or that; my only preoccupation is to do the will of God."

On September 6, 1755, when Gerard seemed to be close to death, Father Caione entered his room and said: "Your superior, Father Fiocchi, has written." And he handed him the letter, which Gerard read with great effort. Then he placed it on his chest and exclaimed: "Lord, may it be done to me according to your will." In the letter Father Fiocchi asked him "to be well and not to vomit any more blood." And so it was.

When the doctor came to visit him, Gerard told him: "I still can't die, because I have to do the will of my superior. I would like to eat some apricots." The doctor didn't know what answer to give his patient. Meanwhile the infirmarian brought some apricots from the garden and Gerard ate three of them. The doctor went off feeling worried, and the next day he came earlier than usual, certain that he would be assisting at a funeral. The room was empty but in order. He ran into Gerard walking around slowly and leaning on a cane. Obedience works miracles, thought Dr. Santorelli.

Another month went by. Now Gerard was impatient to be united with his God, and his God too was impatient to have him with him once and for all. On the night of October 15, upon hearing the *Ave Maria*, he murmured: "Six hours still to go." The next morning, in the loneliness of his last hour, he surrendered forever to the "beautiful will of God."

That night he was alone except for the brother infirmarian, who fell asleep from fatigue. He awoke with a startle when he noticed that Gerard was getting worse and was asking him for water. It was like the "I thirst" of Jesus. The brother ran to the refectory and found it locked. While he looked around for the key, he also woke up Father Buonamano to accompany him back to the sick man's bedside. The brother placed a spoon with a little water to his lips, but the dying man did not react. Father Buonamano began the prayer for the recommendation of the soul: "Depart from this world in the name of the Father and the Son and the Holy Spirit...." Gerard's thirst for love could now be quenched in the ocean of the Trinity.

CHAPTER THREE

Saint Gerard and the Popular Piety of His Time

Angelomichele de Spirito

FROM PIOUS PRACTICES
TO RELIGIOUS LIFE

There was a time when one of the main functions of a mother was the Christian education of her children whom she would teach to pray and to experience the presence of God and the saints, the angels and demons. Faith was transmitted and nourished by maternal communication, many times aided or even replaced by the care of an aunt or older sisters.

Such was the case of Gerard Majella, who had three sisters. One of these, Brigida, fourteen years older than Gerard, went to see him at Deliceto. She was already a wife and perhaps a mother. Gerard was a religious. His sister reminded Gerard about his boyhood days when he was "some seven years old, at a time when the family was very poor, left at dinnertime—perhaps so that there would be one mouth less and one mouthful more at the table—and went outside the town to a place called La Raia [unclear what this place name is. *La raia* is Italian for "skate" (the fish)—PH] and returned home with a loaf of bread in his hands." Gerard told her at their meeting at Deliceto: "Now I know that the boy who gave me the bread was Jesus; and I thought back then that Jesus was a boy like the others." Brigida jokingly suggested: "Let's go to Muro again so that we can return to the same place and you can meet that boy again." To which Gerard answered: "Now I meet him everywhere."[1]

Profound reflections, in both the theological-mystical and the historical-social sense, have been drawn from this episode. But I don't think I'm forcing or twisting the meaning if I try to read it in the key to the popular piety—the sort of popular piety that Gerard lived and with which he expressed himself.

The inclination to the sacred and the search for divinity, which used to be called "knowing, loving, and serving God," was offered to Gerard above all in his own family milieu; and it was developed in him by observing nature according to traditional models, although not without personal originality and spontaneity. The relationship with the sacred was expressed amid the people and through a natural, almost materialized, religious experience. It was characterized by sensible or fantastic elements and responded to concrete and immediate necessities that were close to the magic and superstition which often prevented a purer and clearer encounter with God. Gerard, already a religious, spoke like an angel about the "immensity of the good Lord (...) explaining with expressive examples how we live in God," in such a way that it was a pleasure to hear him.

He surely took those examples from the symbolic-religious imaginative fund that he had acquired in infancy and adolescence, formulating them in the language of the people. In his letters we often find expressions such as "with water or with wind," "to die beneath the millstone of God's will," "I sympathize with you, my sister, because you are alone, afflicted, and disconsolate," "so goes the day: one rises and another falls," "Brother Sulfuric (the devil)," "I entertain myself in the divine immensity."

Now he met God everywhere, even beneath the rocks: "If God were to remove this veil from our eyes, we would see paradise everywhere; God is there, even beneath these rocks."[2] And with all the more reason he found him within himself, as he often sang: "If you want to see God / seek him wherever you wish / and you have to return / for he is in your heart." Beyond the spectacular forms or instinctive sentiments through which the folkloric religious world finds expression, Gerard the Redemptorist—guided by the Rule and advised by his superiors—had encountered a spiritual experience that was more intimate, more sacrificial, and more pure.

This doesn't mean that before, when he was with his family and dedicated to the tailor's shop, he didn't have a deep piety full of asceticism and mystical experiences. But his experience of God shows itself fully, as a paradox of cruelty and sweetness, during the brief period of his religious life. We can recognize as characteristic of his way of life (that is, of his sanctity) expressions like: "By God, I don't love God, but what God loves"; "Take away God's will from me and you will see that nothing is left." On the door of his room, when he was on the point of dying: "Here the will of God is done, as He wishes and for as long as He wishes." That was the synthesis of his sanctity and his piety, which had already arrived at full conformity with the divine will. Piety is, after all, not a momentary calling, but life itself; or as Gerard wrote: "I have resolved to live and die inundated with faith; for faith is life, and life is faith."

GERARD'S CHILDHOOD AND YOUTH

Where did Gerard's piety come from? How had it begun and developed in him? Apart from the Holy Spirit who is the only one capable of scrutinizing the human heart, all the interpretive categories fall short when they try to explain a religious experience in terms of rational, historical, or anthropological principles. In order to try out one path of response, let us take a look at Gerard's infancy and adolescence.

From the first years of his life, San Alfonsus de Liguori went to confraternities and pious associations and had expert spiritual directors. Something like that can be said of Domenico Blasucci, a youth from the same region as Gerard and, like him, a Redemptorist. But Gerard never joined a confraternity and never had, in his life as a lay person, any advisor for his moral and religious formation. Perhaps the spontaneity and exaggeration of some of his behavior, which even his family members and fellow peasants couldn't understand, were due to the lack of clear and continuous guidance. "Spiritual orientation would arrive later, in religious life; and it would be as he wanted it, of iron. For the time being he had to experience all the phases of the progressive invasion of grace, which drew him to the strangest forms, devoid of all logic or opportunistic calculation. It was a spiritual life with no apparent method, without a schedule, always alert to the interior impulses of the Spirit, as if the earth were a needless reality and the body a husk to be cast off as soon as possible."[3]

One might say that the house, the church, and the street were the places and the memory of his religious identity, the models and masters of his devotion. Back in those days that was where the faith of the simple folk was breathed, the faith of those who were, on the whole, ignorant but nonetheless upright and "wise." There the piety of the poor—peasants, shepherds, or artisans, like their fathers before them—was learned by imitation. There, too, one could see the rare cases of "impiousness," of those about whom it is difficult to say if they behaved that way out of desperation or wickedness. In a word, the piety of the people was lived out there.

Still, we cannot simplify the situation with images of an innocent and devout peasant society. The poor were not all kindliness and tenderness. As far as morality of life goes, there are differences between persons of the same age or social class. In his apostolate among men and women, young people and old people, nobles and plebeians, Gerard was far from false generalizations that identify holiness and sin with one stage of life or with a given social group rather than with the free will of each individual. In other words, there are no special groups who have a guarantee of getting to heaven or the certainty of going to hell.

At first glance, youth seems an easy pretext for irresponsibility; at least that is how popular morality judges the issue. But Gerard had a vision of youth "with no naive illusions." To a young man who had tried to deceive a consecrated girl, he wrote: "Someone who is in a state like yours doesn't think of hell or of the infinite loss of God." And finding himself in Castelgrande in June 1753, "the greatest wonder was that he drew to God, with his sermons that were simple but full of fire, some fifteen irresponsible young men. In the end they went with him to make a good confession at Caposele. And they continued to come in a group every Saturday afternoon to make their confession on the following Sunday: they spent the night in a camp near the door of the church. The one most impressed by this was our Father Paul [Cafaro]."

One might suppose that the most surprising fact of all was that it was a group of young men. And Father Cafaro was right to say of Gerard: "Wherever he goes, an earthquake follows."

Gerard participated enthusiastically in popular pilgrimages. It's possible that as a very young boy he went with his mother to visit the shrine at Materdomini. Along with Redemptorist students he went on the nine-day procession to the sanctuary of Monte Sant'Angelo in Apulia, where "he suffered greatly, as much as from the discomforts of the long trip as from the bloody cough that he got." In addition, he made other pilgrimages on his own and spent whole nights in church, far from all sounds, in order to dedicate himself to "conversing with God."

As a young man in Muro Lucano, Gerard "began to frequent a chapel on the outskirts of the town. He went there as if he were going to a place of holy retirement. There he busied himself for three or four days without returning to sleep in his house, and spent all the time in prayer and conversation with God. The little sleep that he allowed himself he took while lying on the bare ground." "Other times he took from home a little bread and a bottle of wine and remained in the chapel for a number of days." The detail about the bottle of wine is interesting, with its touch of feasting and serene joy. That way he could "interrupt" the daily misery of his family. After his father died, the poverty of the house got so bad that Gerard sometimes "had to flee the town because he had nothing with which to pay [the taxes]."

THE WARMTH OF HOME

To find the sources of Gerard's piety we have to go back to his parents. We know extremely little about his father, Domenico, a taciturn, hardworking man, who left him an orphan when he was barely a boy. We likewise know little about his mother: a pious, obliging woman, from whom Gerard inherited his sensitive soul. This can be deduced from the intensity with which he loved the Virgin, whom he called "Mamma Maria," as well as from the purity of heart and intention with which he viewed and treated other women, whether young or old, ugly or pretty, healthy or sick, secular or religious.

His freedom and spontaneity in dealing with the opposite sex was notable, so much so that it attracted the attention of his conversation partners. It was the complete opposite of the "misogyny" that is customarily attributed to the saints, including Saint Alphonsus. The latter's servant, Alessio Pollio, used to say that, "Seeing a woman bothered him so much that when he ran into my ten-year-old daughter at the bishop's house, Monsignor told me: Alessio, I don't want you to bring her back." Another witness at the canonization trial said that "Alphonsus didn't let women, not even illustrious matrons, kiss his hands. He never spoke alone with a woman without having another person along; nor did he make eye-contact, but looked to the side and continually took his glasses off."

By contrast, Gerard could write to a young nun: "Don't be surprised that I write to you with such affection, because we are in truth brother and sister in the Lord; and we always have to love each other *purely* in God." The adverb "purely," underlined by Gerard himself, speaks to the virtue of prudence, one of the most difficult to practice.

It was said of Domenico Blasucci, whose father died when he was three, that "he never looked his mother in the face and much less his six sisters or other women." A companion of his relates that "returning one day from a walk, he inadvertently stumbled over the silhouette of a woman and immediately cried out two or three times: "Jesus and Mary!" as if to drive off the dangerous fantasm."[4] Gerard, who was the same age as Domenico, who came from the same region and social class, had resolved: "As often as I see a woman I will honor the Virgin with a Hail Mary." This was not praying to avoid temptations, but to praise God through Mary.

We have no direct knowledge of the memories that Gerard had of his mother. She died on April 10, 1752, while Gerard was making his second novitiate in Deliceto. Six days later he wrote, in deep affliction, to a nun at Ripacandida: "God's will wants me to go forward with water and with wind; it points out this path to me, and so I love it." There is no mention here of his mother's death, because deep sorrows lose meaning when one tries to explain them to others.

Saint Alphonsus said: "During my childhood the good that I did and the evil I avoided were both owing to my mother." We don't know if Gerard said anything like that, but we can't help thinking that he remembered the sufferings of Mamma Benedicta for this son who "grew in years and also in the desire of becoming a saint," and whom the others, Caione tells us, "considered a 'lunatic' because of his natural simplicity and spontaneous heart. For this reason, they made fun of him, not only in words, but they went so far as to strike him and mistreat him without measure (...); and he gave no sign of resentment, but took it all in jest, because of his natural inclination for sufferings and the cross."

We don't know how his mother reacted to seeing her son tied up and dragged all the way down the street. Nor when she saw him hanging from a cross, in the Passion drama presented in the cathedral; or her response to Redemptorist missions in Muro, when Gerard insisted on going away with the missionaries. "His relatives knew this and locked him in a room. But he found a way to get out; he wrote a note about his destination, knotted sheets, and let himself down through the window."

Some years later, Gerard wrote to a woman novice: "We have all been tried in our vocation; and God tests us so as to see our fidelity." One would have to think of the filial love of Gerard and the sustained struggle to choose between dedicating himself totally to God or waiting still more years by the side of his old mother. This must have been the strongest temptation of his religious vocation, because Gerard had clear ideas and definite feelings about the attractions of the world and about himself. In his account of conscience (which Gerard called his "examination of the hidden interior"), he declares: "I trust and hope in God alone. I have never trusted in myself and I never will, because I know my wretchedness well; if it were not so, I would have lost my head." He was quite different from the "town fool," as some of his fellow peasants thought him or as some pseudo-scholar might consider him today. To his mother Gerard was never a madman, to be sure, nor was he one to the patients in the Incurables Hospital in Naples, to whom Gerard "used to bring some candy or food" in order to "encourage them to support cheerfully the cross that the Lord sent them, to offer up to God the hardships imposed upon them by the shift chief."

It's impossible to know fully how and to what extent a son loves his mother or inherits her physical or spiritual traits. But the popularity of Gerard among families during his lifetime, and the special protection he afforded mothers and boys has to be connected, in a subtle but consistent fashion, with this experience of maternal and familial affection. Various episodes in his life join in this perspective of generous availability to families, whether his spontaneous simplicity in the face of the mystery of life or his natural sense of sacrality in the face of motherhood and infancy. These are very particular characteristics of peasant culture and piety—which is not to ignore the fact that there were also abuses and violence.

It was the summer of 1754; Gerard was about to be set free from the "horrible imposture," that is, the accusation that he had "sinned with Signorina Nicoletta Capucci, an honest and pious young woman from Lacedonia." His fellow townsman and friend Alessandro Piccolo, who had married for a second time, went to visit him at Materdomini. Gerard told him: "Live in contentment and with a good heart with your wife. She is forty days pregnant and will give birth to a boy." All of which proved true. And "master Alessandro esteemed Gerard so greatly that he wished to give the boy that same name even before he was born. The most amazing thing was that every time the father placed his hand over the belly of his wife and said 'Gerard, Gerard,' he felt the baby move within the womb of his mother and pound at the place of his hand."

BELONGING TO A PEOPLE WHO PRAY

It's not possible to have exhaustive knowledge of the mechanisms for transmitting qualities from parents to children, any more than we can readily see the stages in the acquisition of the culture of belonging, in the anthropological sense. We can only capture something, and obliquely, through the history of popular piety in southern Italy. In recent years there has been a sharp increase in investigations and interpretations of this area.

Giuseppe De Luca says that in Basilicata, Gerard's region, "people went very early to church, when the dawn was still no more than something sensed by the roosters. They walked in silence, accompanied by the grandmother, to the church of Santa Maria. And the parish priest, before Mass, read the meditations of Saint Alphonsus by the faint light of a candle. The women, wrapped in their black shawls, knelt down in the middle of the church, while the men were on the side of the presbytery. And we, the children, sometimes were with the women and sometimes with the men, awake—but the way one is awake during the night. And we all listened to those words, even the oldest in the group, who knew them practically by heart (...). And again, in the afternoon, at the hour of the *Ave Maria*, the bell of the same church began once more to fill the humble village with its ringing; these are sounds that I remember and recognize from far off with so much emotion. And then again, on the way back from church, the procession of mothers and grandmothers, of boys and old men. But not the men: they stayed in the fields to work till late at night. You couldn't miss, not for one day of the year, the visit to the Blessed sacrament."[5]

This was going on at the end of the nineteenth century, but it was also the scene two hundred and more years ago in the days of Gerard. Those were the pious practices of everyday life, the "devout life" of Christian people. In the year when Saint Alphonsus was publishing his *Visits to the Blessed Sacrament,* Gerard "was passing hours in church in front of the tabernacle." When Alphonsus edited *The Glories of Mary,* Gerard was writing: "I choose the Holy Spirit as my only consoler and protector in all things....And you, my only joy, Immaculate Virgin Mary, you will be my second protectress and consolatrix." When he heard Father Caione read the *Counsels on Religious Vocations,* Gerard, who was sick in Pagani, remained in a state of divine rapture for half an hour. In 1755 Gerard died; that same year saw the publication of Alphonsus's *Conformity to the Will of God,* which was for Gerard "the most heroic virtue; he spoke divinely about it, he wrote admirably, and he practiced it to perfection."

The writings of Gerard suggest that he drank from these works of Alphonsus for his own spirituality and for that of others. He also read other authors because Gerard liked to read. In the afternoon, when his confreres were taking their siestas, he "spent those times in prayer or in reading holy books." And during his travels he carried a packet of books, many of them on the Passion of Christ, which he later gave to priests or to lay people. His readings began and ended with the Passion. The first book that he read, as a young lad, was *The Sorrowful Year,* the work of the Capuchin missionary Antonio da Olivadi; and the last, a few months before he died, was *The Life and Virtues of the Servant of God: Sister Maria Crocifissa della Concezione* by Geronimo Turani.[6]

THE MADNESS OF THE CROSS

O ne cannot talk about popular piety, especially in the past, without stressing the place occupied in it by the cross of Christ and the "insanity of his love," with its salvific suffering, neither sadistic nor fanatical, but intense and anguished. Only in that way can one understand the spirituality of Gerard, which was constantly marked by the weight of the cross. "Now I do not walk nor move, because I am on the cross and saddened by unspeakable sufferings. The lance has been lost that should have brought my death. It is my gallows. I obey in order to find it, to have life in suffering....This is the will of my heavenly Redeemer: to be nailed on this bitter cross."

In the monotony of the daily occupations of a precarious life, men and women were more given to the marvelous and the monstrous than they are now. It was a culture of "certain and essential" values where the capacity for love and suffering was more widely diffused. In this context, Gerard and many other men and women in love with God went to extremes in imitating the suffering Christ that our modern sensibility fails to understand.

One example is the penitential rites, more specifically the collective flagellation to the point of blood, which the faithful practiced almost everywhere. This can be seen even today in Guardia Sanframondi, a little town in southern Italy, on the occasion of the feast of the Assumption. (....) It is an expression of worship, propitiation, and supplication, that until recently was a central element in religious experience, particularly in the heyday of popular missions.[7] It is a vivid representation of the human being as a creature, nailed to his time and to his space, who visualizes suffering with Christ and at the same time expresses, amid tears, groans, and blood, the hope for a new heaven and a new earth.

All these objects, symbols, gestures, and uses of social and religious experience have to be contextualized if we are to understand them. If we are impressed today by the long prayers of the pious men and women of the past, we must not forget that, until recently, as many as five hours of prayer were held every day in novitiates—just about the same amount of time that many people today spend in front of the television. If we are frightened by the skeletons that Gerard kept in his room at Deliceto, we need to remember that in the past the relation between the living and the dead was much more intense and frequent. Death was "domesticated" in the bones and skeletons that could be seen in the churches and cemeteries, as well as in the pictures of the saints and even on the cups that people drank from.

POPULAR PIETY AND THE OFFICIAL LITURGY

To say popular piety is practically the same as saying Marian piety. And it would seem easy to recognize and interpret it. But not all authors succeed in capturing its deeper dimensions. One instance of this is Carlo Levi in his well-known book, *Christ Stopped at Eboli*, which looks at the religious life of the poor more through the lens of literature than of history.

Recalling his stay in Lucania, Levi writes that the Black Virgin of Viggiano "is neither good nor bad for the peasants; she is much more. She dries up the crops and lets them die, or nourishes and protects them; she must be adored [sic]." In the local feast-day processions, "between the grain and the animals, amid the roar of trumpets and rockets, it is not the merciful Mother of God who is being venerated, but a subterranean deity, black with the dark color of the entrails of the earth, an infernal goddess of the harvest...the fierce, unpitying, and obscure archaic divinity of the earth." [8]

Apart from the fact that Levi borrowed these reflections from a text written a century before, [9] it's not hard to discover that this is the vision, or rather the erudite interpretation, of a doctor from the north and does not reflect the complex reality of southern peasant class that Gerard belonged to. It was precisely in one of these processions "in honor and for the love of" the Virgin that Gerard placed a symbolic ring on the finger of the statue. From then on, when he was asked why he didn't get married, he always answered: "I have wedded the Virgin."

Gerard received Marian devotion with his mother's milk, and in this "soil" his spirituality sent down roots and sent forth branches till his dying day. In the final delirious vision of his life, he pointed and said to Brother Andrea: "Look, look how many scapulars there are in the room." We don't know the exact meaning of this phrase, says Caione, but we do know that Gerard was greatly devoted to the Virgin of Mount Carmel and had greatly promoted this devotion.

It will be said that this is a popular devotion, and it certainly is. In the eighteenth century Tiepolo painted the Virgin of Mount Carmel; Pope Benedict XIII extended the feast of Our Lady of Mount Carmel to the whole Church in 1726, and in 1752 Gerard made his religious profession on July 16, which in that year coincided with the feast of the Most Holy Redeemer.

Some experts in pastoral theology or historical anthropology describe popular piety as an inferior or degraded state of faith when in reality it's a matter of expressing the relations with the Transcendent in a different way. It might seem that popular piety is somewhat deficient and can find its legitimization only in the liturgy of the Church and in the official cult. But that argument forgets that liturgy, too, is the result of the influence of theological currents on a given epoch and environment. In other words, liturgy, too, is a cultural product.

What is meant by popular piety? There are two usual definitions: religious practices, insofar as they differ from the official cult and are capable of being subdivided into three categories: proposed, proscribed, and tolerated; or else it is the piety of the people understood in socioeconomic terms, insofar as it differs from the culturally more advanced elite. Each of these definitions is matched by a different analysis in the biography of the saint. In any event, it is the historical vision that can take a more objective view of the phenomenon, precisely because history doesn't follow our "logic" and cannot be locked into a priori schemes.

The popular piety of southern Italy—and of Gerard Majella—is characterized by "a profound sense of transcendence, unlimited confidence in a provident God, perception of the divine by way of the heart, experience of the mystery of the cross in all its drama and salvific power, filial attachment to the Virgin, and a great sense of the intercession of the saints."[10] This popular religiosity, with its "symbols and naturalness" can be converted into the "poor people's alternative to the liturgy." But, like any other experience of faith, without hearing the Gospel it "can be reduced to a question without an answer, the cross without the resurrection, a gesture with no content, a memory of emotions and solidarity without communion."

MAGIC AND THE MARVELOUS IN A WORLD OF SURVIVAL

A propos of a nun who had died, Gerard wrote to the Carmelite sisters at Ripacandida: "In my unworthy fashion, I have taken communion for eight days for her soul. I wish to do the same for all of you that you may get to heaven. So tell all of those who are still alive to pray to God for me, and let them also take communion for eight days, so that I may pass to a [glorious] eternity." Seven months before he died, upon sending a list of indulgences to the Redemptoristine nuns at Foggia, he told them: "Pray to the Lord for me and get me all the indulgences you can to intercede for my soul after my death, along with eight days of communion on the part of all the sisters."

When he went to Castelgrande to persuade the parents of a young man murdered in a quarrel to pardon his killer, he told them: "Your son is in purgatory on account of your obstinacy. If you wish him to get out, reestablish peace [by pardoning] and have five Masses celebrated for him." He said something similar to a young woman of Lacedonia who was disconsolate over the death of her mother: "Courage, she is in purgatory. Make forty communions for her soul and she will go to paradise."[11]

Such practices, which were widespread in the eighteenth century and later, provide some theologians with the opportunity for showing how superstition crept into participation in the liturgy and sacraments. Believing that a specific quantity of Masses could free a soul from purgatory moved people to become more interested in numbers than in personal, sincerely convinced participation in the celebration. That, however, was not the spirit of Gerard. A well-informed and unbiased reader will discover clear expressions of piety in all this, above and beyond the mnemonic technique and ordering role of numbers. If the numerical combination were considered efficacious in itself, that would be magic. Here we have rather the true faith of the devout person in the efficacy of the sacrifice of Christ and in the communion of the saints. It is also a matter of the so-called "Gregorian masses," which were promoted for centuries by the official Church. If anyone was promoting this devotion with its fixed and uninterrupted number of Masses, it was the teaching and learning Church, the clergy and lay people, theologians and liturgists, in a word the "whole people of God." One has to ask: must such a practice be considered superstitious, magical-religious, popular piety, or simply religious piety?

There is no denying that there are elements of superstition and magic in popular Italian piety, just as there are in other parts of the world, above all when one looks at the social and economic history of southern Italy.[12] In the symbolic and religious universe of the peasants from this region, strengthened by historical memory and the "collective imagination," and marked for centuries by an economy of survival, miracles have an important place and a special function. The same must be said about magic or rather the magical mentality. For this reason the saintliness of the "men of God" best known and loved in the South, from whom people expect prodigies—including Gerard—has an influence on the grieving and disconsolate vi-

sion of existence. Such holiness does not elude the human framework in a person who is maturing nor the magical-folkloric
attitude that revolves around it....Gerard would take it upon
himself to evangelize this reality.

There is an interesting episode concerning a young man
searching for a treasure in the forests of Deliceto. The wide
diffusion of tales about treasures (Plutonic legends), so typical
of the southern regions of Italy, marvelously colored the in-
genuous infantile world and awakened new illusions in the
monotonous continuity of the adults. The young man was
dazzled by the appearance of Gerard "with his cape and wide
hat," and above all by the thought that the conditions had
been met to make his lucky find. The legends about treasures
had a precise ritual, and among the important requirements
was the presence of a curate or monk. Gerard went along with
the game...and wound up converting the young man, speaking to him about the treasure that is Christ crucified.

In that context of poverty and "psychological misery," we
can also understand the story of the man who "lost the use of
language after marriage": one day Gerard entered his house
and the people there explained to him that "someone had cast
this spell by black magic." To which the saint replied, "What
spell! I will make him talk." He turned to the mute and asked
him to speak in the name of God. And the man, Caione concludes, "began to speak, as he does to this day, because he is
still alive."

CONCLUSION

In summary, certain tones, certain aspects of Gerard's spirituality put in an appearance from the first years of his life:
naive and passionate traits, sweet and strong, like the popular
piety with which he was imbued, but without swerving aside,
that is, without transforming it into a refuge, when it ought to
be a stimulus for human and Christian growth.

At the time, the highways of Europe were plagued with

drifters, crazies, troublemakers, beggars, pilgrims, gypsies, and adventurers. Gerard had no qualms about being mistaken for one of them. He went about the roads like a good madman and good poor man.[13]

In the imitation of Christ he could not do as Saint Francis or as Saint Alphonsus had done, that is to pass from being rich to being poor. From his first to his last breath, Gerard was always poor. That is why he imitated Christ in madness, the madness of the cross, which is not mental disturbance, but perhaps "love's ultimate port."

CHAPTER FOUR

The Penitential Piety
of Gerard Majella

Gabriele De Rosa

SANCTITY, PENANCE, AND EVERYDAY LIFE

The privileged saints of southern Italy, the best known and most loved, are wounded saints, examples of physical mortification, completely and totally surrendered to adoration and prayer. In general, these are saints who restore health and who have a clear sense of belonging to a specific geographic area. [...]

In the southern Italian saint, even in the modern era, piety and prayer were born from the humiliation of the body, considered almost as an obstacle for lifting oneself up to God. That was the teaching of the Desert Fathers, whose books were found everywhere in the religious houses of Calabria and Lucania. The era of penance went back much further than the history of the self-flagellating confraternities and continued to endure in southern Italy when it had already disappeared in the north. In the Naples of Saint Alphonsus, a curate named Genovesi was concerned that there should be an educated clergy who would teach the rural plebeians and be an integral part of social life. At this same time, the popular saint was still living like a medieval monk, in a constant tension against the risk not only of temptations, but of the comforts and little weaknesses of his body. Nevertheless, this saint with his miracles did not represent a history apart. His life was not met with outside of the daily life of the local populations, nor was it an evasion or a folkloric appendage; he formed an integral part of the social structure, which he penetrated with himself and manifested in his own way.

The penitential piety of the old religious structure was intimately mixed up with the social and cultural life of the peasants in southern Italy, including the period from the seventeenth through the nineteenth century. There was no separation between, on the one hand, the economy with its price curve, its markets, and its taxes, the towns with their house and parish registers, the fiefs, the properties, and monasteries, and, on the other side, piety with its saints, its devotions, and even its superstitions, placed there as an afterthought, as a sort of curiosity for ethnologists and sociologists. All this moved conjointly in the life of the peasant and the life of the merchant. It was the same person who went to the notary to deliver a written promise to build a chapel if the Virgin drove off a spell afflicting him, or begged the saint to kill the mice that had invaded his field. The same person appropriated the lands of the episcopal curia and then made a pilgrimage to a mountain shrine. Holiness belonged to the same historical context in which a person moves that way, forms part of his culture, lives within his day-to-day world, inspires his opinions, reveals his deepest and most unconscious aspirations.

There is, nonetheless, an area in southern Italy where this interdependence between local culture and sanctity is particularly evident: Muro Lucano. It is a region greatly loved by the Redemptorists and rich in the names of the venerables and blesseds who were active there. The most important saint from this zone is Gerard Majella; but before him there were other religious who seem to have opened a path for his harsh asceticism: Fra Domenico Girardelli, who became a Franciscan in Muro, and Fra Bonaventura of Potenza, a Conventual in Ravello. [...]

THE SAINT AND THE IDEAL OF SAINTHOOD

Despite the fact that he never left his stamping ground, Gerard Majella stirred up a devotion that was very great and sweeping, and that soon overflowed the frontiers of his homeland. His name, even during his lifetime, spread over the area that stretches from Muro Lucano to Caposele, Conza, Lacedonia, across into the region of Foggia and Bari. After his death, his memory extended all through the Salerno region and around the end of the nineteenth century it crossed the Atlantic with the emigrants: peasants, workers, and priests.

At first glance, it would seem that one has to exclude in Gerard any relation to the ascetical tradition of the Desert Fathers. There is no evidence of a direct connection; and yet they clearly share the same mental wavelength, a special approach to practicing penance.[1] That is because the form of asceticism that eventually prevailed in southern Italy was that of heroic, superhuman virtues.

We don't have any writings by Gerard that can help us to understand the birth of his ascetical vocation. He was practically illiterate, never having studied. He entered the Congregation as a coadjutor; his letters are linguistically rustic, full of dialect, although expressive of a strong religious temperament. "This is the will of my heavenly Redeemer, to be nailed to this bitter cross, with head bent."[2] Nevertheless, the [penitential] culture was in the very environment in which he lived; it could be seen in the names of the places and the monasteries, which repeated the Greek and Byzantine traditions. He breathed in the constant example of a severe asceticism, brought by the monks to people accustomed to calculate life more by the movement of the stars than by the swing of prices. He found himself in the vigilant presence of so many convents and shrines that, along with the pilgrimages to them, constituted the only sign of social mobility in the demographic history of southern Italy.

Whom did Gerard listen to when he was a boy? What were his relations? Here we are not so much interested in the life of the saint as in his contact with the devout and, in general, with the people of Basilicata. We would like to try to grasp how he was a saint for the townsfolk of Murano, for the peasants of the Sele River valley, for the inhabitants of Apulia; that is, we would like to know what the devout asked of him, and if his piety was like that of the bishops and the Tridentine

Church; and if one may not speak of a comparison or parallel between the popular piety that grew up the figure of Gerard and the sort that might be called the official religion of the Church.

How can we reconstruct the popular collective feelings that correspond or make reference to the sainthood of Gerard? To see more clearly into the history of this relationship we have referred to the minutes of the canonization trial of Gerard Majella. The minutes, although they were collected ninety years after his death, and hence were based on indirect testimony (that is, from persons who didn't know the saint personally), still evoke the voices of those who knew him, the echo of what they told their relatives and friends. There is a unanimous will in these testimonies, just as in the trials of Fra Domenico of Muro and of Bonaventura of Potenza, in the sense that Gerard absolutely had to be a saint because that was the conviction of the majority. Those who bore witness were above all peasants, laborers, notaries, doctors, landowners. There were also friars, priests, and monks, but they don't make up the majority.

Among those who testified in the trial were Michele (a priest), Raffaele (a lawyer), Giuseppe Santorelli (a doctor), all of them grandsons of Nicola Santorelli, who was the physician to the Redemptorist community of Caposele and assisted Gerard on his deathbed. The name of Nicola appears very often in the biography of the saint as a "rich source of information." Tannoia himself, in his monumental biography of Alphonsus, frequently resorted to him. Thanks to the prestige and fame enjoyed by this doctor, the testimony of his grandchildren wound up constituting the most abundant and interesting part of the trial.

The documentation began in Conza and Muro.[3] The judges wanted to find out if the witnesses had been "coached or catechized" by the Redemptorist missionaries, who were very much interested in seeing their confrere canonized. This was not least of all because of the fame that would then redound to the shrine of Materdomini, where the saint had worked and died. Their caution was unnecessary. The depositions were faithful to the original milieu, to the popular feelings that had made Gerard, by the nineteenth century, the best-known and most invoked saint in southern Italy.

SAINT OF BREAD AND EARTH

Gerard Majella is the saint of the inland regions, which in his time were still afflicted by endemic poverty. He was the saint of a place where everyday life was miserable. He was active in areas of extreme poverty, where the inhabitants very often had more trust in miracles than in their individual capacities and recourses. He was the saint most called upon when people were hungry or sick or doing penance, the saint of the peasants and workers. He protected women in labor and animals as well.[4]

The miracle with which the holy life of Gerard begins makes reference to a "little white loaf," which was offered to him by the Child Jesus, who came down from the arms of the Virgin to "play with him." Gerard was just a little boy. One morning he left Muro, covered the two kilometers of road to get to the little church of the Virgin on the other side of the stream, called Our Lady of Capodigiano, which is still open today for the devotion of the faithful.

But in those days it must not have been easy to reach, judging from the testimony at Gerard's canonization trial that the road was "extremely rough and uncomfortable." After their games, the Boy Jesus gave him a loaf of white bread, which he brought to his mother. "She was surprised," we read at many points of the trial, "by the whiteness of the bread, because it was rare in that town." All the witnesses insist on the exceptional quality of the bread. The mystical significance of the offering of bread is evident, but its whiteness is also a material fact, which shows how rare white bread was in Muro Lucano. In the oldest account of this miracle, the one left by the Redemptorist Gaspare Caione a few years after Gerard's death, there is no mention of the whiteness of the bread nor of the little church of Capodigiano nor of the Boy Jesus.

Caione writes: "At the age of seven, when the family was very poor, he left the house around the hour of breakfast and went to place outside the town called 'Over La Raia,' and afterwards returned with a loaf of bread in his hands. When his mother asked him who had given him the bread, [he answered] that he had gotten it from a certain boy. And so it continued for a long time. [Years] later his sister Brigitta went to visit him at Deliceto, when he was already in the Congregation, and he told her: 'Now I know that the boy who gave me the bread was Jesus, and I thought that it was a boy like me.'"[5]

We are not interested in verifying the accuracy of this or that version of the facts, since we are not writing the biography of the saint. We are interested in the real meanings that the people gave to the miracles of the saint, the sense that they attributed to them, how they transform and enrich the reports of tradition and the role that they assign to sanctity.

The saint is represented, more often than not, distributing bread or grain to the poor. In many ways, the canonization trial is an interminable chronicle of loaves of bread distributed at the doors of Redemptorist houses, of storehouses miraculously full of grain, of promises of good harvests in the future. And when the saint went into ecstasy (which happened often enough), in the milieu around him, it is easy to catch a glimpse of people begging for bread or flour.[6] Gerard's miracles were never gratuitous; as unusual as they may appear, they were always useful and correspond to requests from the people.

The witnesses have passed down to us the image of a saint whose religion was lived in close connection with the earth and the mentality of the peasants. These people, the trial transcripts make clear, transform the words of the saint into miracles and imagine the saint's extraordinary qualities with a fully material corporeality.

Staying with the series of bread miracles, we read that one time in Materdomini the distribution of bread to the poor had ended, when Gerard was told that a "poor gentlemen" remained without bread. Since the bread had run out, Gerard "went up to the convent and shortly afterwards they saw him return and give the poor man a large round loaf of bread, which he pulled out from his chest still steaming. Since at that moment the community's oven wasn't functioning nor was bread being made in the house, everyone considered it a prodigious deed."[7]

There is also talk of grain. Gerard distributed it to the poor, without regard for the needs of his fellow friars. When the rector protested, Gerard answered by invoking divine Providence, which filled the larder anew to meet the needs of the community.[8] Evidently the zone in which Gerard worked was rather monotonous, limited to the cultivation of only a few products, especially grain, on which the fate of the peasants absolutely depended.

A similar miracle is told of a certain Fra Antonio of Cosimo, who had first been a Redemptorist and then became a Benedictine. In Ferrandina a woman named Donna Lucrezia, a landowner, found it impossible to give Gerard the alms of grain because of the poor harvest. This was, then, a year of want. Lucrezia showed the saint "some three measures of flour, apart from which she had nothing else to sustain her family. Despite that, Gerard told her that if in other years she had given half a measure as alms, this time she had to give the whole measure of flour, because the Virgin would see to her needs." Gerard took the whole measure and "hundreds of workers" ate from it. The remaining flour was enough for Lucrezia and her people, until the next harvest, just as Gerard had predicted.

Here the miracle is different: Gerard doesn't fill the larder, he makes a deal with Lucrezia, who has only a little flour, but enough to feed a large group of workers. Lucrezia believes the words of the saint, in his "prophecy," as the trial says; and everything is resolved in a kindly agreement, based on mutual trust and on the legitimate expectation of a good harvest.

It is obvious that these miracles became more pronounced in periods of scarcity. In the trial we read that the excess of charity toward the poor happened in the "year that was so hard, I believe it was '53."[9] But there is a scarcity that is endemic, that can occur at any moment: a frost is enough, a more or less serious dry spell, the invasion of mice in the crops. Thus it was difficult to stockpile for a future critical year. In the miracle of Donna Lucrezia, we are evidently looking at a situation of scarcity, which Lucrezia fears and tells Gerard about.

We also know that supplies of grain fell short because the merchants of Barletta were hoarding it. All the protests by the peasants and the authorities were futile: "Everyone has to be free in the use of his own things" was the answer from the Naples liberals. In the lands traversed by Gerard, grain was cheap and there was also a great deal of speculation on the part of the merchants. This "monopolist practice continued throughout the century, beyond the crisis of 1764 and the thousands of deaths that year."[10]

PROTECTOR OF THE CROPS

There is another earth-related miracle in the account of Fra Antonio of Tricarico. The site was no longer Basilicata but Apulia. Gerard headed to the coastal towns of Bari to receive the first fruits of cotton, and he passed through Corato. The trial transcript relates:

"As the servant of God was passing through some fields sown with crops, a field worker from that same town came forward and told him: 'Father, the rats are ruining my fields; put a curse on them.' Gerard asked, 'Do you want them to die or to go somewhere else?' The poor peasant replied, 'They will do harm elsewhere; it's better for them to die.' And Gerard raised his right hand toward those fields and made the sign of the cross. No sooner had he done that than one could see an immense number of dead rats on the surface of the ground, lying belly upwards. The peasant thought he had met a simple priest, so that, at first, he remained astonished and then thought to walk ahead of the servant of God on the road to Corato, shouting as he did so to everyone he met that a saint was coming. Thus he roused the entire town, as he told the marvelous event that had occurred."[11]

This account, too, is revealing. We know that rats were one of the most dreaded plagues of southern farming, an "old terror of the peasants."[12] Wherever the rats appeared in large quantities, whole harvests of grain and barley were wiped out. Gerard performs the miracle by making a sign of the cross over the land. The peasant was expecting "a simple priest," but discovered a saint who freed him from his anxiety over the nightmare of the rats.

Once again we are in the domain of "lived religion," that is, of the religious experience that is a part of the day-to-day history of the people, which is embodied in the repeated events of the "hard life" of the country, a life of poverty, hunger, and plagues.

Let us pause for a moment to look over the miracle of the rats. The struggle of the peasants against these animals goes back to time immemorial. Everyone knows the story of the Pied Piper of Hamelin. Rats were carriers of the plague and formed part of the fantasy of medieval horrors. This miracle by Gerard in Corato belongs to the pre-bourgeois history of the land, when the peasant struggled for vital needs and was bound to the soil. Over the paths of the eternal vagabondage, religious or otherwise, of monks, devotees, and scoundrels, the miracle of the rats could be repeated in the most distant and distinct places, and could even arise as the result of the same mental automatism. In depressed economies, always on the edge of survival and with no system of incentives, the link between scarcity, misery, and plagues allowed only one freedom, the same everywhere: the freedom of the miracle, which broke the web of condemnation, even if only for one day.

Gerard wasn't the sort of saint who does nothing but stand in adoration before God. He himself was integrated into this history of sacred wandering, with its roots in the medieval fears that continued to be present in southern Italy all through the eighteenth century. Gerard didn't wait in the convent for people to come ask him for a miracle. He was the pilgrim who crossed the fields, met the peasants, spoke to the workers in his and their coarse rustic dialect. And in his traipsing around he, too, ran into problems. He was an ascetic doing penance—in Apulia, which is hot and dry. The landlords were no friends of the saint and denied him water.[13]

DIFFERENT CLASSES OF THE DEVOUT

The peasants, day laborers, and workers spoke of Brother Gerard and his miracles when they went through the fields, during their work, and in the streets of the town. They did not write, but they remembered. Memories of Gerard remained confined to oral tradition, because peasants can't read.[14] In the rural regions of the ancient Kingdom of Naples where Gerard lived, he continues to be the saint invoked for every sort of ailment. Quite often, the account of his miracles concludes with a prayer calling on him "for particular and general necessities."[15]

Recourse to the saint, naturally, is not a fixed ritual nor is it always organized. The language used is spontaneous, confidential, dialectal. As with the processions, there is discussion over who goes first, despite the sacred character of the ceremony; and there can be conflict or harsh words if the miracle is slow in coming.[16]

The behavior of the middle class and the nobility toward the saint was very diverse. We are speaking of behavior, that is, of atmosphere, of ways of acting, of customs. The saint was received and put up in the house. When word got around of his presence in the villages, many priests and nobles came to visit him. Miracles also occurred among the well-to-do class, which certainly increased the family's prestige in the eyes of people.

Gerard was invoked for women in labor, which is understandable, given the high mortality rates for newborns and mothers. Father Angelo de Rogatis testified as follows in the trial: "Not just the town of Caposele, but all the nearby towns and even the distant ones have great devotion to this servant of God; and these are good and religious people. This devotion is widespread among everyone and consists especially in having recourse to his powerful intercession before God in time of need and particularly in serious illnesses and difficult births."[17]

The cult of the saint's image was very widespread in all the social milieus. A doctor from Calitri recalled that in the exercise of his profession he had seen "all the sick persons invoke the help of Gerard," whose picture was kept "devoutly in every family." Still more, he added, "I have seen not only a great faith in Brother Gerard on the part of the women in labor, but also a special protection supplied to them by the servant of God."[18]

The prints of the saint were widely distributed. They were considered to have miraculous powers, even for animals. The already quoted Michele Santorelli tells of a miracle obtained by a copperworker in Sanseverino, who had a "seriously ill" horse. The man placed a little picture of Gerard in its ear, and "the horse rose immediately, as if it had never been sick."[19]

Notaries, doctors, and lawyers describe the miracles of the saint without the least excitement. The learning of a lawyer or doctor in the mid-eighteenth century in the deep south of Italy was not at odds with expectations and beliefs in miracles and sainthood. Pietro Falcone, a doctor from Grassano, went so far as to say: "I no longer practice because Brother Gerard does it for me; there is no sick person or woman in labor who does not find relief or get prodigiously better when I give him or her the image of the saint."[20] Religion, when it is lived up to the point of sacrificing reason, wipes out, so to speak, the social roles: everything moves in the climate of the exceptional accepted as the general norm, in such a way that the prodigy becomes a fully integral part of everyday life.

If we have the voice of nobles and priests in the trial, there is still something missing: the voice of the bishop, especially that of Angelo Anzani. It would have been interesting to know what the bishop of Campagna thought about Gerard Majella and his miracles. Anzani certainly was in the convent at Materdomini. He was a bishop of ascetical temper, a man of vigorous and rigorous piety, an enemy of magical-religious syncretism. The few letters of his that have been preserved don't say much, apart from the fact that several pages seem to be missing.

Even so, wouldn't it be possible to glimpse a contrast between a popular piety, verified by a collective mental consensus, alien to all profane and modern science, and, on the other hand, an institutional religion, severe and anti-magical, concentrated in the theology of sin, supported by a purified kind of prayer, contrary to the excessive cult of images, to the materialization of the sacred? There is no doubt that the first kind was more consoling, more earthly, more anthropologically adapted to the simple people, with their roots in the traditions of the rural environment.

Not that Gerard didn't have any contact with bishops. We are told than when he was young, he was in the service of Monsignor Claudio Albini, the bishop of Lacedonia. But which elements accent the texts and the legend of this period in the life of the saint? The tremendous obedience and humility of Gerard, who had to put up with an "angry and impatient"[21] bishop who mistreated him. In other words, a bishop is an authority, like the superior of the Redemptorist community, an authority to whom one owes obedience, whatever the cost and under whatever circumstances.

OBEDIENCE AND MORTIFICATION

Obedience is the fundamental and most notable characteristic cited by the witnesses and in the biography of Gerard. Total obedience, with no reservations, is the most complete renunciation of rationality, that is, obedience in the literal sense, even when the order is only a hint. The story about the oven in Caposele was the example most frequently brought up at the trial. The rector, in a moment of impatience, had turned to Gerard, telling him literally, "Hey, stupid, go stuff yourself in the oven!" which would sound nowadays like, "Oh, go to hell!" But Gerard actually did put himself in the [unheated] oven, where he stayed till they found him there, and made him get out.[22] Relations with his superiors, then, were relations of submission, reasonable or otherwise.

Obedience forms part of the mortification of the saint. He also translates it into reality outside of all logic, up to the point of the ridiculous—but ridiculous only for us: Gerard accepted becoming a madman for the love of God: "It is true," one witness says, "that he had himself treated as a madman by the boys of Muro, in order to be mistreated as Our Lord was." From his early youth Gerard chose the sacred madness of Christ. In the trial we read: "He was impressed when he read in a book that Jesus had been called mad: and so, moved by the Spirit and an inner impulse, he too resolved to pretend to be mad, so as to share the contempt shown Jesus."[23]

The ecstasy and swooning into which he often fell increased Gerard's fame as a "man of God." In one way, the descriptions of his ecstasy sound like a form of epilepsy.[24] But, in another way, we have to remember that he was considered a protector of people affected by convulsions and diabolical possession.[25] It was said that he could subdue the devil and make him do his bidding.[26] A world of madness revolved around him; but it was a madness that the saint dominated, controlled, and directed along the paths of piety and prayer.

The passage from sacred madness to the mortification of the body is instantaneous. "Then he took the whipped Jesus as his model and had himself struck many times with a twisted, moistened cord."[27] He subjected his body to cruel penances, as one witness reports: "He was so extreme in his penances that he looked like a living skeleton...and so enthusiastic to whip himself for Jesus Christ that in his disciplining he made blood pour from his body."[28]

There is no need to insist on the well-known penances of Gerard; they displayed a disconcerting rigor. Francesco Spadola, a bricklayer from Caposele, declared at the trial:

> The public fame of his penances caused him horror. Always fasts, always hair shirts, always vigils. And if some times he went to sleep, he did so on a bed of

branches with a large rock as a pillow. The continual whippings till the blood flowed caused *me* horror, above all when I recall the secret room that Brother Stefano showed me one day where Gerard did penance. After many years, its walls were still covered with the blood of this man of God.[29]

The appearance of Brother Gerard was that of a hermit, a penitent, emaciated, covered with rags.[30] There seemed to be renewed in Gerard, as in Domenico of Muro and Bonaventura of Potenza, the penitential asceticism of the ancient anchorites.[31]

This eastern tradition also becomes transparent in the particular piety of a saint, apparently independent, with no intellectual training, but faithful to his land, as Gerard Majella was.

From what the fieldworkers, the notaries, and the priests and nuns of the town said at the canonization trial, it seems we can deduce that Gerard subjected his body to rough mortifications through a wish to imitate the "patient Christ," through an effort at reparation and expiation of the sins of human beings paid with the blood of Christ, through a wish to take upon his own shoulders the sufferings of the people.

Penances, humiliations, and sacrifices made the figure of Gerard charismatic in the eyes of the people. No doubt we are far from the manifestations of the "free spirit" (quietism), that species of mythical sanctity which presumed to make soul and body, even on earth, unscathed by sin. With Gerard we are rather in the sanctity of the "martyrs' tortures" and of the first monks: penance and more penance in the total, active adoration of the crucifixion. Not so much the words, but the whole body of Gerard and everything that this body, with its fibers and substances, touched—all that became sacred to the people. The mortifications weren't just the proof of Gerard's love for God; they themselves were, in his martyrized body, a divine relic, a materialization of the sacred. What happened at Gerard's death confirms this, when so many people from the surrounding villages came to Caposele.

"They fought to get a piece of his clothes or any other object belonging to the servant of God, to keep for their devotion. And they even went so far as to soak handkerchiefs in the blood that spurted from the vein that was deliberately cut in the cadaver many hours after his death."[32]

PENITENTIAL PIETY
AND ILLUSTRATED PIETY

This holiness of Gerard, so penitential and ascetical, full of blood and renunciation, is surely not the kind that would have pleased Lodovico Antonio Muratori, the great contemporary priest-historian: it involved too many little images, too many miracles, in a word, an exaggerated materialization of the faith. Gerard Majella lives in the circle of Redemptorist piety, the circle of Alphonsus Liguori, but with a distinct connection to the past and to the people.

The devotional line of Saint Alphonsus is closer to that of Muratori, and for that very reason, contrary to the materialization of the faith, always indulgent, but sober in its expressive manifestations. Saint Alphonsus moves in the direction of the new spirituality of the eighteenth century. This had its guidelines in the Synod of Benedict XIII, in the treatises on "the good bishop," in the pedagogical appeal of the popular missions to the peasants, with which the Church responded to the "Age of Reason" and the mockery of the "intellectuals." In Saint Alphonsus, piety follows the line of the heart: it is patient, human, optimistic, but it never passes through the door of madness. The devout person in the Alphonsinian style knows the instruments of faith, which are logical means to help in prayer.

In the Redemptorist congregation, Gerard wasn't the only one who wounded himself with flagellation. There were other religious, such as Domenico Blasucci (1732–1752), who also was born in the diocese of Muro and was a close friend of Gerard. At his beatification trial, we read: "The use of mortification, although prudently controlled by superiors, frequent prayer, and continuous union with God, had weakened his health so that he contracted tuberculosis, which then carried him off to death. This was the reason why he suspended his studies."[33] Blasucci was a student who had taken his vows, but he didn't make it to the priesthood. The witnesses claim that he had, as the original text says, an "erotic temperament,"[34] that is, affectionate, docile, amiable, extremely sensitive, and noble. Nevertheless, Saint Alphonsus would not have wanted his disciples to take mortification too far. As one of the witnesses said: "The only defect [of Blasucci] was an excessive anxiety about penances....His flagellations were horrific; in winter he wouldn't go near the fire, so that his hands remained wounded by the cold; he mingled bitter herbs in his food, and so on."[35]

The recommendation of Saint Alphonsus to his Redemptorists not to abuse their body with penances, not to punish it as an obstacle to the love of God, to protect their health, was alien to the mentality of Majella or Blasucci. It was alien to that more ancient tradition of monastic asceticism, which had such deep roots in southern Italy. And yet the sanctity of Gerard was not opposed to that of Alphonsus. It was different because it was old; in its original foundations, it did not correspond to the humanistic culture of the fathers of the Council of Trent. In other words, the holiness of Gerard was not a product of his own century, but it reached a place where Saint Alphonsus would have had a hard time reaching with his pastoral strategies. Gerard got to the immobile rural world of the south, where the destiny of the human being is bound up with a religion of the earth, with cosmic comprehension of daily facts; where the signs of the ancient oriental cultures and of ascetical monasticism itself (contemplation, resignation, flagellation, eremitical life) continued to be present in Gerard's day. To those who struggled with the earth, with drought, with rats, with usurious traders, to those who continued to be defenseless and degraded by scarcity, by swings in prices, by the epidemics of the field, to all those people Gerard offered miracles. The peasants, the day laborers, and the gentlemen too accepted miracles. They were convinced of them, lived them fully as an extraordinary element that materialized in daily life.

These miracles were not a step toward the kind of religion proposed by the Counter Reformation, nor did they propose or stimulate a more spiritualized or organized piety. The saints from southern Italy had names like Manuel Ribera (also a Redemptorist and a "madman of God," martyrized in his flesh by flagellations. Their names were not Don Bosco or Don Murialdo. Nevertheless, Gerard's miracles accompanied the expectations, the hopes, and even the protests of the mass of devout persons who read the lives of the saints as a sort of Cabala, who demanded from the saint, in disconcerting or cruel forms of piety, the help that nature or fate denied them, who still could not manage to separate science from mystery, nor economic mechanisms from the action of divine Providence. Miracles belonged to the spirituality of the masses, they followed the footsteps of the wonder-working saints, and they attracted people without distinguishing between roles in the rural world of the south, a world of vital and spontaneous impulses, always oscillating between anarchic rage and resignation.[36]

Gerard Majella, one might say, was a saint imposed from the bottom up. He was not a saint of the hierarchical Church. His figure does not fit into the questionnaires of Roman canon law. The witnesses speak about a saint who belonged to them; a saint who does not educate, does not transform, does not organize, but who accepts their material and spiritual conditions as they are. The spirituality of the Counter Reformation, with its requirements and canonical codifications, remains in southern Italy a religion of the elite. It rarely emerges from the bishop's house; it barely peeks out in the seminaries; and it has a hard time finding expression in the synods. Gerard is present where ecclesiastical documents and tribunals have yet to reach. From the other and more risky front of a popular piety close to magic and superstition, he also struggles for the experience of faith, but he makes it easier, closer to those who don't trust the intelligence, but without confusing it with obscure or demoniacal natural forces. And, for this reason, the Church remains grateful to him, accepts him, and elevates him to the honor of its altars.

Under the religious aspect, to say that *Christ stopped at Eboli* is to stress only one model of spirituality, alien to the rural world of southern Italy. It is an unreal and exclusionary definition, which unites piety to the religious culture and tradition of the West, which is rational and dialectical.[37] In reality Christ did go beyond Eboli, although covered and hidden beneath the mortifications, the miracle-working, the asceticism of a superhuman religious practice, originating far away in the east. The Church of Rome is to be found at once in the indulgent and cultivated piety of Saint Alphonsus and in the penance of Gerard Majella.

CHAPTR FIVE

Gerard's Letters
and Rules for Living

Introduction and Notes: Sabatino Majorano

LETTERS

Introduction

Those who really love seek to know better the person they love. This isn't curiosity, but a sincere desire to grow in communion and to journey together. No one can get away from this law, not even the saints. Anyone who loves them and feels their near presence, anyone who takes inspiration from them in day-to-day decisions, will feel a strong desire to explore more deeply their personality and their life in order to know the most profound truth: the secret of their sainthood.

The careful reconstruction of events by biographers opens the path to this truth. But the truth often remains nearly paralyzed beneath the weight of all the acts and situations that have to be considered, of important figures who have to be described, of often divergent interpretations that need to be clarified. Attentive analysis of all these factors is indispensable, but one also has to go further and try to approach the secret that the saints bear within themselves.

Hence, the desire to read for ourselves their personal notes, diaries, and letters. In them, the saints have expressed themselves with greater closeness and spontaneity. They have, in some fashion, confessed "their truth." Holding them in our hand is like looking out an open window into the secret of their lives.

In Saint Gerard Majella, we notice the overwhelming presence of grace; we remain impressed by its luminosity, made up of total surrender to Christ and of happy availability to the brothers. We intuit the deep truth of the prodigious deeds that have been passed down by popular memory. Nevertheless, we still have a strong desire to know him more and better.

The brief twenty-nine years of his earthly career (Muro Lucano: April 6, 1726, to Materdomini: October 16, 1755), the few documentary sources, the fact that the people very quickly laid claim to his life, emphasizing the aspects and gestures that were closest to their own sensibility, justify such a desire.

Unfortunately, not very much of Gerard has come down to us. He was a humble lay religious, wholly preoccupied by the thousand concrete emergencies of the gospel and of charity to the poor. His writings were not many, and some of them very quickly got lost, because he wasn't an important person. All this means that whoever wants to know him thoroughly will find particularly precious the few writings that we do have: some forty letters and a set of rules for living. Along with the testimony of those who were closest to him, collected immediately by the Redemptorist priest Gaspare Caione,[1] they constitute a passage one must go through to get closer to the truth of Gerard Majella.

It is not a question of opposing this knowledge to the one that the people have developed over the last two centuries. It must be said at the outset that the true book about Gerard is everything that popular memory has transmitted. This memory was, in other respects, a fundamental protagonist in the trial that brought to the altars the humble Redemptorist brother.[2] Here it is rather a question of establishing an account that manages to integrate, correct, and develop what we know.

These are the motivations and ultimate purposes of this edition of the spiritual writings of Gerard Majella.[3] It seeks to establish a more direct and immediate contact with the sources, so as to capture something of his "truth." If it is a fact that the "secret" of Gerard cannot be discovered merely by reading the documents, it is just as much a fact that we cannot do without them when we wish to hear him.

The following pages will offer a translation of all the texts by Gerard that have been preserved.[4] The original Italian text has many dialectical forms, with words written the way they sounded, with incorrect use of articles and prepositions, abbreviations, and abrupt transitions from the intimate to the polite form of address, all of which cannot be conveyed in English. In general, an effort has been made to offer a clear and legible text.

Gaspare Caione notes that during the years spent in Deliceto, just after he entered the Redemptorists, Gerard "never rested, but extended the effects of his charity to those outside. He continuously wrote letters to troubled and tempted souls, who received marvelous consolation from his replies, which were full of a singular unction and a doctrine learned solely in the school of prayer. One cannot read his letters without being amazed, especially knowing that Gerard was a poor lay brother who could barely read and write, and nothing more."[5]

These were not hurried statements, nor were they dictated by fraternal enthusiasm. Caione was very close to Gerard and got to know him very well, since he was, among other things, his superior. Caione was a man of culture with a sharp critical sense. Saint Alphonsus had full confidence in him and had recourse to him in particularly difficult moments. In gathering documentation about Gerard, he shows a notable attention and concern for the truth.

As far as the extent of Gerard's correspondence, Caione is echoed by the other contemporary biographer, Antonio Tannoia,[6] and the testimony gathered for the beatification trial. These same sources likewise acknowledge that many of Gerard's letters were lost. Nowadays we know of forty-four, apart from one other brief fragment. But we have the originals of only nineteen; the others were passed on to us by Caione and Tannoia or by transcripts from the beatification trial. The authenticity of these sources seems beyond the shadow of a doubt, when we compare the transcriptions with the originals that have come down to us.[7]

The authors of the transcriptions, nevertheless, were concerned to some extent with improving the style and language that Gerard used. This is more obvious in Tannoia, less so in the beatification trial. For his part, Caione stands, so to speak, halfway between the two.

The Addressees

The addressees of Gerard's letters are fairly well known: some Redemptorist confreres, some Carmelite nuns, Maria Celeste Crostarosa, lay people, and a priest who were particularly good friends of his. There are only five letters whose addressees are unknown, but it can be inferred that three were sent to nuns and two to lay people. By contrast, the date of many of the letters is more approximate.

The largest body of correspondence was sent to the nuns of the Carmelite monastery at Ripacandida: sixteen to Sister Maria of Jesus, who was the superior until 1753; seven to Sister Michela of Saint Francis Xavier, who succeeded her in office; five to other sisters (Battista of the Most Holy Trinity and Maria Celeste of the Holy Spirit).

"Gerard's favorite place," Caione observes, "was the monastery of the Teresians [Carmelites] at Ripacandida, and his favorite souls were, of course, those exemplary nuns with whom he had a very special friendship. Gerard almost never let a week go by without sending them some spiritual message or receiving one from them, as they inflamed and encouraged one another in the love of God and in the acquisition of the most heroic sanctity."[8]

Having been founded recently, the monastery was at a high tide of fervor. Tannoia makes a significant statement in connection with April 5, 1750, when Saint Alphonsus went to Ripacandida:

> He moderated the voluntary and excessive austerity that they practiced, to the detriment of their bodies. He wanted them to use less rigor, especially in eating; he induced them to take some rest for their body and spirit. Admiring the holiness of that place he said: "I never would have thought to find a carnation like this on such a cliff."[9]

The meeting with these nuns, above all with Sister Maria of Jesus, was extremely intense. Gerard would make with her the particular commitment of receiving Communion and saying prayers, which he would indicate in the letters by the phrase "holy faith."

"In this monastery," Caione again recalls, "while Gerard was conversing with Mother Maria of Jesus and was engaged in spiritual discourse, particularly about how God deserves to be loved and about divine goodness, transported by a sacred enthusiasm, he struck several times three of the thick iron points that come out from the grille, with such force and violence that he twisted them as if they were made of soft wax. And to this day the bars may still be seen, somewhat twisted and different from the others."[10]

Between 1751 and 1753, the monastery of Ripacandida went through a delicate problem. Considering the environment excessively austere, as Saint Alphonsus had already pointed out in 1750, the bishop, Teodoro Basta, moved to introduce a mitigation of the Carmelite rules. In the face of this, the Sisters, led by Sister Maria of Jesus, put up stiff opposition. At that point, the bishop took over direct control of the monastery, gave full power to a Carmelite priest from Naples, and forbade all epistolary contact with outsiders. Sister Maria of Jesus was declared to be a visionary. The storm lasted until the beginning of 1753. This state of affairs must not be forgotten if we wish to understand adequately the remarks in the correspondence that Gerard sent to the monastery.[11]

The letters to Gerard's Redemptorist confreres number eight in all. Two were written to say thank you for the profession of religious vows in July 1752; one to Saint Alphonsus and another to Giovanni Mazzini, the consultor general. The letters to Fathers Francesco Margotta, Francesco Garzilli, and Gaspare Caione are very different from one another. To the first, Gerard writes asking for cooperation to put together the dowry needed by a young woman who wanted to enter a monastery. To the second, Gerard writes to comfort him about the scruples and spiritual anxiety he was facing; to F. Caione, to inform him about his worsening health while he was collecting alms in mid-1755 and to request "a strong obedience." There are also two brief messages to Father Celestino de Robertis about orders received from him.

As for Sister Maria Celeste Crostarosa and her monastery, Caione notes: "The other place Gerard prized was the monastery of the Most Holy Savior in the city of Foggia. Since it belonged to our same institute and since the rule was being observed there exactly and lived with the highest example, Gerard, so to speak, continuously kept his heart there. With the permission of his superiors, he went there frequently to encourage the nuns with his most fervent discourses on the acquisition of the most solid virtues and of regular observance."[12]

And Tannoia adds: "Whenever he went down to Foggia, whither he often traveled, the first thing was to see Mother Celeste. She liked to talk with Gerard, and Gerard enjoyed sharing with her the feelings of his own heart. And I don't know if it was Gerard who encouraged the nun to love Jesus Christ more, or if she was the one who stirred up Gerard's fervor to cling more tightly to God.[13]

The only letter to Sister Maria Celeste that we have is barely an echo of this profound communion, since the greater part of the text is a list of indulgences for the monastery that Gerard had managed to obtain in Naples. Tannoia himself felt obliged to lament that "the letters between Sister Maria Celeste and Gerard are missing."[14]

Then we have two letters sent to the Santorelli family from Caposele, who were very close to Gerard. In the first, he exhorts Father Gaetano not to let himself be overcome by scruples in his priestly ministry. In the other, he gives a sharp tug on the ears of young Geronimo, the protagonist of youthful frivolities toward a consecrated girl (a nun living at home). The last letter that we have, written by Gerard in the course of his last illness, was sent to the young Isabella Salvadore from Oliveto; although written by a dying man it overflows with life, as do all the rest of Gerard's letters.

The letters are given in chronological order. That way it

will be easier to follow Gerard's spiritual evolution. When it is not possible to know the actual date, we have been guided by the sense of the text.

Fundamental Contents

It doesn't seem very elegant to offer the reader a synthesis of the contents of Gerard's letters before he or she has read them. That would also run counter to the purpose of this present volume, which aims at leading to direct and personal contact with the writings of the saint.

By contrast, it is useful to indicate synthetically the principal themes that constitute the framework of these pages by Gerard. This is not just to facilitate comprehension of the contents of each letter, but also so as not to remain, from the outset and by force of tradition, a prisoner of the rigid interpretive schemes of his spirituality. This traditional reading surely has valid elements that have to be rescued and developed, but it must also be animated by what Gerard says about himself. Only in this way is it possible to arrive at "his truth."

What emerges immediately from the letters is a profound sense of communion that unites Gerard with his interlocutors. It is a sincere, spontaneous love, charged with solicitude and affability. The expressions even seem at times too strong; here and there Gerard himself makes a point of spelling out this affection in God. It is impossible not to be impressed by the profound human burden of tenderness and communion that shines through in his pages.

The assimilation to Christ crucified is another aspect that frequently returns here. Gerard was strongly convinced of the centrality of the mystery of the cross in all Christian life, although everything also seems rich with Easter-consciousness: he feels himself the grain that must die so as to come to be a blade of wheat (see Jn 12:24). The cross, therefore, does not frighten him, but is viewed as a grace: a grace that permits him to carry forward salvation for his brothers.

The will of God makes up something like the refrain, which becomes particularly insistent in some letters, above all when the cross is mentioned. But Gerard asks us never to forget that we are face to face with the will of the Father: a will that wants only our happiness. It is beautiful. Therefore, the "yes" is not spoken with reservations or fears, but with "great spirit" and "gaily."

Confidence in prayer is another theme particularly prized by Gerard. He insistently begs prayers for himself and for the needs of others; he promises to pray for others; he projects them for after death. At bottom, one sees the countenance of his "dear God" with the infinite love revealed in the gift of the only begotten Son, and the simple and hopeful warmth that wells up from the certainty of the constant presence of *Mamma Maria*."

The path proposed by Gerard is a path of deep faith and deep generosity. Communion with Christ is necessarily linked to assuming the burden, with him, of the sins of the whole world in order to defeat and finally overcome them. But it is a path on which he proceeds with serenity, confidence, and joy. Even when he is beneath the weight of the cross, Gerard doesn't cease to recommend optimism. In this way, human values are not denied, but brought to fulfillment, permeated by the force and clarity of Christ.

The mystical depth thus runs into daily life and its thousands of emergencies. Gerard lives concretely, as the people do, amid so many problems and so many hopes, always guided by the light of faith. The features of popular piety, to which he always remains faithful, are animated and strengthened by the profound intensity of his relationship with the Redeemer.

In these letters of Gerard, one is surprised by the strong esteem he nourishes for religious life. Without losing spontaneity and warmth in the brotherly relationship, he never tires of reminding the nuns of the particular dignity that is proper to their vocation. This does not mean, however, that he looks down on other life options. Although there are not many letters written to lay people, it is clear that what counts for Gerard is the "yes" to one's own vocation and the consistency with the Gospel in different situations: living joyfully and with great energy the beautiful will of God.

1. [December 17, 1751]

To Sister Maria of Jesus[15]

"Gerard greatly prized this nun and Sister Maria had the highest opinion of him. Once they met, they began to share their feelings. When they got together, it was like seeing two coals on fire, each setting the other aflame."[16]

From October 1751 on, Father Cafaro was no longer the rector of Deliceto, and Gerard had more freedom of movement. Then he visited the nuns of Ripacandida and returned full of profound joy. But he feared that they had formed too high an opinion of him. With the letter that he sends he wishes to humbly place himself in the light of the truth.

The communion of prayer that was established with the monastery was a source of profound joy in charity.

Jesus + Mary

O Divine love, may you always be in the heart of this, your beloved and dear spouse.

I am writing to you in haste, my dear and blessed Mother, with the goal of putting myself once again at your feet, and at the feet of all those dear sisters of mine: I wish they may always be in the wide open side of Jesus Christ, and in the afflicted heart of Mary Most Holy, where all sweetness and repose are to be found.

So many are the graces and the kindliness of your Reverence that on the one hand they have given me supreme consolation, and on the other they have brought me mortification and sorrow when I see how I am full of unworthiness in comparison with the true spouses of Jesus Christ. I have shown little humility and thoughtfulness before your Reverence. I realize that I am guilty of these great faults.

I am forced to declare myself guilty and to exclaim everywhere: mercy! I wish to humbly beg your pardon for the love of Jesus Christ, if because of my past, or rather present, madness, in what I told you. That is true even if in other ways it was all for the just purpose of declaring myself as I am, so that

Your Reverence might be moved to pity with all those Daughters of yours, since I am asking help from the Reverend Mother for my continuous imperfections, while hoping for her holy prayers, so that by means of those prayers I may rightly do the will of my, and everyone's, Father.

Finally, I thank you for your holy prudence in having supported me with so much charity, and this not for myself, but for the love of Jesus Christ.

Meanwhile I tell you that if you didn't realize what I remarked, I beg you to reflect on it, because I was speaking with the just purpose of being helped by Your Reverence.

For a while, I lamented those words that were said during recreation the morning after my departure, because you had taken the wrong way what I told you, while I had spoken to you in simplicity of heart. Thank goodness I have never had any confidence in myself, since I could certainly be deceived.

And so great was the pain in my heart that I remained beside myself, and as I was returning on the road to Melfi, the horse took the road to Foggia, taking me around four miles out of my way. Upon realizing this, I left everything to the divine Passion of Jesus Christ.

The communions [according to the pact we had made] were in a way a source of great consolation, but in other ways a source of great confusion, as I thought of the infinite goodness of God who had employed his dear Spouses for the salvation of someone who had so often offended him.

Oh excess of charity, oh stupendous prodigy, oh love of a true shepherd, who searches with such industry for his little lost sheep.

For myself, I can only say that may the charity shown me be recompensed by the blood of Jesus Christ united with the pains of Mary: May the pact agreed on be in your heart, and in the hearts of all your dear daughters.

I beg you, for the love of Jesus Christ, to say to that sister of mine that, unworthy as I am, I will make holy communion as she desires, so that she may become a saint with the help of

God. And I say to all the rest: I remain embracing you within the sacred side of Jesus Christ.

Melfi, today December 17, 1751

Will you do me the favor, for the love of Jesus Christ and of Mary Most Holy, to greet Father Confessor for me and Don Tommaso Rendina: tell him that I would like to see him at the holy exercises in Deliceto.

The most unworthy servant and brother in Christ
of Jesus Christ and then of Your Reverence,

GERARD MAJELLA OF THE MOST HOLY REDEEMER

2. [January 22, 1752]
To Sister Maria of Jesus[17]

In an attempt to get the nuns of Ripacandida to accept the mitigation of the Camelite rules, Monsignor Teodoro Basta isolated the monastery, making even correspondence difficult. Sister Maria was left with no other form of communication than "being in the most sacred side."

Gerard stresses the profound reality of this sort of communication and invites Sister Maria to read all events, even those that are full of difficulties, in the light of faith. Only in that way will it be possible to remain firm. But "joyfully," because the "yes" to the will of God leads us to continuously "grow greater."

My dear sister in Jesus Christ:

It surely was the deepest consolation for me to hear that you were so strongly engaged on my behalf with your Divine Spouse, and to read the letter in which you told me that you had no other way of speaking alone with me except within his most sacred side.

Consider, Your Reverence, what contentment was mine in hearing you speak so sweetly. And for this reason I felt the desire to confess my truth to you. And so may it please you, dearest one in Jesus Christ.

I, unworthy as I am, do not cease to pray to the Lord for Your Reverence and for all your holy community so that you may be true spouses and true lovers of his most holy will. Every time that I go to the Lord, in truth I tell you, I always see you within his most holy side, and I always offer myself entirely to the most sacred heart, wounded for you.

And God knows the feeling you cause in me because I see you so afflicted. This is not true distress, of course, but envy. Blessed be the Lord forever who keeps you in such a state to make of you a great saint. Come now, be joyful and do not fear. Be strong and have courage in the battles, so as to conquer and have a more glorious triumph in our heavenly kingdom.

Let us not be frightened of anything except what the evil spirit sows in our hearts, because that is his job. And our duty is not to let him triumph in his works. Let us not believe him, because we are not what he wants and says. This is just to terrify and frighten us, and in that way to make us believe that he is the conqueror in his evil works.

It is true that sometimes we find ourselves confused and weak. But there is no confusion with God, there is no weakness with God's power, because it is certain that in our battles the divine majesty helps us with his powerful arm. And so we can be joyful and grow in strength [by accepting] God's will. And we bless his most holy works for all eternity.

So I say to your Reverence, [do not] forget me in all your holy prayers. Thus I beg, for the love of Jesus Christ and of Mary Most Holy, all your holy community.

And let us remain in the sacred side of Jesus Christ.

Consolazione, January 22, 1752

Your Reverence's Most Unworthy Servant
and Brother in Christ,
          GERARD MAJELLA OF THE MOST HOLY REDEEMER

3. [February–March 1752]
To Sister Maria of Jesus[18]

Tannoia has handed down to us this fragment of a letter, claiming that it was sent to Sister Maria of Jesus, but he doesn't specify the date. The unfolding of events in Ripacandida and the comparison with other letters from Gerard lead Domenico Caione to propose the most probable date as the months of February or March 1752.[19]

"I find myself full of sins." Gerard was living deeply the words of Christ: "Be you perfect as our heavenly Father is perfect" (Mt 5:48). But he felt, nevertheless, a deep sense of solidarity with sinners. At this point, he lost his usual joyousness and relived for them the mystery of the Passion of Christ.

I find myself full of sins! Pray God to pardon me.

Everyone is converting and I continue being obstinate. Ask all your daughters: continue doing mortifications for me, so that his Divine Majesty may pardon and receive me.

I am full of afflictions and I can't find anyone to believe me. That is how God wants it for me. He wants me to die without compassion, abandoned by everyone. Thus I wish to live and die to give pleasure to my God.

4. [April 1, 1752]
To Sister Maria of Jesus[20]

The difficulties of communication for the monastery of Ripacandida worsened in the first months of 1752. This, however, must not cool their brotherly and sisterly relationship. Gerard asks Sister Maria to intensify communion in prayer, centering it in the Eucharist and in Mary. But he also knows how to appreciate the simple gestures of popular piety. "When he assisted during the day at the exposition of the Blessed Sacrament, despite the care he took to hide himself continually from the eyes of strangers, Gerard's face became radiant. His chest heaved and became agitated. His mind was fully concen-

trated and as if out of his senses so that one saw in him a seraph in the act of adoration."[21]

Jesus + Mary

May God make holy, my dearest in Christ.

It is something about which I cannot be mistaken, which I know very well: our passionate Lord is there, and in the prison of love he is most frequently visited by his spouses and by Your Reverence, who have been the first "jailer."

For this reason, I beg of you that with the authority of motherly charity you order all your most obedient daughters to make just one visit on my behalf to their divine spouse, Our Lord. All they need do for me in this visit is say one "Glory be to the Father." That is all. And in the end let everyone often say for me, "Lord, have mercy."

And in the future never forget to recommend me to our divine Lord wounded for me. For my part, unworthy as I am, every morning I will surely remember to commend you. And as for the Hail Mary, I will say it most punctually. And I say the usual prayers such as the visit to the Lord in his divine will to ask that he make you a saint. And I hope to console you with what He knows and does.

Do me the kindness, for the love of Jesus Christ and of Mary Most Holy, to send me a copy of the little statue of Saint Teresa, because I don't have the one you gave me. It was taken from me by a monastery that wanted it, and so as not to make them lose their devotion, I had to give it to them.

Of all the letters that I have sent you, I have not received a single answer except for the first one that Brother Gaetano brought me.

I insist again: do not forget me because I have a very great need. And God knows my usual needs.

I remain kissing your holy hands.

Santa Maria della Consolazione, April 1, 1752

Your Reverence's most affectionate brother in Christ,

GERARD MAJELLA OF THE MOST HOLY REDEEMER

5. [April 16, 1752]

To Sister Maria of Jesus[22]

The joy felt by Gerard when he finally received correspondence from the monastery of Ripacandida was tremendous. He still did not know that at that precise moment that the prohibitions of Monsignor Basta had been extended to himself.

He was in the middle of his novitiate period and intensifying the preparation for his profession as a religious. He had to avoid contacts with the outside world in order to deepen the climate of recollection, reflection, and prayer. The communion with Sister Maria and the other nuns of Ripacandida bursts in with force and spontaneity. Nevertheless, Gerard invites his correspondent to remember that his love is born from the fact that he considers the sisters "true beloved spouses" of Christ and, for this reason, a "memory" of the Virgin.

The joy that he feels in writing the letter makes him forget for a moment the spiritual sufferings he is going through. His "yes" to the will of God does not lose its impulse; still better, it convinces him all the more to beg that he may continue on his way "beneath water and wind."

Jesus + Mary,

The grace of divine love be eternally in the soul of Your Reverence. Amen.

O God, what supreme contentment I had in my heart today when I received your letter, your highly esteemed and long desired letter. But because I speak with truth before God, this desire of mine is not from my will, but from the Most High, who always makes me ask help from others, because I can't do it by myself. Even though his divine will wishes me to walk beneath water and wind; that is how he wishes, and I wish; therefore let everything be done perfectly in accord with his holy will, if only God makes me worthy.

Meanwhile I am consoled that Your Reverence and all you

daughters are so strongly engaged in praying for me at the feet of the Divine Majesty. And I certainly hope and wish that God may repay you abundantly for my sake. Because my only patron Jesus Christ has given me all his infinite mercy, which I offered to his Eternal Father. And I repeat, I hope you may be paid double with the same mercy given me by his Son, and with endless glory for all eternity.

Do not be surprised if I write to you so affectionately. The sole reason for this is that I esteem you as true spouses of Jesus Christ, which moves me to devotion in conversing continually with you. But the sole reason that touches me to the quick in my heart is that all you spouses remind and represent for me the Divine Mother; and I esteem you as such. I do not know if...God forbid that any sister think otherwise. For this reason, I would like this present letter of mine to be read in common as testimony.

Therefore, my dearest sister in Christ, I thank you enormously for the little copy that you sent me of the statuette of Saint Teresa, and that I was so much looking forward to.

I advise you that that I have had the bad fortune not to have come there. This is an obvious sign that God did not wish it. I wanted to go at least some day, because it was for God's glory and commanded to me by my superior. But my lord Don Benedetto Graziola has kept me by force in his house, which meant that I didn't have time to come there. In order to obey my [spiritual] director, who was in Melfi and with whom we traveled together from Deliceto, I betook myself back to Melfi. But there I found to my mortification and by the will of God that he had left for Caposele.

Your Reverence commands me to send greetings to our brother Gaetano. I can do nothing else to discharge my duty of obedience but to have him read your most respected letter because I myself have not actually spoken to him for a long time, by the will of God: This was what my superiors commanded, that I speak to no one outside our community. That applies only when I am outside of it.

And so I beg you to pray to the Lord to rid me of this false opinion that they have of me, and may they all forget to speak and deal with me, when this clear truth that they have misinterpreted comes into the clear.

Let this letter of mine serve as a reply to your letter of today. I tell you that our brother Gaetano is persevering in his holy hermitage and loves Jesus and Mary Most Holy as much as possible. What consoles me the most is that one can see in him a great purity of heart, which does everything for God alone.

As I write to you one more time, I beg you to tell me how far you have come on the paths of sacred perfection with all your daughters, to my utter confusion.

Of your three letters sent to me I have received neither the second nor the third, which is a clear sign that God's will has not wished me to. May his will be done, so that we may remain in the heart of Jesus and of the Blessed Virgin Mary.

Melfi, April 16, 1752

I place myself at the feet of your most worthy Spiritual Father, so that he may remember to pray to God for me.

Your Reverence's most unworthy servant
and brother in Christ,

GERARD MAJELLA OF THE MOST HOLY REDEEMER

6. [April 24, 1752]
To Sister Maria of Jesus[23]

The tone here is totally different from that of the preceding letter. Gerard has learned about Monsignor Basta's ban and hastens to declare his full compliance, exhorting Sister Maria and the sisters to live these difficult moments too with deep faith.

"The most zealous bishop of Melfi," Caione writes, "being fully aware of this exchange of letters between Gerard and the good nuns [...], forbade them to have any correspondence with anyone, including Brother Gerard. The brother came to

know of this not from the nuns themselves, but through a third person, who was a holy priest, whom by order of the bishop they had to make use of to write any indispensable message. Gerard, perhaps sensing the shadow of a complaint in one of the nuns about the prohibition mentioned, writes them a letter that is worthy of eternal memory and that shows what was the virtue and perfection of our brother."[24]

There is no need to dwell on the surface of the daily events, but rather, to scrutinize them with the eyes of faith: the project and the loving presence of God are real, even beneath the crust of events that at first glance seem too harsh. Then it is possible to live always in serenity, knowing well that in God's plan lies our happiness and our fulfillment.

If my dear and most illustrious Monsignor has forbidden you to write, he has done well, since this is the will of our dear God. And I rejoice greatly that the Lord is putting these hindrances in your way, since they are all signs that he loves you greatly and wants you entirely restricted to him, and wants you to spare yourself so many labors. So let Your Reverence be joyful and in good spirits, because these are not things to cause you pain, but ready joy. When the will of God is at stake, accept everything. Your Reverence knows better than I or anyone else.

What would you have me say? I have spoken and I shall speak with confidence with a woman who is my teacher on this point. I have not yet been able to understand how a spiritual soul, consecrated to her God, could find bitterness on this earth, by not accepting always and in everything the beautiful will of God, since this is only the substance of our souls.

Ah, accursed self-will, which bars souls from such an immense treasure, an earthly paradise! A God! O truly great thing, worthy of infinite consideration! O cowardice of human ignorance, when it makes us neglect such a great gain!

Is it not perchance this supreme God ruling all things who permits this? Is it not perhaps his sacrosanct will here, although it does not appear as such? Is there perchance a better way of acting to lead us to our eternal salvation? O God, could there be a better means of saving us? And what better thing can be found to give him pleasure except always and in everything to do his divine will? And what else does he want from us but that his divine will always be done perfectly, as he wishes, where he wishes, and when he wishes, and that we be always ready for the slightest sign from him?

Let us remain, then, completely indifferent in everything, so that we may always and in all things do the divine will, with that supreme purity of intention that God wants from us.

What a great thing is the will of God, oh hidden and priceless treasure! Ah, if I understand you rightly, you are worth as much as my dear God himself, and who can understand you, if not my dear God?

I surely live at the height of consolation because Your Reverence is one of those souls who are nourished only by the lovely will of my dear God, since your heroic virtue on this account is well known to me. Continue then to be always transformed into a perfect union, into one and the same thing in the lovely will of God.

We wish to do on earth what the angels do in heaven. The will of God in heaven, the will of God on earth; and consequently, paradise in heaven, paradise on earth.

Read these few lines to all the Sisters. I believe, as I have already believed, that the most illustrious Monsignor has not only given the prohibition to your Reverence, but to all the sisters, against writing [letters] to other persons. He has done well, and one must abide by it.

I beg you not to be afflicted by this, because that would be the same as complaining about God. And so let his most sacred will be done. And I declare myself supremely content that you not write to me anymore, and I say the same to the sisters. And yet if sending me greetings, you were to reveal the least shadow of a fault against obedience, please do not do it, for the love of God; because I am happy with everything. It is enough that you commend me to the Lord.

This is what I want, because I know well the intention of

this holy prelate, who wishes you all to be united to Jesus. And if I pass that way, I will refrain from asking him for permission to speak with you, now that we cannot write. And if my superior at some point commands me, I will not go to see you, because we will see each other afterwards in paradise. While we are on earth, we wish to become saints with the will of others and not our own.

Given the twenty-fourth day of April.

GERARD OF THE REDEEMER

7. [Before April–May 1753]
To Sister Maria of Jesus[25]

In transcribing this letter, Tannoia affirms that it was sent to Sister Maria of Jesus, without specifying the date. Gerard's language presupposes that Maria is still the superior. We know that she was in charge until April or May 1753. The letter is best read in conjunction with the preceding letter on the generous and unreserved "yes" to God's will.

Gerard's "yes" is filial, governed by confidence in Christ's promise: "He who believes in me will also do the works that I do; and greater works than those will he do...Whatever you ask in my name, I will do it" (Jn 14:12–13). For this reason he can dialogue with the power of God: "this time may he dispose things as we wish."

Tannoia adds that the nun, for whom Gerard asked prayers, was in fact cured.

I wish you to strive firmly in praying to God for a nun who is very seriously ill.

I do not want to see her dead. Tell my beloved God that I want her to become more holy, and may she die in old age, so that she may enjoy the service of God for many years.

Courage, strive with the power of God. And this time may God dispose of things as we wish.

In the name of God, I give you the order not to let her die. I wish to make a novena to the power of God for the health of this nun.

8. [July 26, 1752]

To Father Giovanni Mazzini[26]

"In mid-June, Gerard was finishing the second semester of the novitiate, the consultor general, Father Giovanni Mazzini, who had gotten to know Gerard during his canonical visit to the community of Deliceto in June 1571, recommended that Saint Alphonsus admit him to the profession of religious vows. In fact, on July 16, the third Sunday of the month and the feast of the Most Holy Redeemer, Gerard took the vows of poverty, chastity, and obedience."[27]

The brotherly relationship that he felt bonded him to Mazzini had a profundity and clarity which Gerard could not explain. "Only God knows." Now he is enriched with the joy and gratitude of the religious profession. The deep perspective is and continues to be one of generous fulfillment of God's will.

Sister Maria Celeste, to whom he refers at the end of the letter, is certainly Crostarosa, whom Mazzini knew in Scala in the early days of the Redemptorist Congregation.

Jesus + Mary

The grace of the Holy Spirit fill and always be in the soul of Your Reverence and may the Immaculate Mother keep it for you. Amen.

My dear Father,

How much I love you in Jesus Christ and Mary Most Holy. I hope that it is a pure affection in God. I do not know how to explain this. Only God knows how.

I thank you greatly for the pity and charity that you have shown me before his divine Majesty, to get our father to let me make my holy profession.

I have already made it, on the sacrosanct day of our Most Holy Redeemer. I hope that his Divine Majesty may never leave me and always assist me and help me to do his holy will.

My father, for the love of Jesus Christ and Mary Most Holy, may this soul of mine be commended to you: do not forget to present it always before God; and I, unworthy as I am, will never never never forget Your Reverence.

I kiss your sacred hands. And let us remain always in the heart of Jesus, and of the Blessed Virgin Mary.

Consolazione, July 26, 1752

Your Reverence's most unworthy servant and brother,

GERARD MAJELLA OF THE MOST HOLY REDEEMER

Note on the back: Sister Maria Celeste greets you most affectionately and would very much like to see you: she hopes that your Reverence will not forget her in your holy prayers, and she is waiting for a response.

I would have much to tell you about myself, with confidence and in secret, but I cannot: at this moment I am leaving the house.

9. [July 28, 1752]
To Saint Alphonsus[28]

This letter, too, is a clear and convincing testimony to the joy and profound gratitude with which Gerard lived his religious profession. It goes beyond a simple formal gesture of gratitude to authority.

The sincere respect for his "holy" Rector does not make Gerard lose his spontaneity. He is living "without light" in "eternal clarity." The deep sense of obedience, always noted, even in the most difficult moments of his life, is enhanced by this clarity. He can, therefore, write in his Memories (number 15): "I will correct everyone, even if it were the Father Rector, when he speaks ill of his neighbor."

Jesus + Mary

May the grace of divine love always be in the soul of Your Reverence and may the Immaculate Mother keep it for you.

My Father:

Here I am prostrate at the feet of your Reverence, and I greatly thank you for the goodness and charity shown me, so contrary to what I deserved, when Your Paternity accepted and received me for one of your sons.

Blessed for all eternity be the divine goodness that has shown such mercies to me that I am barely aware of, since on the sacrosanct day of our Most Holy Redeemer I made the holy profession and in this way consecrated myself to God.

O God, who was I and who am I that I dare to consecrate myself to God? I would actually like to speak of my unworthiness. But no, this does no good. For when one has not seen the eternal clarity, he who wishes to speak of the eternal truths is mad. At present it is useless.

My Father, for the love of Jesus Christ and Mary Most Holy, send me your holy blessing and put me at the feet of his Divine Majesty. I kiss your sacred hands.

Consolazione, today July 28, 1752

Most unworthy servant and son,

GERARD MAJELLA OF THE MOST HOLY REDEEMER

10. [February–March 1753]

To Sister Maria of Jesus[29]

The epistolary isolation in the monastery of Ripacandida lasted until the beginning of 1753. "The clarification had to take place in December of 1752, or, if there were more delays, in January 1753, keeping in mind that on the twelfth of December Saint Alphonsus wrote about the 'difficulty' with Monsignor. Later, in February, he rejoiced with Sister Maria because 'she was bringing back the observance.'"[30] Hence the date sug-

*gested, given that the letter bears witness to the joy over the
end of the prohibition, which was lived in faith amid profound
suffering.*

*The letter is a hymn to faith: faith in God, the faithful
guide on everyone's path, which comes to be fidelity and true
love of the neighbor. Gerard is profoundly determined "to live
and die saturated with holy faith." And on this point he does
not tire of exhorting all those whom he meets.*

*The joy over the recommencement of the correspondence
is masked with humor. Thus Gerard manages to avoid opening
up a conversation about the problematic aspects of the recent
past, which were just about to be resolved. The important thing
is to continue the path with great courage and freedom.*

Long live our beloved God. May God protect you.

Our dear and loving Jesus be always with you, my dear
mother, and Mother Mary Most Holy, keep you always in the
lovingness of our dear God. Amen.

Here is the answer to your attentive letter. I tell you that
one has to write to all the universe and make everyone understand...and that it counts as one of the most famous marvels
of God, the fact that after so much time, Your Reverence remembered me, your servant. I thought that the woman I knew
before was no longer with me. Although, despite everything,
I'm still not sure. But I'm not worried; it is enough to have had
the honor to see you again. I rejoice infinitely and I give glory
to the Supreme Creator. Enough for now. Whatever may come,
I offer everything to my beloved God, and I pardon you.

If afterwards Your Reverence complains of me, I tell you
that at least I am not Sister Maria of Jesus, who promises so
much and does not come through. Because I am incapable of
forgetting what I have promised. I wish to make sure that I
satisfy my obligation, because I want to do everything that I
promised you. Because he who does not meet his obligations
doesn't meet them with himself either.

That is how I am: the more I see myself far from Your

Reverence, that much more do I hasten to journey toward you, to meet with my beloved God once more.

Long live that holy pact that was made, which illumines so great a mystery for me! Faith is needed for loving God. Whoever has no faith misses God. I am now resolved, with all this, to live and die kneaded in holy faith. Faith is my life, and life to me is faith.

Oh God, who would want to live without holy faith? I would like to shout, so that I might be heard by the whole universe, and so say all the time: Long live our holy faith in our beloved God!

Only God deserves to be loved. And how will I be able to live if I miss my God?

Ah! I will have to put a brake on my pen and live buried in silence. And rest there in the sweet rest of eternal fusion. Oh inexplicable divinity, speak for me, since I cannot. I surrender to you, my God! Ah, I rest with you.

Your Reverence's most unworthy and beloved brother,

GERARD MAJELLA OF OUR BELOVED REDEEMER

11. [May 1753]
To Sister Maria of Jesus[31]

To leave a post of responsibility one has occupied for many years is never easy. Sister Maria of Jesus found herself in this situation, since the community had elected a new superior, Sister Michela of Saint Francis Xavier. Gerard approaches her, exhorting her not to cling to any thoughts of sadness or discouragement: "Do not be afflicted, for you afflict me too." It is necessary, instead, that she strive to make the most of all the opportunities for doing good that are available in her new situation.

Above all, Sister Maria must not doubt his brotherly affection. This is not based on the office that she used to hold: it is the transparency of love that is faithful to God. For his part,

*Gerard is convinced of the loyalty of Sister Maria and so he
insistently begs her for prayers.*

May divine grace fill the heart of Your Reverence and may
Mother Mary (*Mamma Maria*) Most Holy keep it for you. Amen.

My blessed mother in Jesus Christ, glory be to God, that
the new prioress has been designated. I want you to do me the
kindness of greeting her for me, for I greatly rejoice in her new
office. I hope from the immense God that with this office she
may become a great saint. Amen. And when God wishes, because he does wish it, I hope to write to her.

You tell me to go there. Yes, my blessed mother, when God
wishes me to go, I shall go with all my heart to console you.
Therefore be joyful; do not afflict yourself, for that way you
afflict me too.

You tell me that now that you will no longer be superior,
everyone will forget Your Reverence. My God! How can you
say that? Even if all creatures were to forget you, your divine
spouse Jesus Christ will not forget Your Reverence. As for me,
I have never forgotten and I will never forget. And I would
wish Your Reverence never to forget me, because you know
well the meaning of a pact and faith.

Come now, have great courage in loving God and in becoming a great saint; now you will have more time, because
you do not have so many matters to deal with as before.

Pray a great, great deal to God for me, for I have a great
spiritual need, and God knows how afflicted and disconsolate
I am now. If you wish, you can help me a great deal with God.
Do me this favor, which God knows…God knows what I would
like to say to you.

Many greetings to Sister Giuseppa, to Sister Teresa, to Sister Olivia, and to all the holy community. And let us remain
united in one, transformed into the being of God. Amen.

Foggia, May 7, 1753

I find myself in Foggia taking care of our affairs.

Your Reverence's most unworthy servant
and brother in Jesus Christ,

GERARD MAJELLA OF THE MOST HOLY REDEEMER

12. [June 11, 1753]
To Sister Maria Michela of Saint Francis Xavier[32]

*After having written to Sister Maria, Gerard takes up the pen
once more and turns to the new superior of Ripacandida. His
congratulations and best wishes arise from the his awareness
of the "holy election" by which Sister Maria Michela has come
to be in charge of the community. This is another element that
bears witness to the esteem which Gerard nourished for the
monastery.*

*The vigilance to which he exhorts the new superior must
be such that it permits all the sisters to be "seraphs of the love
of God."*

*The memory of the prayers of the community, which he
begs for himself, is accompanied by a delicate gesture toward
Sister Maria of Jesus that profoundly reveals Gerard's personality: "May it be in your heart."*

Jesus + Mary

May God's grace fill the heart of your reverence and may
Mother Mary (*Mamma Maria*) Most Holy keep it for you.
Amen.

My dear sister in Jesus Christ:

For a long time I have been wanting to write to you so as
to satisfy my obligation. I have not been able to do so because
of a lack of opportunity. Now I can and so I am writing to
you.

I tell you that I am greatly consoled by your holy election
as mother superior. I pray the Lord that he may make you
exercise this office of yours so that with the utmost attention

you may watch over so many spouses of Jesus Christ. I hope that his Divine Majesty may wish to give you the same spirit that he gave that seraph of love, Saint Maria Magdalena dei Pazzi, the great servant and beloved of Jesus Christ and of Mary Most holy, so that with such a grace and spirit you may animate those spouses with the perfection that his Divine Majesty deserves (insofar as a creature may be capable of this). And may all of you remain so many seraphs inflamed with the love of God.

My mother, I beg you for the love of Jesus Christ and Mary Most Holy not to forget me in your prayers, and to order all your daughters to pray to God for me, as I do for all of you.

Within a short time I shall be there. I come under command of God's will. And if you wish to answer me, do as you please; I might be in the house of Don Benedetto by Thursday. I beg that Sister Maria of Jesus may be in your heart, because you know well that she was a mother to you from the beginning and nursed you with the milk of the love of God.

Send my greetings to Sister Maria Giuseppa and Sister Maria Battista and to all the holy community. And I remain kissing the holy walls of the convent.

Deliceto, Santa Maria della Consolazione, June 11, 1753

Your most unworthy servant and brother in Jesus Christ,
GERARD MAJELLA OF THE MOST HOLY REDEEMER

13. [July 11, 1753]
To Sister Michela of Saint Francis Xavier[33]

Gerard had a profound respect for religious life. He strove to get everyone who was called to this vocation to respond with generosity and haste. "Whenever he got to know any young woman anxious to become a saint, he would immediately propose to her one of the monasteries of Ripacandida or Foggia, and went to all the trouble he could to persuade her to enter them, provided that she had a sufficient dowry. When he met an aspirant who was well intentioned but poor in material goods, he did everything possible to help her, getting his friends to cooperate with a generous donation to provide her with a dowry."[34]

Signora Nuncia to whom Sister Maria was supposed to write was the wife of Don Benedetto Graziola, from Atella. Her house was always open to Gerard on his travels.[35]

The decisions regarding a vocation—Gerard was convinced—must not be put off. Hence his insistence with Sister Michela "to be quick, quick, and with the greatest solicitude."

Most reverend sister:

I am writing to you from Foggia, and I write in haste. My God, I would really like to know what is going on there. I don't know anything, because I have gotten no answer to any of my letters. It seems to me that you must not have paper to write to me. For mercy's sake, if that is true, send me word of it, so I can send you a notebook and you can reply rapidly. Enough for now.

By the grace of God, I have gotten new alms for a matter that you know about. But you are keeping me in suspense. Let it be for the love of God!

Have Mother Maria of Jesus write to Signora Nuncia, and ask her too about the matter already mentioned. But her husband is not to be informed of this; and let it be quick, quick, and with the greatest solicitude. And let her know further that other contributions have been received, so that she can join in.

If there are letters for me, send them to me.

I am unwell. Greet everyone from me. I kiss your hands.

Foggia, July 10, 1753

Most unworthy servant and brother in Jesus Christ,

GERARD MAJELLA OF THE MOST HOLY REDEEMER

14. [July 1753]

To Sister Michela of Saint Francis Xavier[36]

This brief letter is passed on by Tannoia, with no indication of the date. Its contents allow us to place it in the month of July 1753.

Despite the difficulties, Gerard wouldn't stop trying to collect what was needed for the dowry of the sister of Sister Maria Giuseppa. His confidence in those who he felt were his friends allows him not just to be sure of their contributions, but to set the amount as well.

Send a letter to Don Benedetto for the purpose of soliciting a large contribution for Maria Giuseppa. He himself will be able to request [further help] from the prince of Torella. We will satisfied with an alms from the prince and Don Benedetto in the amount of one hundred ducats.

I have a scruple that prevents me from collaborating as I would like. But if I get permission from Father Fiocchi we will finish off the matter. I have also written to Sister Maria Francesca in Muro so that she can ask her brother for a contribution.

15. [July 21, 1753]

To Sister Michela of Saint Francis Xavier[37]

From the reply of Sister Michela, Gerard has been disappointed to learn that the problems persist in accepting the sister of Sister Maria Giuseppa. To set up the dowry, Gerard continues to ask for and receive contributions.

He continues as ever to count on the communion of prayers that link him to the community, especially now when he is "very afflicted." He begs for prayers in a special way from Sister Celeste, one of the daughters of Don Benedetto Graziola. He doesn't fail to make special mention of Sister Maria of Jesus.

My Mother Prioress:

I reply to your most revered letter, in which I have heard things that have saddened me. May the will of God be done!

I have gotten three gold sequins for Your Reverence, and the person who gave them to me doesn't want this known; for this reason I will keep it among my things...if God wills, I will send them to you.

I am very afflicted; hence I beg you to pray a great deal to God for me. I believe that Your Reverence will not forget to have your daughters also pray to God for me. As for myself, I do not forget Your Reverence. God knows how I love you in God. I would like to see you a seraph full of the love of God, so that when they see you all your daughters may catch fire.

Be well and keep yourself in the pure love of God. May God bless us. Amen.

Long live the beloved Lord God. May God keep you.

Melfi, July 21, 1753

Your Reverence's most unworthy servant and brother,

GERARD MAJELLA OF THE MOST HOLY REDEEMER

Greetings to Maria Celeste and may she not forget me in her holy prayers, for I do not forget her.

My mother, what do you want of me, who continually thinks of you in my frozen prayers? I am always close to you, begging you not to forget me.

I hear that there are still obstacles for the sister of Sister Giuseppa, but "who is like God?"

Imprison Mother Mary of Jesus: tell her that she deserves it. When God wishes, we will see each other. Now God has not wanted us to....

16. [July–August 1753]

To Sister Michela of Saint Francis Xavier[38]

In the face of the difficulties in getting the sister of Sister Maria Giuseppa accepted in Ripacandida, Gerard would not surrender. He made contact with Celeste Crostarosa in Foggia. The insistence on living on Divine Providence is meant to be an admonition, with seriousness and respect, for Sister Michela, who appeared to be too worried about the dowry.

As for changing the purpose of the offerings he had received, he flatly rejects the idea. The commitment taken on would be lost. It is yet another aspect of that fidelity and loyalty that Gerard shows in all his activity. Hence his desire to meet personally with the young woman, in order to speak "with the utmost sincerity" and better understand her real intentions. But everything has to be done discreetly so as to avoid any misunderstanding.

Doing the will of God demands that all the talents be put out to make a profit. But evangelical simplicity is always accompanied by prudence (see Mt 10:16).

My Mother Prioress:

As for the difficulties with the sister of Sister Maria Giuseppa, you tell me that I should content myself with the will of God. Yes, Lord, take that away from me and then see what remains in me, yes.

And about the money that is in my power, which I have obtained from friends, you tell me that you want it kept in deposit, so that if she doesn't succeed in becoming a nun, the funds will serve to get her married.

My mother, what are you saying? This is something neither I nor anyone else can do. It would be the same as harming our congregation, because the people I sought help from were asked with the commitment and purpose of making her a nun and not of getting her married. And if I don't succeed in doing this, the money ought to be restored to those to whom it belongs.

But I hope in God that it may not turn out that way, because here we are trying to place her in the girls' orphanage in Foggia, since less money is required there, and surely it could work. Although they are of the middle class, they live by divine providence, they say the office of the Virgin, and they live without making any distinctions between one another.

Oh my God, I would like to have this girl here; so speak to her with the utmost sincerity. And I would like her to express her wishes. That is how—quickly, quickly—to do things well. And we could send her to somebody so that she might come to the house of Mamma Victoria, with the excuse of going to see [the sanctuary] of Saint Theodore. And don't speak with anyone in Berilli, much less in Melfi.

And if she came here, let no one mention what house she is coming to, because if it would be known, it would prompt criticism. As for the expenses of the mount that brings her, I will pay everything here.

Long live God, love God.

Your Reverence's most unworthy true servant,

GERARD MAJELLA OF THE MOST HOLY REDEEMER

If you are in agreement, then let it be immediately, tomorrow morning. But in order to make sure that the matter is more secret, send her word, by means of the woman employed, not to say anything in her house to anyone; otherwise I will have her tongue dried. Our director blesses you, and so do I.

17. [End of 1753 or Beginning of 1754]
To Father Francisco Margotta[39]

Tannoia, who has passed on this letter to us, provides no indication of its date. We know that Gerard was in Deliceto, during the period when Father Fiocchi was the superior, until April of 1754. He made the acquaintance of the sisters at Ripacandida in December 1751. The letter says that it has been three years since Sister Maria Giuseppa recommended him to her sister. Hence, this letter is placed between 1753 and 1754.

Gerard continues with his efforts to get the dowry together. He begs without blushing, moved by true charity: it's a question of allowing a vocation to be realized. He exhorts Father Margotta to do as much.

My father:

Three years ago Sister Maria Giuseppa recommended me to her sister in Ripacandida. I could not help her, because I was not free; but now the Lord moves me to take an interest in her.

Father Fiocchi is in agreement. And he too wishes to give me some alms and wants me to look for others. The first time I opened my mouth I got fifty ducats. The Lord makes me find all doors open. I have thought of sending it to Foggia, committing myself with the prioress for three hundred ducats.

Come, my father, seek out those who may have an alms, without respect to persons. I seek it without blushing. Speak with the Berillis and others. You can do everything if you wish.

18. [Summer 1753]

To Sister Michela of Saint Francis Xavier[40]

Tannoia notes that "most of the letter is missing, because it has been lost."[41] But the part that has remained can make us understand how Gerard saw the ministry of authority in a religious community.

As we saw in the previous letters, he was always ready to help the monastery. But his main concern was the authenticity of religious life. For this, with complete freedom, he doesn't hesitate to give his advice about running the community.

It is necessary, first of all, that the superior consider the charge that had been confided to her as willed by God: in everything "one must be ruled by the spirit of Jesus Christ." Hence the accent on humility, on the bustling solicitude for each one of the sisters, and, above all, on true prudence. Gerard was convinced that "it is because of a lack of prudence that so many problems exist in some religious houses."

My Mother Prioress:

Be indulgent with me, for the love of Jesus Christ and Mary Most Holy, and if I didn't serve you immediately so as to send you these regulations, which Your Excellency asked for, as I have been continually occupied in my usual idleness. May God's will be done. And now that I am writing you in haste, pardon me, out of charity.

First, the mother prioress, who is in the place of God, has to carry out her office with extreme rectitude, if she wishes to please the supreme Lord, whom she represents. Be full of infinite prudence. In all her doings she must be guided with the spirit of Jesus Christ. She must be full of fine virtues and good examples and not give her daughters the least grounds for scandal. She must be a pure vessel full of holy virtues, and let all the virtues pour out from her so as to communicate them to her daughters. In this way, all the same virtues of the mother grow.

Whoever is superior must continually look at her unworthiness, considering that she cannot do anything else but evil, that God in his goodness has placed her in the office where she finds herself, because there are so many others who could do it better and give him more pleasure. She must, therefore, humble herself, recalling her imperfections, and understand the defects of the others.

She has to carry out her office completely full of love for God and not with annoyance, as if it were something that did not come from God. She must think that God prepared it for himself for all eternity. For this reason she must exercise it with extreme angelic perfection and conform herself in all things to the divine will. And she should stay in her position with indifference, without becoming attached.

In the matters that leave her confused, that is, the ones she doesn't know how to resolve or what course to follow in this or that question, she should take counsel with a person illumined by God. When the case is over, she must place before her eyes only God's glory and execute it without any more worries. And for God she must risk her blood and her own life because it is God's cause.

For the love of this same God, she must look down, especially, on her own personal opinions, as if she didn't have any. She should consider only that she is the superior and say: God wants me to be in this state, and therefore I must do his will in all things. I must take care of everyone. I must always console everyone and satisfy everyone. I must always give the best things to the others, and always make use of the worst, so as to give pleasure to God. And, finally, I must suffer in all things so as to enjoy the holy imitation of my dear spouse, Jesus Christ.

The thought of the superior has to be a continual wheel, which turns by thinking of her daughters' needs. She must purely love all of them in God, without making any distinctions. She has to think that her daughters cannot seek what they need, since holy obedience gives it to them. For which reason she must not be concerned for herself, but all her thought has to be occupied in her daughters. When food is given to her, or clothes, or any other thing, she must not take it unless she has first pleased the others.

She must give her trust to all her sisters, above all when she sees that one of them does not have complete trust in her. Then she must use all her energy and prudence to win over the other's heart, receiving her with kindness, although she does not feel it internally. And she must use all force upon herself in order to overcome herself, for the love of God. If she does not do so, showing the familiarity of a mother, she will certainly enlarge the distance separating her from her daughter, who, seeing herself despised, may give in to despair or, at least, not advance in the love of God, because she will continually have that thorn in her heart. This is frequent among women.

Strength and sweetness are demanded of the superior. Placed as a representative of God, she must make herself obeyed and must punish the disobedient who do not wish to hear the will of God, but she must punish them with prudence.

Correction must begin with sweetness. That way you are left with a certain tranquility, which helps to recognize the mistake. For example, the correction must be made in this manner: "You are not doing well, and your unworthiness can no longer be borne by me and by so many good souls who know you. My God, what can I do with this imperfect soul? My daughter, do you not see that with your bad example you are the cause of scandal among so many holy souls? It would have been better for you to remain in the world and not to have come to occupy this place, where another might have come who would now have become a saint. I tell you this and I must tell it to you because I am your mother. God knows how much I love you and care for you and how much I desire your holiness. My daughter, decide to become a saint and promise God that you wish to get rid of these imperfections. Do this and see how I can help you, and come [to talk] with me with the confidence of a daughter."

I am of the opinion that when correction is made in this way, the daughter will have recourse to the mother; and the mother, by showing confidence in her, can disabuse her and make her walk on the true path of perfection.

It is done better with sweetness, when that is appropriate, than with harshness. Intransigence brings with it disturbances, darkness, and discouragement. Sweetness brings peace and tranquility and encourages the daughters to love God.

If all superiors behaved this way, all their subjects would be saints. Because prudence is lacking, there are so many problems in some religious houses. Wherever there are disturbances, the devil is present and God is not.

19. [October 1, 1753]

To a Nun[42]

We do not know the addressee of this brief message. Its tone allows us to suppose that it is one of the two daughters of Benedetto Graziola, who were nuns in Ripacandida.

The radiant holiness of Gerard causes his presence to be a consolation in the house of his friends. But it is also a consolation for him to communicate with so many women servants of God. And he is happy to share all this with anyone who will take from it new incentives for goodness.

Most Beloved in Christ:

I was in your house one night, because your lord father asked me there, so as to console everyone in your respected family. There was much success, and I remained most consoled for having spoken with so many servants of God.

Pray for me, as I do not forget Your Reverence. And let us remain in God.

Ruvo, October 1, 1753

Your Reverence's most unworthy servant
and brother in Jesus Christ,

GERARD MAJELLA OF THE MOST HOLY REDEEMER

20. [Around the Middle of 1753]
To Sister Maria of Jesus[43]

The letter has no date. In all probability it should be placed in the summer or autumn of 1753: Gerard's state of soul seems to be the same as described in the letter of July 21 to Sister Michela; he also refers to her in this letter.

The "complaint" of Gerard aims to be more an incitement than a chiding. With the joviality that is characteristic of him, he insists that the communion of prayers not break down. Sister Maria must not doubt Gerard's fidelity, despite all the difficulties.

Jesus + Mary

I have received your most esteemed letter, which I greatly lament: first, the style was so cold; second, you are always telling me that I do not pray to his Divine Majesty for Your Reverence.

My sister, God knows and sees my spirit! But you do not see results because God does not hear my prayers on account of my great unworthiness.

Tell me, then, what you want me to do about this; but don't tell me anymore that I forget to pray to God for Your Reverence, because that would be against our pact.

Greet the other prioress for me and tell her that I have to call her to account since she doesn't wish to pray to God for me.

Very well, very well. I have informed myself sufficiently about your person. Your Reverence is making fun of me. Pray for me. If you do not, you will have much to answer for to God.

Your Reverence's most unworthy servant
and brother in Jesus Christ,

GERARD MAJELLA OF THE MOST HOLY REDEEMER

21. [Second Half of 1753]

To Sister Battista of the Most Holy Trinity[44]

This dense but brief message to Sister Battista of the Holy Trinity, eighteen years old, a nun at Ripacandida, does not have a precise date. Perhaps it comes from the summer or autumn of 1753, given that Gerard is still near Ripacandida and his state of mind here seems to be that of his letters from this period.

Gerard had not been able to meet Sister Battista in the parlor of the monastery, possibly because she was ill. But he does not cease to give her words of encouragement and exhortations. The condolences over her sickness are backed up by the certainty that she has lived in the light of the cross of Christ. All this is possible when we do not lose sight of the fact that "the center" of life is in giving oneself totally to God and conforming to his will.

My sister in our beloved Jesus Christ:

I regret very much to hear about your sickness. But I was greatly consoled by the fact that you have suffered it for our beloved God.

My sister, let us be conformed to the divine will, insofar as his Divine Majesty has not permitted you to come speak with me. Because the center of true love for God consists in surrendering completely to God and conforming in all things to his divine will and then remaining there for all eternity.

Let us be attentive, my sister, so as never to commit voluntary defects, which greatly displease God.

Pray to God for me, since I am not a man, but a man transformed into a beast, since I let myself be conquered and swept along by my own passions.

Most unworthy servant and brother in Jesus Christ,
GERARD MAJELLA OF THE MOST HOLY REDEEMER

22. [Second Half of 1753]

To Sister Battista of the Holy Trinity[45]

This brief note is found in Tannoia, with no indication of the date; it can be attributed to the same period as the preceding letter, given that Gerard's state of mind and the personal situation of the sister seem to be the same.

When it is read with the eyes of faith, everything comes to be a motive for uniting oneself with God, even one's name. Then communion with others develops, along with the mutual support of prayer, a wellspring of trusting hope.

My sister:

Recommend me to God, and now more than ever, because I have a great need.

I do not forget Your Reverence, because your name, which is that of the Blessed Trinity, always reminds me of God and carries me to him. My sister, God knows how much I esteem you because you are a faithful spouse of Jesus Christ.

Love God with your heart, and become a saint. The sufferings do not matter. Courage, suffer for God, because that way your pain will become a second paradise here on earth.

23. [March 1753–April 1754]

[To Sister Maria Celeste of the Holy Spirit][46]

In giving us this letter, Tannoia "tells us that Gerard writes it for a novice at Ripacandida. Ferrante suggests as a mere probability that this may have been Sister Maria Celeste of the Holy Spirit. This is very likely, since she would make her profession in October, 1754....This letter would have to be placed in the year running from March 1753 to April 1754."[47]

The novices' vocational difficulties lead Gerard to compose a hymn to the beauty of religious life and to insist on the "dangers of the world." The decisive options for life have to be chosen while keeping our eyes fixed on the right horizon: God and eternity. And the fidelity to one's own vocation, whatever it may be, has to be seen as a fundamental element of Christian life.

My Sister in Jesus Christ:

I tell you on the part of my dear God to put yourself in a solid and holy peace, because this is all the work of the devil to cast you out of this holy place.

My daughter, be attentive, because the iniquitous evildoer is full of envy and deceits; and he will be disgusted if you stay there, as he wishes to prevent you from becoming a saint. We were all tempted about our vocation. It is God who sends the temptation so as to see our fidelity. For this reason, remain cheerful and always offer yourself to God without any reservation, for he will help you.

How is it possible that Your Charity would wish to forget the beautiful resolutions that you have made so many times, to offer yourself and wish to be the spouse of Jesus Christ? If you desired it then, why do you wish to reject it now?

My sister, who will be able to give us peace except God? When has the world filled the human heart, whether of a princess, a queen, or an empress? This has never yet been heard or read in any book. We only know that the world always sows thorns and tribulations in their hearts, the richer, the more honored and esteemed they were, with a life completely full of satisfactions, they suffered just as much inside.

What do you wish me to say? I would like to make you speak with the most joyful person in the world, so as to see whether if what appears in his or her exterior is genuine. But believe, for I have experience: what an ugly thing it is to live in the world! May God free you from it, my sister. God loves you well and for this he has permitted you to be tempted, so as to test your fidelity.

Therefore, be joyful and take heart! Overcome, overcome every temptation with generosity, declaring yourself always the spouse of our greatest Lord Jesus Christ. To be a spouse of Jesus Christ is beautiful. In him is met all happiness, all peace, all good. What good are the brief appearances of the world in comparison with that celestial and eternal beatitude that someone who has consecrated himself to Jesus Christ enjoys in heaven!

I do not say that people who are in the world cannot be saved, but I say that they are in constant danger of being lost. And they cannot become saints as easily as in the convent.

Consider, I beg you, the brevity of the world and the lastingness of eternity. Think that everything comes to an end. Everything is finished for those who live in the world; it's as if they had never been there. As a result, what good does it do to lean on what cannot sustain us? So, all these things that do not carry us to God are all vanity, and they can be of no use to us for eternity. How poor is the person who trusts in the world and not in God.

I beg you, my sister, to go for a moment to your cemetery, where the remains of so many holy nuns from the monastery lie buried. Reflect above all on what would have happened if they had been important people in the world. Oh, how much they were helped by living poor, mortified, despised, and locked up in this little convent. How much peace must they have had, seeing themselves die in the house of God. Everyone would like to be a saint at the moment of death, but then it is not possible: in the end we are left with only what has been done for God.

If the storm has not passed, I have much faith and much hope in the Most Holy Trinity and in Mother Mary (*Mamma Maria*) that Your Charity has to become a saint where you are. Don't make me look like a liar. Crush the head of the great infernal beast that seeks to throw you out of this holy place. Despise him: tell him that you are a spouse of Jesus Christ, so that he trembles. Be joyful, love God with your heart, always give yourself generously to him and make the demon burst and die.

Pray for me, and I will do the same for you.

24. [First Months of 1754]

To Sister Maria of Jesus[48]

This is a cry for help directed to Sister Maria. The name of the sister is written in the lower margin. The communion reflected in the text is the same one attested to in the other letters sent to the nuns at Ripacandida. The date is not certain. The one given above is suggested by Capone, based on Gerard's spiritual evolution during this period. Furthermore, we know that in the month of September 1754 Sister Olivia had already died.[49]

"I see myself totally downcast and in a sea of confusion: almost in despair." And the reason, at bottom, is that he seems to be suffering abandonment by God. The process of assimilation to the Crucified for the salvation of his brothers was becoming more pronounced. This relates to what the witnesses remembered in the beatification trial: "Gerard was almost always happy even in his most painful sicknesses: and he felt in pain and downcast only in the days of the Passion of Jesus Christ, as he considered the sufferings of the Redeemer."[50]

My God, have pity on me:

Ah, my mother, how do you make fun of me? Do you know why you write to me in this way? To cause me more pain for my sins.

Your Reverence is glad and for this you make fun of me. What do you wish me to do? That is how God wishes it, and I rejoice greatly in your happiness. May God maintain you and keep you, since you are loved of God.

That is how things are going nowadays: one rises up and another goes down. I have descended in such a manner that I have no way out. And I think that my sufferings have to be eternal.

But I would not care if they were [eternal]: it would be enough that I loved God and that I pleased him in everything.

This is my suffering: I believe I am suffering, abandoned by God.

My mother, if you do not help me, I will have more problems, because I see myself totally downcast and in a sea of confusion: almost in despair. I think that for me God no longer exists and that his infinite misery has been exhausted for me. Only his justice has remained over me.

Observe and see in what a miserable state I find myself. And if in truth you are keeping that pact between us, now is the moment to help me and to pray hard to God for me, wretch that I am. I beg you to have pity on my soul, because I am ashamed to appear before God's creatures.

Greet Mother Superior for me, Mary Magdalene, Giuseppa, Battista, Olivia, Maria of Divine Love, Teresa, and all the holy community.

Your Reverence's most unworthy servant
and brother in Jesus Christ,

GERARD MAJELLA OF THE MOST HOLY REDEEMER

25. [Before March 1754]
To Sister Maria of Jesus[51]

This brief message for Sister Maria is passed on by Tannoia, with no indication of date. Gerard refers to Luigi Mercante, a penitent of Father Fiocchi's, whom Sister Maria wanted to be-

come a Redemptorist. On March 24, 1754, writing to Sister Maria, Saint Alphonsus laments the lack of news about Mercante "for a long time" and concludes that "surely he will have gone cold by now."[52] Gerard's letter cannot be later than this time, since he says that "our dear Don Luigi sighs for Jesus Christ."

Our dear Don Luigi cannot find rest and sighs for Jesus Christ. He has been seen totally immersed in God and cannot separate himself from Jesus Christ. He sees the world as nothing and looks upon all creatures in God. He loves God and is transformed into him. That is all that I can tell you.

26. [Undated]

To a Nun[53]

In transmitting this short letter, Tannoia doesn't offer us any information, either as to the date or for specifically identifying the addressee. The latter must have been a nun suffering from scruples.

Gerard's habitual recommendations return here insistently: be joyful and confident. There is no need to let oneself be terrified by the difficulties. The certitude of the presence of Mary lets every obstacle be overcome.

Be joyful and do not lose heart. Trust in God and hope for every grace from God.

Do not trust in yourself too much, but in God alone. When you believe you are serene is just when the enemy is closer. Do not trust peace, because in moments of quiet war can come.

Live with caution; at every moment you must trust in Mary Most Holy, so that she can assist you and overthrow your every enemy with her power.

What you are suffering is no reason to be afflicted, but rather to humble yourself before God and to trust even more in his divine mercy.

Reflecting on the things that you tell me is a work of the Evil One so as to make you lose time.

Be joyful; trust in God, who will make you a saint.

27. [April 1754]

To the priest Gaetano Santorelli[54]

We are in Easter Week (April 14–21). Gerard is at the point of heading to Pagani, where he has been summoned by Saint Alphonsus, on account of the calumny spread by Nerea Caggiano. Despite this, he takes up the pen to write to Gaetano Santorelli, a priest at Caposele, whom he got to know a few months before, and who had opened up to him his conscience full of perplexity and scruples, which had ended by blocking him in his pastoral activity.

For Father Gaetano's peace of mind Gerard adopts an authoritative tone: "On behalf of the Most Holy Trinity and my mother Mary Most Holy." He reminds him of the "rules" that he, a humble religious brother, has drawn up for him. Scruples, whether in the past or the present, should not block him in his priestly ministry, above all in hearing confessions: "It is enough that your will not to offend God remains firm."

As for himself, Gerard limits himself to ask for prayers, "because I am greatly in need."

Jesus + Mary

The grace of the Holy Spirit be always in the soul of Your Reverence. Mary Mother (*Mamma Maria*) Most Holy keep it for you, Amen. I write to you in haste.

My dear and most venerated Father Gaetano,

To my supreme consolation I received a most lovable letter from you. I thank you very much for your great kindness to this servant of God. May God himself reward you for it, as I certainly know he will.

Listen to me and listen with the utmost attention to what I say to you, because I say it in the name of the Most Holy

Trinity. Consider this as the last reply you will have from me and that I will no longer speak to you as I do now.

As for the scruples of your past life, your conscience has been examined more than once, as I know. Therefore let Your Reverence no longer think about it. Your anxieties and doubts are all tricks of the infernal enemy, who tries to make you lose the beautiful peace of your conscience. Hence, you must not attend any more to such thoughts; reject them as a real temptation. Try rather to keep true interior peace, so that you can advance better in holy perfection.

Concerning the rules that you want, let Your Reverence use the first one that I made for you and none other.

About the continual scruples that you have about confessing, in truth I tell you that this lament of yours is a temptation to make you leave the office that was assigned to you by God from all eternity for your supreme spiritual profit. Be attentive.

I tell you on behalf of God: never give in to such a temptation, because if Your Reverence were to leave [the ministry of] confession, it would be your great ruin and impediment in the spiritual life. And if you leave it, God would not give you that great future reward. It would be the same as not doing the divine will.

Once again I insist that it is God's will for you to strive with the utmost zeal in the vineyard of my Lord and not have doubts about what may happen in confession. It is enough that your will not to offend God remains firm, and don't worry about the rest.

As for knowledge, God has given you as much as you need for your task.

I do not think it feasible that Your Reverence and Don Nicola should come here, because I am about to leave for Pagani, as the superior tells me.

I thank you for your affection, without merit on my part.

I beg you to pray for me always to God, because I am greatly in need.

Blessed be the divine goodness forever, which bears my so many miseries.

I greet attentively all those of your house and Don Nicola. I remain embracing you in the heart of Jesus. I kiss devotedly your sacred hands, as I do those of Don Nicola.

Your Reverence's most unworthy vile servant
and brother in Christ,
                    GERARD MAJELLA OF MY BELOVED REDEEMER

28. [Undated]

To Father Francesco Garzilli[55]

In transmitting this letter, Tannoia doesn't provide any information about its date. In its motivations and contents, it is analogous to the preceding one. The Redemptorist Francesco Garzilli, a priest and thirty-six years older than Gerard, was likewise going through a period of scruples. And by thinking and rethinking all this, he was running the risk of becoming more entangled.

Gerard invites him to play down the drama: it is a game by which God wants to show us that everything comes from him. Hence one has to be joyful. Confidence and hope in God must help us also to accept our limits and make us understand that the "saints were not pure spirits on earth."

May God's grace fill the heart of Your Reverence and may Mary Most Holy keep it for you.

My dear Father:

I rejoice greatly and I am consoled by the game that his Divine Majesty is playing with Your Reverence; let us hope that he wishes to grant you an ideal victory.

Now, let us go; up, fear no more, but be joyful, for God is with Your Reverence and I trust that He will not abandon you.

Your Reverence has doubts about your confessions. This state of anxiety is a small mortification that God wishes to give you. You tell me that you are [judging] in your own case.

Yes, sir, this idea is one that you must necessarily experience. If it were not so, there would be no anxiety. His Divine Majesty is accustomed to do this with his lovers, because he wants them to be anxious so as to let them know that everything comes from him. If Your Reverence recognized that everything comes from God, surely you would not have anymore sufferings; rather it would be for you like a paradise on earth. And if afterwards we have some little defect and we fall, let's think that the saints were not pure spirits on earth.

Trust and hope in God, my dear father. And for charity's sake, I beg you to recommend me to Jesus Christ and to Mary Most Holy. May they wish to bless the two of us.

29. [Toward the End of July 1754]
To Sister Maria of Jesus[56]

That this letter was directed to Sister Maria of Jesus may be inferred from its tone and contents, as well as the outside address: "To Mother Maria of Jesus C.S." The date proposed (Gerard's first stay in Naples, after the case of the false charges was settled) comes from Domenico Capone: Gerard was far away; it was before the profession of Sister Maria Celeste (October); and the text "has all the air of a letter that finally breaks a long silence and that has been awaited for some time. In addition, it seems to allude to the recent trials undergone by Gerard."[57]

The thanks for "the help" burst out sincerely, along with the prayer that "the Lord may reward you on my behalf" and the confirmation of the communion and reciprocal effort: "I would have given blood and life."

The jovial tone prevails, full of hope. The difficulties in the correspondence are due to "Fra Zurfo" (Brother Sulphur = the devil); but he can't be given the victory. "May God make you a great saint" is, in Gerard's letters, an exclamation of reproach said in a positive way.

My most reverend sister in Jesus Christ:

I have received your most venerated letter, and I was greatly, greatly consoled by it.

And for this consolation that you have given me I bless you a thousand times in the name of the Most Holy Trinity. May you be blessed a thousand times. Be blessed by God himself and by Mother Mary Most Holy and by the whole celestial court.

Your Reverence complains about my saying that I have answered none of the many letters you sent me. For the love of God, Your Reverence is saying to me what I wished to say to you. In truth, I have not received a single letter from Your Reverence, except for this one, and I have gotten no answers to any of the ones I have sent. I believe, as I have judged, that many of your letters and mine have been blocked by "Brother Devil" so as to make us suffer and cancel our pact. Let hell do what it wishes, in this it will never conquer.

I also excuse that mother prioress who, despite all letters I sent, has not answered a line for my consolation. I have her marked out: I wish to accuse her before Jesus Christ himself, so that he may imprison her.

I thank you for the assistance that you have afforded me. I trust that God will repay you on my behalf; I beg you not to speak of this to anyone. And do not let this business of yours become known.

Only God knows how many sufferings I have felt for your love. What do you want me to say? I would have given blood and life if it had been necessary.

May God make you a great saint, since you have not been willing to heed me.

Greet all my sisters affectionately for me and beg them not to abandon me, now that we are far apart.

Greet mother prioress especially for me. I am not writing her because she doesn't want to answer me. Do not imprison her anymore. Greet Maria of the Divine Love, Maria Giuseppa, Maria Teresa, Maria Magdalena, and Maria Celeste, whom I believe you have received.

Pray to God for me, for I shall not forget Your Reverence.

Finally, be well and commend me, and let us remain in the holy pact of Jesus Christ.

Long live Jesus, Mary...and my crazy [Magdalena] dei Pazzi

Your Reverence's most affectionate servant and brother,

GERARD OF MY DEAR REDEEMER

30. [August 28, 1754]

To Sister Maria Celeste of the Holy Spirit[58]

Gerard was in Naples with Father Margotta. "Most of the day he spent praying in one church or other, learning the art of making large crucifixes of papier-mâché. After shaping them with the plaster molds, he painted the Christs, but in a manner so pitiful, with the flesh torn and bloody, that they moved to tenderness everyone who looked at them."[59]

But he also had time for the booklet of songs that Sister Maria Celeste, the daughter of Don Benedetto Graziola, asked him for, shortly before her profession. She had to sing in order to become a great saint.

My Celeste:

I deeply regret that I can't write to you at length because of the hurry I am in, since I have to go out and they are waiting for me in the church. May God's will always be done.

Dear sister, I have recalled that since last year Your Reverence has wanted a little book of songs; I haven't sent them to you because the opportunity didn't arise. I have been waiting for a chance. Now that I find myself in Naples, I remembered. Here it is, I send it to you. Sing in your room, so that you may become a great saint, and always pray to God for me.

Your brothers greet you and are well. Greet my prioress for me and Maria of Jesus, Magdalena, Battista, Teresa of Divine Love, Giuseppa, your sister, and all my other sisters, and I remain saluting them.

Naples, August 28, 1754

Your Reverence's most unworthy servant
and brother in Jesus Christ,

                GERARD MAJELLA OF THE MOST HOLY REDEEMER

31. [August or September 7, 1754]
To Sister Maria of Jesus[60]

*Gerard forgot to indicate the month when he put the date at
the end of this letter. He remained in Naples until the last days
of October, but at the beginning of this month he wrote another letter to Sister Maria. It's likely, therefore, that this letter
comes from August or September.*

*The restrictions imposed after the calumny had ended, and
hence the stay in Naples was a period of serene joyfulness.
And in reality Gerard was living it up with his God and radiated joy and hope even into the poor corners of the hospital of
the "Incurables."*

*But at the same time, he continued his assimilation to Jesus
crucified: a painful process, but one charged with faith. "Blessed
forever be he who gives me more victories over life, so as to
give me more torments that I may be an imitator of my divine
Redeemer."*

Dear and most venerated sister:

I am writing to you from the cross, and because I have no
time to live, I am obliged to write you in all haste.

Have pity on my agony. I have little [spirit] now. And if I
had not forced myself, I would not have written this letter
because of the tears. My sufferings are so bitter that they give
me spasms of death. And when I think I am dying, once again
I find myself alive only to be more afflicted and desolate.

I do not know what else to tell you; I am not capable of
sharing my bile and poison so as to embitter you; I know that
you are happy. And because you are happy, that is enough to
encourage me and strengthen me in God.

Blessed forever be the One who grants me so many graces,

and who, instead of making me die beneath his holy strokes, gives me more victories over life, so as to give me more torments, that I may be an imitator of my divine Redeemer. He is my master, I am his disciple. It is just that I must learn from him and follow his divine steps.

But now I do not move or travel, being with Him on the height of the Cross, saddened and in inexplicable torments. The lance that could give me death has been lost. It is my gallows. Here I obey so as to obtain life in suffering.

It seems that everyone has abandoned me. And then, so that I may not remain in this state, I tell myself: this is the will of my heavenly Redeemer, to be nailed to the bitter Cross. I incline my head and say: this is the will of my dear God. I accept it. And I rejoice in doing as he commands and disposes.

It is possible that I might go there. But I mortify myself and I make no effort to succeed in doing so. My will is placed entirely in the hands of my superiors; let them do what they wish with me, for I am content.

God knows the desire I have to see you, perhaps more than you do [me]. Because I am urgently driven to breathe the living faith in that place of our holy mother Teresa.

Do me the kindness of greeting Sister Maria Giuseppa for me, along with Teresa, Battista of Divine Love, Magdalena, and all my other sisters.

Remain in peace. Farewell, my sister.

Naples, the 7th, 1754

It is no use speaking of your sufferings, because I know them and I see them in God, who praises you.

Your Reverence's most unworthy servant and brother,

GERARD MAJELLA OF THE MOST HOLY REDEEMER

32. [October 4, 1754]

To Sister Michela of Saint Francis Xavier⁶¹

"I am very sick, and within a few days I am going to live in Caposele." Despite this, Gerard finds all the power of his faith confident and full of hope of finding favor. The tone of his letter breathes joviality, rich in the sincere gratitude to the Lord that is typical of his way of life.

The affection and mutual commitment to prayer should not surprise Sister Michela, since, as brother and sister in the Lord, "it is right that we must love each other purely in God." For the rest, Gerard is counting greatly on the prayers of the sisters of Ripacandida: from time to time Sister Michela must remind them of this (renew the recommendation to respect it).

Jesus + Mary

Long live our dear God and our Mother of God.

Most venerated mother, my dear prioress:

With great consolation for myself, I received your dear letter. May my Lord be blessed and infinite, infinite number of times, he who has consoled me. And for your charity and kindness with me, despite my little merits, may the Lord repay you.

I was resolved to quarrel with you before my dear God. I was justified in doing this on account of my letters, which had not been answered. You have done well to write to me, because Your Reverence was in danger of falling under censure, as Your Reverence had once written me.

Do not be surprised that I should be so affectionate in my letter, because I have three reasons: the first is that you are a spouse of Jesus Christ, and as such I esteem and venerate you; the second is that you are a daughter of my dear [Saint] Teresa, and for the high esteem in which I hold her, I would give my blood and life to always defend and proclaim the glory of my dear God; the third is that we are brother and sister in my Lord, and so it is right that we must always love one another purely in God.

Enough: I am not asking you for anything else but that with some frequency you order all my dear sisters to always remember me in their holy prayers, for I, unworthy as I am, will always do the same for all of them.

As for what Your Reverence has asked of me for your aunts and uncles, I will pray for their souls till I die.

I am very sick, and within a few days I am going to live in Caposele. Pray for me, poor wretch.

It is true that if I went all the way there, I would console you, because I know your troubles. It is nothing: endure them all joyfully for God alone. And tell me how I can serve you, useless as I am. Command with complete freedom.

Do me the kindness of greeting every single one of my sisters, especially Sister Maria Teresa. I remain saluting you.

I thank you very, very much for the novena you made for me in honor of our Most Holy Trinity.

Naples, October 4, 1754

Your Reverence's most affectionate servant
and brother in Christ,

GERARD MAJELLA OF THE MOST HOLY REDEEMER

May God's will be done. I can't find the letter I had written for Sister Maria of Jesus. Night is coming on; I cannot write another, and the mail is about to go out. Wednesday, if God wills, I will send it to her. Greet her for me.

33. [October 4, 1754]
To Sister Maria of Jesus[62]

This is the letter that Gerard referred to at the end of the previous one to Sister Michela. It was already finished on October 4 and was sent on the ninth.

Gerard was sure of the loyalty of Sister Maria in the mutual commitment to prayers. In the same way, Sister Maria must not doubt his loyalty. For this reason he feels the sister's sufferings as his own: "If I say that I suffer them more than you, I am not lying." But rather than words, it is the Holy Spirit who must make Sister Maria understand this.

Personally Gerard was on the cross, but he blesses the divine will. He insists on asking for prayers, because "I fear I will not persevere." This depth of mystical assimilation to the crucified Christ and of brotherly communion is linked with intercession for the dying, lived in the forms most dear to the people: for Sister Olivia "I did eight days of communion."

To Mother Sister Maria of Jesus Christ the Savior:

Long live, long live our dear God, and our blessed Mother, in the unity of our holy pact. Amen.

My dearest sister:

I am replying to your most esteemed letter, and I tell you that I am very, very grateful to you for the holy novena you made for me to our Most Holy Trinity.

It is true that with Your Reverence there is no need for expressions, prayers, or doubts; and I know that what I wrote you in the most divine presence of God has remained confirmed by us. And the witnesses are our Most Holy Trinity and Mother Mary Most Holy. Yes, for my part I fulfill my obligation to Your Reverence before my Lord; and I do not cease to pray to him, unworthy sinner that I am.

My sister, I sympathize greatly with you, because you are alone, afflicted, and disconsolate, because you have no one to whom you can pour your heart out and be consoled. I know from personal experience the pains that you have gone through and are still going through; but I tell you that I feel them more sharply in my heart than Your Reverence does. You cannot imagine with what clarity and sharpness I understand them: if I say I do so even more than you, I am not lying.

I do not explain anything to you, because I know that, while Your Reverence reads this letter, the Holy Spirit is making me understand everything for my part, better than I could explain to you.

Oh, if only God would let me go there to console you, more for Your Reverence's sake than for mine.

I am very afflicted and disconsolate, wounded by divine justice to the maximum. Blessed be his divine will forever. And what makes me tremble the most and creates the greatest horror for me: I feel that I will not persevere. God forbid, because it would be the same as debasing myself. On this point I wish you to say all the prayers.

For my part, I tell you that, with respect to your sufferings, not to think of them anymore so that they may not cause you even more pain. Rather leave them in the arms of God's pity. Conform yourself to his divine will. And value highly what you have suffered for God, because this merit of yours will serve to make you a greater saint.

I beg you the favor of greeting for me mother prioress and Sister Maria of Divine Love, Maria Battista, Teresa, Giuseppa, Magdalena, Celeste.

You say that Olivia greets me. That is true, but from paradise, not from here. Unworthy as I am, I have offered her eight days of communion for her soul and all that I have done in these days. I wish to do the same for all of them, so that all those who are alive when I pass into eternity may pray to God for me and make eight days of communions for me.

Our Father Margotta is making the holy exercises. I know that he would have wished to send you greetings as well.

Your Reverence's most unworthy brother in Jesus Christ,

GERARD MAJELLA OF THE MOST HOLY REDEEMER

34. [November 1, 1754]

To Sister Maria Celeste of the Holy Spirit[63]

It is a "great consolation" to learn that the young sister has made her religious vows. In congratulating her, Gerard invites her to deepen her awareness of the gift that has been given to her, so as to proceed generously to the response: "Become a great saint, since by God's mercy you find yourself in such a holy circumstance." From this perspective, the time is coming to be a precious treasure so as to understand and bring forth fruit.

The desire to hide becomes stronger. Now that he is about to leave for Materdomini, Gerard will plead with his "holy Rector" to be locked in a room.

Most venerated sister in Christ:

Your dear letter gives me the utmost consolation, as I heard that now, by the grace of the Lord, you have made your holy profession. Long live God and Your Reverence, who have obtained the grace of consecrating yourself more completely to God by means of the holy vows.

Now more than ever you have greatness, because you are a new spouse of my Lord.

Ah, may you be a thousand times fortunate, if, while reflecting night and day on your great good luck, you humble yourself and put into execution the perfect customs that your great state demands.

In truth, you are in a state more dear to God than any other. Open your eyes and each morning venerate this divine goodness that grants you so many graces.

Courage, become a great saint, since, by God's mercy, you find yourself in such a holy circumstance.

Always, always pray to God for me and tell him, for kindness's sake, to make me a saint, because I am losing time. Oh my God, what bad fortune is mine, that I uselessly let pass so many moments and hours and days, without knowing how to make good use of them. Oh how much I waste. May God pardon me.

I already knew about the death of Maria Olivia. But I see that now Maria Antonia is in her place. Tell her for me that this greatly consoles me. For greater satisfaction I would like her, now more than ever, to put into practice the holy sentiments that she had before entering, and to become a saint like Sister Olivia. For if she does not become a saint, God will hold her to account for it. I greet her attentively and I beg her to do me the favor of commending me always to my Lord.

I consider going there impossible. I do not ask it of my superiors, because such is the path that my Lord has taught me. And now that I am withdrawing, as God wishes, I will ask my holy Rector to have them lock me in a room so as never to leave the house. I hope to obtain it.

I attentively greet the mother prioress, Maria of Jesus, Maria Teresa, Maria Giuseppa, Maria Magdalena, Maria Concetta and Scholastica, Maria of Divine Love, Maria Battista, and all the other sisters. Let them pray to the Lord for me, poor wretch, because I still do the same for those sisters, and God is my witness.

Remain in peace with the grace of my Lord. Farewell.

Naples, November 1, 1754

Your Reverence's most unworthy servant
and brother in Jesus Christ,

GERARD MAJELLA OF MY DEAR REDEEMER

35. [Undated]
To a Nun[64]

In giving us this brief text, Tannoia provides no information about the date or the individual nun to whom it was sent. "In the monastery of Ripacandida alone there were three nuns who had the appellation 'of Divine Love': Sisters Maria, Teresa, and Maria Battista."[65] This letter is placed here because it has a certain affinity with the previous one.

In a few lines we see synthesized some of Gerard's most beloved themes: love, prayer, the constant "yes" to God's will, and sincere brotherly communion.

Dear Sister in Jesus Christ:
I remind you to remember me when you love and pray to God. In truth, I tell you that you can help me, because you call

yourself "of Divine Love." And I believe that you are totally transformed into the loving essence of God and into his divine power. Become a saint, and quickly.

36. [March 1755]

To Sister Maria of Jesus[66]

In the Summarium *the addressee indicated is Sister Maria or another nun. The contents and tone of the letter undoubtedly lead us to think of Sister Maria of Jesus. It is hard to give a precise date. Capone suggests Gerard's second stay in Naples, in 1755, after two winter months spent in Materdomini, where the correspondence with Ripacandida was more problematic because of the rigors of winter. This would explain the break in communication to which the letter refers.[67]*

The tone of the letter is particularly cheerful: "I place in God all the contempt you have shown me." Everything is interpreted on the basis of its positive elements. Only in that way it is possible to make one's way joyfully. Gerard serenely accepts being considered, for no reason, an ingrate.

Long live our dear God.

The Holy Spirit, our loving Lord, be always in the soul of Your Reverence, my dear sister in Christ, and may Mother Mary (*Mamma Maria*) Most Holy keep you. Amen.

I am responding to an attentive letter of Your Reverence. I was greatly consoled to learn that you are well and that you have remembered me; I thought that Your Reverence had already given up praying for me to God. Even so, I am not very sure. But I place in God all the contempt you have shown me. God forgive you, for I have forgiven you.

As for that lady that Your Reverence writes to me about, you have not told me when [I would be able to meet her]. And Father is not here to ask permission from him, if he does give it to me, which I see as very difficult. Enough: let us trust in the Lord; pray a lot that he may do what we cannot do.

According to what you tell me, you were suspended from being portress for a little while. This was nothing; they suspended you on account of your being sick and for your own good. For this be joyful and take care to look after your assignment when you can. Love God and become a great saint.

Give my greetings to everyone, and continue to pray to God for me, as I do for Your Reverence. And may God bless us. Amen.

Our father cannot reply to mother, but he will send a reply tomorrow morning.

I believe that you take me for an ingrate. May God's will be done. That is how God wants it, because of my sins. But if you wish to be far from me, at least be close to me so as to always commend me to God.

Our Father asks the mother prioress to do him the favor of allowing Your Reverence to speak with the servant of Don Luigi and with Gerard.

Your Reverence's unworthy servant and brother in Christ,

GERARD MAJELLA OF THE MOST HOLY DEAR GOD

37. [March 8, 1755]

To Sister Maria Celeste of the Most Holy Savior[68]

This is the only letter that we know of from Gerard to the foundress of the female branch of the Redemptorists. The announcement of the indulgence obtained for the monastery of Foggia, "also for the young ladies who are their pupils" is accompanied by the pressing request for prayers, particularly "to intercede on behalf of my soul after my death." Perhaps Gerard felt that the moment of his meeting face to face with the Lord was not far off.

Like him, Maria Celeste would die a few months later, in September of that same year. "One day, the 14th of September to be precise, [Gerard] said to a lay person: 'Today in Foggia

Maria Celeste has passed over to enjoy God.' This was taken for a delirious comment; but in fact, as was later learned, on that day Maria Celeste had passed into eternity in the odor of sanctity... And it was at the same hour as he said. There must have been some link between him and the servant of God that we did not know."[69]

Jesus + Mary

May the grace of God and the consolation of our Holy Spirit always be in the soul of Your Reverence and of all your daughters, and may Mother Mary Most Holy keep it for you. Amen.

Our dear and most venerated Mother:

After my insistent pleas to the Rev. Father Francesco Pepe of the Company of Jesus, who, as you know, has all the authority granted by the Supreme Pontiff to grant any indulgences, I have now obtained, thanks to our dear God and Mary Most Holy, the following indulgences, which will be applicable to all your daughters, as well as to the young ladies who are their pupils. They are both for you and for all the other women who will be accepted later on, in perpetuity, the only obligation being to receive communion. And they are:

1. Plenary indulgence on the feast of the Most Holy Trinity.
2. Plenary indulgence on all the feasts of Jesus Christ.
3. Plenary indulgence on all the feasts of Mother Mary Most Holy.
4. Plenary indulgence on all the feasts of the Holy Apostles.
5. Plenary indulgence on the feast of Saint John the Baptist.
6. Plenary indulgence on the feast of Saint Anne.
7. Plenary indulgence on the feast of Saint Joseph.
8. Plenary indulgence on the feast of Saint Michael the Archangel.
9. Plenary indulgence on the feast of Saint Joachim.
10. Plenary indulgence on the feast of Saint Isabel.

I ask you only that you keep the present letter so that those who succeed you may profit from the indulgences mentioned.

Along with this, I remind you that all the sisters are under the obligation of praying to the Lord for me and to apply to me the indulgences that may occur to intercede for my soul after my death. The same thing is recommended to all of them, to all the superiors during their time in office, so that they may apply to me some communion on behalf of my soul....And I especially remind the prioress who is in charge immediately after my death that for eight days, on behalf of all the sisters who are there, she have them apply to me the indulgences that occur for my soul, and I too shall remember to pray to the Lord God for them so that he may make them saints. Amen.

Your Reverence will do me the favor of sending my greetings to all my sisters who pray to God for me, as they have promised me so many times. Impose this obedience on them.

And I remain with all of you in Jesus Christ.

Naples, March 8, 1755

Let our sisters note that in order to gain the indulgences mentioned, they have to make the intention in the morning or before going to communion.

Many greetings to my dear Don Nicola. I commend myself greatly to his holy prayers, as I already do for him.

38. [April 8, 1755]
To Father Celestino de Robertis[70]

Availability for the needs of others accompanied Gerard throughout his life. Beginning with his entrance into the Congregation, Caione observes, "he was especially in love with toil, so much so that he never wasted time. When he didn't have anything to do, he tried to help others with their work.... When the bread had to be baked for the community, he did the work of four men; he brushed aside the other brothers, saying: 'Let me do it; you go rest.'"[71]

He tells Father de Robertis in Pagani that he has followed
the work of making the statue of the Virgin. It was "most
beautiful," he said; but money was needed to cover the ex-
penses.

My dear Father:

I advise you that the statue of the Virgin is almost finished.
The only things lacking are the halo and the colors. It has really turned out most beautifully, as Your Reverence wished.

The master tells me that he wants money and that around
the end of this month you can send to get the statue.

I have obeyed you by assisting and serving the aforesaid
sculptor.

I commend myself to your holy prayers and I remain devotedly kissing your sacred hands.

Naples, April 8, 1755

Your Reverence's most unworthy servant
and brother and son,

GERARD MAJELLA OF THE MOST HOLY REDEEMER

39. [1754–1755]

To Father Celestino de Robertis[72]

We have no information enabling us to date this note precisely.
"It must be thought of as belonging to one of the two periods
when Gerard was in Naples (summer/autumn of 1754 or spring
of 1755)... From Pagani, where Father de Robertis was living,
it was normal to consider Naples the center for small jobs.
Materdomini and Deliceto were far away; Ciorani was closer
to Salerno than to Naples."[73]

My dear and most venerable Father:

I send you what Your Reverence ordered me to.

I commend myself to your holy prayers.

Have patience with me, for I am writing in haste.

I prostrate myself before Father Minister and all the others. I remain kissing your sacred hands.

Your Reverence's most unworthy servant and son,

GERARD MAJELLA OF THE MOST HOLY REDEEMER

40. [May 16, 1755]

To Geronimo Santorelli[74]

Young Santorelli "had tried to seduce with presents a certain Catalina, a 'house nun'—and, when he failed, he had poured out abuse on her confessor and the one who had placed the black veil on her,"[75] *a sign of the wish to consecrate oneself to the Lord through private vows lived within the family. These consecrated lay women or "bizzoche" were very common in this era. It was equally common to insult other people by cursing their dead parents.*

The tone used here is strong. Gerard appeals to the dignity of the family: "These are not things that a decent man does." And, above all, he appeals to the power of God, who defends the weak who trust in him. Still, Gerard knows well that this is an error due to the immaturity of Santorelli's years. Hence, he assures him of his pardon and his love.

My respected lord, Don Geronimo:

I ought to have written to you before, but God did not wish it. Now I am writing to you and I tell you that I never thought that your lordship would have committed that reprehensible act, so hard to believe.

How is this? Is your lordship so ill? Enough now.

Thus unconscionably do you set about sending, by means of this worthy person, ribbons and crowns to Catalina? What madness is this? To tell you the truth, I didn't believe it. Because I tell you that she is defended by God and by me. Furthermore, why do you wish to test the power of God?

Think and note that these are not things that a decent man

does. And if I am far away, you will know that nothing is impossible to God...you understand me.

Besides, are you so impudent as to curse the dead of the man who hears her confessions and who placed the black veil on her?

Oh God, you already know how much I appreciate you, and you go to such lengths? But I pardon you, because you were swept away by your youth; anyone at such an age does not think about hell nor the infinite loss of God.

Naples, May 16, 1755

Your Lordship's most unworthy servant
and brother in Christ,
                GERARD MAJELLA OF THE MOST HOLY REDEEMER

41. [Undated]

To a Gentleman[76]

In transmitting this letter, Tannoia provides no information about the date or the identity of its addressee. He limits himself to saying: "Upon being tempted, a nobleman was not resigned, but almost desperate amid all his problems. Gerard writes to him, encouraging him to show patience."

All difficulties and sufferings are included in those of the Crucified. This is the gift of the Spirit which must be begged insistently. Christian life, then, will have the "consistency" of the trusting yes to God's will. Thus, with prayer, we can obtain anything from God.

I have received your most valued letter. If your lordship is faithful to God, he will help you. God knows how much I regret your sufferings. May the Holy Spirit be the one who shows you how much more must be suffered out of love for him who suffered so much out of love for us.

My brother in Jesus Christ, have patience in your tribulations, because God permits all this for your welfare. God wishes to save your soul and for you to change your life.

One thing is necessary: suffer everything with resignation to the divine will, since that will help you for your eternal salvation. Go to the fundamentals, which are the best weapon against temptations. Hope with living faith that you will obtain everything from my dear God.

42. [Undated]

To a Gentleman[77]

This is another letter where Tannoia does not provide information about the date or the addressee. He stresses that it was sent to an impatient person who had turned to Gerard in search of a "recommendation."

Gerard tried to intercede, without success; the duke "has no way of placing you." He is sincerely saddened by this, but he is still more concerned that this difficult moment be lived with faith. It is necessary to enter into oneself in order to understand "what an offended God means." Hence the exhortation to confidence: "In the way that you behave with God, so will he help you."

Have patience if you do not come across what you are looking for. Perhaps Our Lord is blocking the path in order to keep you mortified. God reduces the soul to misery and bitterness to make it enter into itself and make it understand what is the meaning of an offended God. In such cases, there is nothing better to do than to weep continually for our faults and pray to God that he may lengthen our days and have time to weep and suffer for him.

Then, why do you wish to despair, when your pains are little in comparison with those that you would have to suffer for your sins? Would it not be worse if you now found yourself in hell?

Son, be attentive, because the devil is cunning, and if you do not amend and behave faithfully with God, the devil will certainly overcome you. Be of good heart and trust in God, for he will give you the strength to overcome everything.

I have sent a message to my lord the duke to speak to him again, but I regret that he does not have a way of placing you. Leave it to God. Depending upon the way that you behave with God, he will help you.

43. [August 23, 1755]

To Father Gaspare Caione[78]

Returning from Naples to Materdomini in the second half of May 1755, despite being extremely sick, Gerard worked for a short while with the bricklayers on an extension of the building near the sanctuary. Afterwards, beneath the burning summer sun, he began a journey around the neighboring towns: Senerchia, Oliveto, Contursi, Auletta, Vietri di Potenza, San Gregorio, Buccino. He was trying to gather the money necessary to complete the work, but those towns were the stations of his final way of the cross, as narrated in this letter.

One is astonished by the serenity with which Gerard speaks of his suffering. More than anything else, he dislikes being the cause of worry for his confreres. The only thing that really interests him is doing the will of God. For this reason, one more time and in spite of everything, he repeats his "joyfully."

Your Reverence should know that while I was kneeling in the church of Saint Gregorio I vomited blood. I secretly went to find a doctor and told him what had happened. He assured me, more than once, that this did not come from the chest but from the throat; he saw that I didn't have a fever or headaches. For this reason, he told me many times and in many ways that it wasn't anything. He bled a vein in my head, but I didn't feel any discomfort.

Last night, when I arrived in Buccino and as I was going to bed, I got the usual cough and I spat up blood in the same manner. They called two doctors, who prescribed certain medicines for me, and in addition, bled my foot. The blood that I vomited I likewise spat up without pain in the chest and without any discomfort. They told me once again that it did not come from the chest. But they ordered me to go away immediately, the next morning or this morning, from that penetrating air and to transfer myself to Oliveto, both for the air and in order to speak with my lord Don Giuseppe Salvadore, a great man and a distinguished physician.

I could not find him, but the parish priest, his brother, told me that he will be arriving this afternoon. Hence, I inform Your Reverence in order that you may know. Advise me what I ought to do. If you wish me to go [to Caposele], I will go immediately; and if you wish the fund-raising to continue, I will continue it without any problems. Because, as far as my chest is concerned, I now feel better than when I was in the house. I no longer have a cough. And so send me a strong obedience, be that what it may.

I greatly regret having worried Your Reverence.

Joyfully, my dear father, it is nothing. Commend me to God, so that he may help me to always do the divine will, and I remain...

Oliveto, August 23, 1755

44. [September 1755]
To Isabella Salvadore[79]

"He returned home the last day of August, with a pale and emaciated face, but with a serene and amiable expression. Father Caione, upon first meeting him, had to make a violent effort to contain himself so as to hold back the tears that were flooding his eyes. He ordered him to take to his bed immediately, seeing that he had a high fever, despite its being noontime. Gerard obeyed, always cheerful and without losing his accustomed and unchanging tranquillity.[80]

Although he was more and more consumed by his sickness, "He wrote, at this time, various letters to different people he knew, whom he helped in their spiritual needs, never wasting a moment of time."[81]

In the house of the Salvadore family he had met young Isabella. He had understood her desire to make a more radical commitment to God, Gerard writes to her so as to confirm, one more time, everything that he had had occasion to tell her viva voce, to strengthen her in her vocation: "How beautiful it is to belong to God completely."

The words are dictated by a simple and profound love, a transparent love for God: "You can understand, then, how much God loves you." This is the last text written by Gerard.

Jesus + Mary

Blessed be our Most Holy Trinity and our dear and blessed Mother Mary.

My dearest sister in Jesus Christ:

God knows how I find myself. Nevertheless, my Lord permits me to write you on my own: you can understand, then, how much God loves you. But how much more will he love you, if you do all that I have recommended to you.

My dear daughter, you cannot imagine how I love you in God and how much I desire your salvation, because blessed God wishes me to give special attention to your person. But know, blessed daughter, that my affection is purified of any worldly ardor. It is an affection divinized in God. I repeat, then, that I love you in God, and not outside God. And if my affection were to go even a little outside of God, I would be a blackguard from hell.

And as I love you, I love all the creatures that love God. And if I knew that a person loved me outside of God, I would curse her on behalf of my Lord, because our affection has to be purified by loving everything in God and not outside of him.

But let us come to our business. You see how I have gone on. Because I tell you that if you do what I insisted you do, you will give continual consolation to my God and to me.

My daughter, it is enough to love God alone and nothing else. Therefore, I beg you to despoil yourself of all the passions and worldly attachments and that you unite yourself and embrace everything in God.

Courage, blessed daughter, the final step so as to be all God's. How beautiful it is to belong totally to God. The persons who have loved this know it well. Try it yourself and afterwards you will tell me: What good is it to love the world, except to constantly encounter tribulations and bitterness.

Forward! Don't seek anything else. From now on your heart has to be all God's; in it he must not find anyone else dwelling but God alone. And when you see that any passion or other thing that is not God wishes to enter, say within yourself: "My heart is committed; God, my beloved, has taken over as my master. For this reason, there isn't room for others that are not my God. So evaporate, disappear all of you that are not my God, my divine spouse."

The bride must be jealous of her divine bridegroom. For this reason, continually, in all her actions, she has to avoid with great attention any vain appearance. She has to guard her heart, which must be called the temple of God, the house of God, the dwelling of God. That is the name given to the hearts consecrated to our dear God.

Unworthiest servant and brother in Christ,

GERARD MAJELLA OF THE MOST HOLY REDEEMER

45. *[Fragments]*

In Caione and Tannoia there appear some fragments of letters that have been lost. We transcribe them, annotating also the addressee as indicated in the sources. They present the ideas dearest to Gerard, which are repeated insistently in all his correspondence.

a. Let us conform ourselves in everything to the will of God and convince ourselves to suffer always for Jesus Christ and only rejoice in his divine will.[82]

b. Let us love our God, who alone deserves to be loved. How
    could we live if we were not to love our dear God with our
    heart?[83]

c. Most reverend Mother, love God for my sake, for I love
    him but little. And always take me to God. Say this to my
    dear God, etc.[84]

d. I am staying in Naples in order to accompany Father
    Margotta, and now more than ever I will amuse myself
    with my dear God."[85]

46. [Appendix: Pact[86]]

*Returning to Materdomini for the last time, Gerard stopped in
the house of the Salvadore family, from August 22 to 31, forced
to do so by his illness. "It was probably during this stay in the
home of the Salvadores when the archpriest Don Arcangelo,
knowing that he was face to face with a true saint, wished to
assure his protection, in life and after death, for himself, for
his family, and for all the inhabitants of Oliveto.[87] Hence the
pact that Gerard signed, "in the style of civil contracts," also
indicating, for this purpose, his full name, as a sign of the seriousness of the obligation.*

*With Sister Maria of Jesus he had also made a "pact" to
take communion and provide mutual help through prayer: the
"holy faith" [holy pact] which he repeats many times in the
correspondence. With her, nevertheless, there was no need to
set it down in writing.*

*Fidelity profoundly marks the whole life of Gerard. It is
the echo and reminder of the fidelity of the Heavenly Father in
the design of salvation in Christ by the power of the Spirit. It is
the conviction that Gerard invites us to set down as the foundation of our path, to proceed always with great courage and
joy. God's plan for us is beautiful.*

Jesus + Mary

Pacts and agreements between the Reverend Brother Gerard
Majella of the Most Holy Redeemer and the priest Don
Arcangelo Salvadore, archpriest.

In the presence of the Most Holy Trinity, of Mary Most Holy and of all the heavenly court.

I. The abovementioned Reverend Brother Gerard binds himself to pray effectively to the Lord in a special way in all his prayers so that we may see each other for all eternity in the glory of paradise, enjoying God.

II. To help me in all my spiritual and temporal needs, even though from far off, when I commend myself to him with my voice or with my heart.

III. To get me strength to fulfill in a holy manner my obligations, to seek the sanctification of everyone, to flee from offending the Lord, and to purify me of all imperfections.

IV. To pray to the Lord for the spiritual and temporal health of all those in my house and for the tranquillity and universal peace of this region of Oliveto.

V. Furthermore, he obliges himself to all those spiritual helps in this life and the next.

VI. And also to request that all the penitents whom he knows may acquire a perfect obedience.

I, Don Arcangelo Salvadore, who have written the present document, bind myself to respond to all the lights of the Lord and to pray and have others pray to the Divine Majesty for the already mentioned Reverend Brother Gerard.

I, Gerard Majella of the Most Holy Redeemer, bind myself by virtue of holy obedience in life and after death to fulfill all that has been and written above.

RULES FOR LIVING

Introduction

A long with the letters, another precious text for penetrating the "truth" of Gerard is the synthesis of resolutions, maxims, and memories, written by himself at the request of Father Francesco Giovenale. Domenico Capone writes concerning this:

"Called by Saint Alphonsus to Pagani on the 14th of April, after Easter in 1754, Gerard stayed for a month. Afterwards he was sent to Ciorani for ten days, always in penance and isolation. Finally he was sent to Materdomini along with Father Giovenale with "the order to follow him, keeping him mortified, not allowing him to receive communion except on Sunday, and preventing him from having dealings with outsiders."[88] Father Giovenale knew Gerard from a long way back, when Gerard was his novice in Deliceto. He didn't limit himself to "keeping him mortified; he wanted to see clearly his internal motivations. Gerard's response was immediate, and thus was born the beautiful document that Caione called *Rules for Living*."[89]

Unfortunately, we do not have the original version of the *Rules*: two from Caione, another from Tannoia, and the one used in the beatification trial.[90] The one closest to the original text and the most complete one seems to be this last.[91] Furthermore, this version is presented by Father Berruti, the Redemptorist rector from this period, who affirms that it was kept in the archives of the Pagani community.[92]

Content

The Rules are not a uniform text.[93] Although they have a certain structure, with various subdivisions, it is not an organic unit but rather a collection of diverse materials. Perhaps one influence here was the fact that the text written at the request of Father Giovenale and that Gerard includes earlier notes, such as the resolution made on September 21, 1752.

The edition corresponds, then, to what the aforesaid father asked him for: "all the mortifications," along with "other aspirations, feelings, proposals, and the vow" to always do what was more perfect.

The list of "mortifications" is long and detailed. It reflects the penitential spirit so characteristic of the piety of southern Italy in the eighteenth century. One must remember, however, that for Gerard it was a matter of participating in the cross of Christ and of assimilating himself to his mystery of universal redemption. For this reason, one must read this part in the context of what follows: both with the "aspirations" or spiritual desires focused on the loving relationship with God, as well as with the "feelings" and "reflections" that underline the source and radicality of the basic decisions in life.

The "resolutions" or "memories" are preceded by an ample explanation of the trust, not in his own strength but in the "infinite goodness and mercy" of a God who cannot fail to keep his promises. This confidence is likewise supported by the "only consoler," the Holy Spirit, and the "second protectress," the Virgin Mary. Then come the more specific commitments, both in attitudes and concrete actions. It is hard to discover any logical order in them. Gerard, who always moved with a spontaneity free of any schemes, nevertheless knew how to capture the essential element in the little concrete things of life.

The "devotions" show his particular propensity to praise the Most Holy Trinity and Mary Most Holy. Gerard also points to a large gallery of "holy protectors."

The final "affections" open a panorama toward the whole world. Gerard is anxious for all human beings to understand the depth of God's love so that they can be saved.

May God's grace always be in our hearts and may Mary Most Holy keep it there. Amen.

My Father:

Your Reverence wishes to know all the mortifications that I do, and wants to have them in writing, along with other aspirations, feelings, resolutions, and the ultimate explanation of the vow I have already taken.

Here I am, disposed to give an account of everything, not just of the external things, but those of the interior as well, so as to unite myself more with God and to journey more securely toward my eternal salvation.

Everyday Mortifications

A discipline. And a little chain, one hand span, less three fingers, wide and two hand spans long, for the leg. A core of iron with iron points.

Upon arising and going to bed nine crosses with my tongue on the ground. Six Holy Marys with my forehead against the ground in the morning and in the night.

At breakfast and dinner throw bitter herbs on any dish. Three times a day chew wormwood or other bitter herbs.

On Wednesday, Friday, and Saturday and all the vigils [of solemn feasts] eat kneeling and leave the fruit. Friday morning eat only two things and, at night, one. On Saturday bread and water.

On Wednesday, Friday, and Saturday sleep, with a little chain on my forehead and the hair shirt on my leg. Stretch out on a hair shirt one hand's breadth wide and three hand's breadth long, which will serve me as a belt those same days.

Every eight days a discipline till the blood flows.

In all the novenas to Jesus Christ, the Virgin, and other saints carry out the mortifications mentioned, adding each day a flagellation and other extraordinary penances that I will ask Your Reverence for.

Aspirations

To love God greatly.
United always to God.
To do everything for God.

To conform myself always to his holy will.
To suffer much for God.

Warmer Feelings of the Heart

Only once do I have the beautiful fortune of becoming a saint and if I waste it I lose it forever.

And if once I have the power of becoming a saint....

Because what do I lack to become saint? I have all the opportunities favorable to being a saint.

Courage, then, for I wish to become a saint.

Oh, how important it is to become a saint. Lord, what madness is mine.

Am I to become a saint at the cost of others and then complain?

Brother Gerard, resolve to give yourself completely to God.

From now on be more sensible and realize that you will not become a saint just by being in continuous prayer and contemplation.

The best prayer is to be as God wishes you. To break before the divine will, that is, in continuous works for God. This is what God wants from you.

Do not let yourself be subjected to your pleasures or those of the world. It is enough, in what is done, to hold God forever present and to be always in God.

Truly, everything, if it is done for God alone, everything is prayer.

Some are preoccupied with doing this or that. I am simply preoccupied with doing the will of God,

No pain is pain when it is accepted seriously.

The day of September 21, 1753, I became more aware of this maxim: if I had died ten years before, I would now not be seeking anything, I would not be trying for anything.

I wish to act in this world as if God and myself were the [only] ones here.

Some people say that I make fun of the world. Oh God, what would be strange about my laughing at the world? The serious thing would be if I made fun of God.

Reflections

If I am lost, I lose God. And what is left for me to lose once I have lost God?

Lord, make the faith in the Most Blessed Sacrament especially alive in me.

Resolutions

My Lord Jesus Christ, here I am with paper and pen to write and promise to your Divine Majesty the following resolutions, which I had already made and which now I confirm again by reason of holy obedience. May it please you that I can fulfill completely all that I am renewing. Ah, I cannot trust in my own power—and for this reason I do not dare to promise. I trust only in your immense goodness and mercy, because you are the infinite God and you cannot fail to keep your promises.

Ah, then, infinite goodness, if in the past there has been anything unfulfilled, it was my fault. But from now on I wish you to act in me. Yes, Lord, make me fulfill my resolutions exactly. Because it is certain that I hope for everything from your infinite fountain.

Examination of My Hidden Interior

I chose the Holy Spirit as my only consoler and protector in all things. Let him be my advocate and conqueror in all my causes. Amen.

And you, my only joy, Immaculate Virgin Mary, [I hope that] you will be my second protectress and consolatrix in all that must happen to me. And with regard to these resolutions of mine, may you ever be my only advocate before God.

I also invite all of you, blessed spirits, to assist me as my beloved intercessors before our universal Creator. I write all this in your presence, so that from heaven, having read and reread it, you may take an interest before the Divine Majesty so as to help me to fulfill it completely. May your requests be effective.

Courage! Thus I bind myself and promise to the Most High God and to Mary Most Holy and to all of you saints. And may

Saint Teresa, Saint Maria Magdalena dei Pazzi, Saint Catherine of Siena, and Saint Inez in particular come to my assistance.

Every fifteen days, I will make an examination of conscience, to see whether I have failed in anything of which I have written.

Alas, Gerard, what are you doing? You know that one day this text will be thrown in your face. Therefore, think it over and observe all of it.

But, who are you that you chide me in this way? Yes, it is true. But you are unaware that I have not placed my confidence in myself, and I will not do that, not now, not ever. I know my own wretchedness well, and hence I am horrified by the thought of placing my trust in myself. If this were not so, I would have lost my head long ago.

So I trust and hope in God alone, since in his hands I have placed my whole life so that he may do with it what he wishes. I am, then, alive, but without life, because my life is God.

I trust in God alone, and only from him do I hope for help in fulfilling truthfully what I promise him here. Long live Jesus and Mary.

Memories

1. My dear God, my only love, today and forever I resign myself to your divine will. In all the temptations and tribulations I will say: "May his will be done." I will accept everything in the intimacy of my heart; and, raising my eyes to heaven, I shall adore your divine hands that let fall on me the precious pearls of your divine love.
2. My Lord Jesus Christ, I will do whatever holy mother Catholic Church bids me.
3. My God, for your love I will obey my superiors as if I were looking upon and obeying your divine person. I will be as if I were no longer mine, so as to identify with what you are in the mind and will of whoever commands me.
4. I will be very poor in pleasures of my own willing, and rich in all wretchedness.

5. Among all the virtues that gratify you, my God, the one I like best is purity and clarity in God. Oh infinite purity, I hope that you will set me free from the least impure thought that I might fall prey to in this miserable world.

6. I will not speak except under these three conditions:— that what I must say is for the true glory of God;—for the good of my neighbor;—for some necessity of mine.

7. In recreation I will not speak up unless I am asked a question or under any one of the previously mentioned conditions.

8. At every word that I would like to say that does not give glory to God, I will say the ejaculation: "My Jesus, I love you with all my heart."

9. I will never speak well or ill of myself, but I will act as if I did not exist in this world.

10. I will never excuse myself, even though I were completely right; it is enough that in what is said to me there is no offense to God or harm to the neighbor.

11. I will be the enemy of every particular friendship.

12. I will never reply to someone who reprehends me, unless I am asked.

13. I will never accuse or mention the defects of others, not even in jest.

14. I will always defend my neighbor, and I will see in him the very person of Jesus Christ when he was innocently accused by the Jews. I will do this especially when [the persons being criticized] are absent.

15. I will correct everyone, even though it be Father Rector, when he speaks ill of his neighbor.

16. I will force myself to avoid every occasion of making my neighbor impatient with me.

17. When I know of some defect of my neighbor, I will try to correct it, not before others but [in private] face to face, with all charity and in a low voice.

18. When I discover that a father or a brother needs something, I will leave everything to help him, unless there is an order to the contrary.

19. I will visit the sick several times a day, so long as I am permitted.

20. I will not meddle in the business of others, not even to say: That person didn't do a good job, and so on.

21. In all the assignments that they give me as a helper I will obey attentively the person in charge, without replying. When given an order, I will not make bold to say that this or that isn't a good idea or that I don't like it. Nevertheless, in matters in which I have some experience and see that they are not going right, I will say what I think, but without acting the master.

22. In all matters where I have to work with others, although the tasks are little and simple, such as sweeping, loading objects, and so on, my norm will be never to take the better place, or the most comfortable one, or the instrument best suited for the work. I will give the best to others, contenting myself in God with whatever remains. That way the others will be satisfied, and so will I.

23. I will not offer myself on my own for any assignment or other thing, I will wait until I am ordered.

24. During meals I will not let my eyes roam from side to side, except for the good of my neighbor or on account of the assignment that I am carrying out.

25. I will take the plate that they put closest to me, without choosing.

26. When I sense rebelliousness within me, I will try not to vent it immediately. That is how I will act in front of someone who is chiding or accusing me. I will wait until the bitterness passes, so that I react gently.

27. Definitive decision to give myself totally to God. For this I will keep in mind these three words: deaf, dumb, and blind.

28. I will not use this language: I want, I don't want; I would like, I would not like. I desire only that in me, oh God, your intentions and not mine become reality.

29. In order to do what God wants I cannot do what I want. Yes, I, I, I want God alone. And for God I don't want

God, I want what God wants. And if I want only God, then I have to detach myself from everything that is not God.

30. I will not be concerned with seeking things out for my own convenience.

31. In all the moments of silence I will devote myself to reflecting on the passion and death of Jesus Christ, and about the sorrows of Mary.

32. Let my continual prayers, communions, and so on, which are offered to God along with the precious blood of Jesus Christ, always be on behalf of the poor sinners.

33. When I know or am told that some person is being tested by God's will but cannot manage to accept the suffering and asks for help, I will pray to God for him. I will offer all that I do in three consecutive days, so that he may obtain from the Lord holy uniformity with the divine will.

34. Upon receiving the superior's blessing, I will consider that I have received it from the person of Jesus Christ.

35. I will never ask for holy communion in the afternoon [outside of Mass], except in great need, but I will ask for it when it is appropriate for me to communicate, so that I may always be prepared. If it should be denied me, I will make a particular spiritual communion at the moment when the priest communicates.

36. Let the thanksgiving last from this moment till noontime. And after noontime until nightfall let there be preparation [for communion].

37. Practice for the Visit of the Most Blessed Sacrament: My Lord, I believe that you are in the Blessed Sacrament; and I adore you with all my heart. And in this visit I wish to adore you in all the places of the earth where you are present sacramentally. And I offer you all your precious blood for all the poor sinners, with the intention of receiving you now spiritually as many times as there are places in which you are present.

38. Practice for the acts of love: My God, I desire to love you with all the acts of love that Mary Most Holy and all the

blessed spirits have made unto you since the beginning. And with the love of all the faithful of the earth, united to the very love of Jesus Christ [for the Father] and for all those he loves, multiplying these acts each time. And also to Mary Most Holy.

39. From now on, I will treat priests with all possible respect, as if they were the very person of Christ, although they are not, and I will pay attention to their great dignity.

Vow to Do the Most Perfect Thing

Explanation of the vow to do the more perfect thing, that is, whatever seems more perfect to me in God's eyes. This extends to all works, [great] and small, that I will have to do with greater mortification and perfection as I see it in the presence of God. It is understood that I have to have a general permission from Your Reverence, in order to proceed with security.

Reservations about this vow:

1. All things that I do distractedly and without paying much attention and that would be against the aforesaid vow remain outside of it.

2. It does not include asking permission. If I find myself outside the house, I can ask permission from anyone, in order to avoid all confusion or scrupulousness, which would paralyze my activity. I can ask permission of my father confessor to dispense me from this vow, and he can dispense me from it as often as he likes.

Devotions to the Holy Trinity

I promise to always perform this little devotion to you, namely, to offer a "Glory be to the Father" every time that I see crosses or images of any one of the three divine Persons, and every time I hear you named or upon beginning or ending an action.

To Mary Most Holy

In the same way with Mary Most Holy: each time that I see a woman, I will pray a Hail Mary to her purity.

To the Guardian Saints

Saint Michael the Archangel and all the blessed spirits. Saint Joachim, Saint Anne, Saint John the Baptist, Saint Isabel, Saint John the Evangelist, the saint of the day, the saints who protect the year and the month. The saint of my birthday and the saint of the day on which I must die. Saint Francis Xavier, Saint Teresa, Saint Maria Magdalena dei Pazzi, Saint Philip Neri, Saint Nicholas of Bari, Saint Vincent Ferrer, Saint Anthony of Padua, Saint Augustine, Saint Bernard, Saint Bonaventure, Saint Thomas Aquinas, Saint Francis of Assisi, Saint Francis de Sales, Saint Francis of Paola, Saint Felix Capuchino, Saint Pascal, Saint Vitus, Saint Aloysius Gonzaga, Saint Mary Magdalen, Saint Catherine of Siena, Saint Inez, Saint Peter and Saint Paul, Saint James and the venerable Sister Maria Crocifissa.

Before and After Meals

[Say] three "Glory be to the Father's" to the Holy Trinity and three Hail Marys to Mary Most Holy.

Upon breaking the bread, at each piece, a "Glory be to the Father." Upon drinking wine, another "Glory be." Upon drinking water, a Hail Mary. And the same each time that a clock sounds.

Affections

O my God, would that I could convert as many sinners as the sands of the sea and of the earth, as the leaves of the trees and of the fields, as the atoms of air, stars of the sky, rays of the sun and the moon, and all the creatures of the earth.

When I rise and lie down, I will make the customary acts of community thanksgiving.

In the afternoon and the morning, before communion, breakfast and vespers, I will make an examination of conscience with an act of contrition.

Long live Jesus and Mary [and Saint] Michael and Teresa, Maria Magdalena dei Pazzi and Aloysius. Amen.

CHAPTER SIX

The Christocentrism
of Saint Gerard

Domenico Capone

GOD THE FATHER
DRAWS GERARD

We that the most authentic path in describing the spirituality of Gerard Majella is the one indicated by the Church in the liturgical celebration of his "memory." This form seems preferable to us to the schemes of life clearly elaborated by the many "schools of spirituality," according to whatever concept they have of "perfection" and the ascetical means of obtaining it.

The Church prays this way to God the Father who has glorified Gerard: "O God, who wished to draw Gerard, even as a youth, to yourself, and who has made him conform to the image of your crucified Son, grant that we too by following his example may be transformed into the same image."

As we see, this prayer is dominated by the concept of image, which is precisely the theme that interests us in this survey: the fact the image of Gerard matches the image of the Son of God, Jesus Christ, and particularly so in the mystery of the redemption through the cross, as a path of new life in God the Father, through Christ and through the Spirit.

Thus there emerge two truths that suggest the plan of this long chapter: (1) God, evidently, has the initiative in this spirituality, insofar as he calls Gerard and attracts him to himself, so that Gerard finds himself immersed in the immensity of God; (2) Gerard accepts this action of God and responds by progressively transforming himself into the living image of the crucified Christ. This means that his spirituality is a "story of a soul" in dialogue with God and in following Christ the Redeemer.

This pattern also suggests to us the method that we have

to follow in the study of Gerard's spirituality. It seems to us that if we wish to be faithful to his originality, the method of analyzing and describing acts, chopping up the continuity and progressive flow of spiritual life into various aspects in accordance with universal schemes of virtue, will be less valid. Those aspects, in turn, follow an ancient anthropology that proves to be inadequate today. We prefer the narrative-existential method, which considers Gerard not so much as someone who performs acts on the basis of a model, but rather as someone in living dialogue with a Person, toward whom God draws him and into whom he transforms him by the power, an often unforeseeable and unclassifiable power, of the Holy Spirit; from this transformation emanate continual acts of virtue. This person is the person of Christ and Christ crucified, who transforms him into new life, resurrected life.

In this way, the spiritual life in general, but more particularly the spiritual life of Gerard, is a historical-existential path with Christ and in Christ toward God. On this path, Christ is the interior energy and guide with the light and power of his Spirit, which is expressed in the great basic energies: faith and charity in a tension of hope toward the plentitude of the risen Christ. We will return to these foundational ideas, which are not sublime inventions, but come out of the Gospel of Christ as a "mystery of the salvific charity of God the Father" (see Col 2:2; Eph 3:14–19).

Gerard was a great mystic. The Holy Spirit illuminated him from his earliest childhood on and he was able to contemplate the immensity of God, both in his ineffable trinitarian life and in his self-manifestation as the creative will that saves humanity. That contemplation came to be an all-embracing uniformity with this will, a uniformity that was mystical rather than ascetical obedience, that is, sympathy and faith-experience, charity, hope in Christ.

The Ineffable Immensity of God

Immersed in the Ecstatic Thought of God

"Gerard was speaking like an angel of the divine attributes, especially of God's immensity. In the house of the Salvadore family, after dinner one time, he was transformed as he spoke of the immensity of God and explained with expressive comparisons how we live in God; he fascinated everyone listening to him." He said: "If God took away the bandage from our eyes, we would see paradise everywhere. Beneath these or those rocks is God, and so on." He often sang: "If you want to find God / look at him in every object / but seek him in your heart / for there you will find him...." All one had to do, Caione says, was mention God or his lovableness to him, and he would fall into ecstasy; and meditation on the divine attributes was the normal topic of his meditations.

"He was sick in Pagani, and I assisted him as his nurse," Caione continues. "One afternoon I prayed with him, and I intentionally chose as a point of meditation the right that God has to be loved and his divine goodness. At the fourth or fifth paragraph, I saw that Gerard was beside himself: stretched out on the bed, with his head upwards and with his eyes open and immobile, without blinking; thus I saw him throughout the whole meditation: one couldn't even tell that he was breathing."[1]

In the canonical trial at Muro, one witness affirmed that he knew, through a person acquainted with Gerard, that he had the name of the Holy Trinity on his lips, and in its name he worked prodigies.[2] In May/June of 1754 he was gravely calumniated, for which reason Saint Alphonsus recalled him and deprived him of the Eucharist. "To compensate for the privation of communion and to ease the ardor of his spirit, which intensely attracted him toward the sacrament of the Lord, he devoted himself to meditating on the divine attributes. When asked how he managed without the Eucharist, he answered: 'I surrender to the immensity of my dear God.'" [It was Caione himself who asked the question.][3]

A great mystic of this era, and an intimate confidante of
Gerard, the venerable Sister Maria Celeste Crostarosa, who
knew the harsh trial he was passing through, but was unaware
of the calumny, wrote to him: "We see ourselves in God, where
we are and live, and united let us love our only good, Jesus,
who loves us so much."[4]

Gerard lived in God, and the thought of God was his life,
his breath. For this reason, it is impossible to understand why
Father Cafaro, who lived a very ascetical life, once imposed on
him under obedience not to think about God. And as God
drew him, poor Gerard went about the corridors saying: "I
don't love you, I don't love you." It as a wound in the depth of
his heart.[5]

One of the effects on Gerard of this living immersed in the
thought of God's immensity was the capacity to grasp the truth
of God in such a way that when he spoke the most scholarly
theologians were left open-mouthed.

"This marvel...of making comprehensible the most obscure
and difficult parts of mystical theology was not rare in Gerard.
He did it with many people; and they all remained stunned by
his capacity to grasp mystical materials that were very difficult
and beyond their understanding. A holy priest, and a credible
witness, also attests that he could not understand some very
difficult things in a book entitled *The Shepherd of the Good
Night,* a singular work by the great servant of God, Monsignor de Palafox, bishop of Puebla de los Angeles (Mexico);
and that Gerard made the sign of the cross in the name of the
Holy Trinity [and told him] 'let us read now.' At that instant
his mind was so illumined that he was astonished to find he
could grasp what at first he could not understand. Still more,
shortly afterwards [Gerard] wished to explain the difficulties
and other things they had read, in such a way that these words
remained stamped on him, just like the sign of the cross that
he had made over him."[6]

Gerard not only gave him a prodigious grasp of things by
making the sign of the cross in the name of the Holy Trinity, he
himself explained the text they had read that had been incom-

prehensible. He was transformed into a theologian and teacher. That is because knowledge from experience, in contact with the light and being of a God, utterly triumphs over our reasoning as a foundation for ideas about God.

In the Presence of God He Feels Himself to Be Darkness and Sin

It might be thought that the experience of contact with the being of God had to be a continual joy, which could be felt even within himself. Even in his harsh tests, he used to say: "I entertain myself with the immensity of my dear God." In reality this mystic experience was also, and perhaps quite often, heartrending suffering in the depths of his spirit. How? It is hard to say. Even the one who was subject to it didn't know how to express it, and sometimes his words and gestures strike us as disconcerting. Persons who believe that they can capture and judge by having recourse to sublimations and projections that are sensory, psychological, and metaphysical, on the Freudian basis of transfigured sex, merely arouse our pity, because they are displaying their genuine ignorance. In this case there is no denying that certain peripheral manifestations, "caused by superabundance of spirit," said Celeste Crostarosa, can and should be explained psychologically. But the deeper truth of Gerard's mystical and often lacerating experience is theological, and therefore ought to be judged with a rigorous mystical theology.

The experimental contemplation of the being of God, infinitely holy and pure, strips bare the fragility of one's own human essence, exposed to the temptation of nonbeing. On the other hand, the knowledge that we have of our daily fragility, which is often morally culpable, means that in contact with the holiness of God's being we feel ourselves not just full of limitations but of sinfulness as well. These were the two dimensions of the heartrending experience of the mystic Gerard Majella: to feel himself small, nothing, in the face of God's immensity, and to feel himself a sinner in the presence of God's holiness.

But one must add that the experience of both dimensions, limitation and moral fragility, is produced by the Holy Spirit. Along with grace, the Spirit communicates a profound loving abandonment in God, even when it is not felt in the spiritual zone where the mystical experience is located. Nihilism does not obscure the mystical night.

Gerard felt the distance that exists between the infinity of God and the solitude, the limitation, and the night that wrapped him round. The Rev. Camillio Bozio reports: "Shortly before [Gerard] became fatally ill, as we spoke together, he asked me about the interpretation of some phrases from Psalm 17, which says: 'I love you, O Lord.' Verses 5–8 must have been for him the object of special meditation, amid the mystical night."

We believe that it is important to read the abovementioned verses, since Gerard meditated on them especially in the stage of the dark night of the soul: "Death's terrors were near at hand, deep flowed the tide of wrong, to daunt me; the terror of the grave was all about me, deadly snares had trapped my feet. One cry to the Lord, in my affliction, one word of summons to my God, and he, from his sanctuary, listened to my voice." The spirit, inundated by the strong light of God, feels itself to be darkness; it feels the solitude and experiences death. But in the depth of being, amid the crisis, the Holy Spirit communicates a latent condition of security and abandonment to God, already known as Father and hence the tested soul lifts up its voice to "its God" and prays.

In the conversation with Bozio, Gerard stopped at verse 10: "He bade heaven stoop, and came down to earth, with darkness at his feet," and asked the priest for an explanation. The latter continues: "From that point on I realized that he was referring to the prayer of darkness, which the mystics call contemplation of God by the negative way, and which is more noble and eminent than the affirmative way; in fact, the light of this contemplation made God appear before the external senses as enveloped in total obscurity. About the phrase itself [verse 10], he gave some response, but he was accustomed to this sort of exercise and spoke with more experience than I."[7]

Bozio noted that this state of harsh mystical testing also caused the darkness to appear externally, that is, on the countenance, in the gaze, which perhaps appeared to be absent. For this reason others considered him someone of little sense, even stupid. Instead of "Poor Gerard!" we have to say, "Poor us, so ignorant and so arrogant!"

Starting from the experience of "infinite" imperfection in the face of God's perfection, Gerard, swept forward by the Holy Spirit, also passed on to the experience of himself as a being distant from God's infinite holiness. He experienced this distance from holiness as sin; he saw himself as a sinner, unworthy of being in the presence of God and even in the presence of human beings. A state of inexpressible heartbreak became manifest in his spirit: from the depths of his being he felt moved to unite himself lovingly with God; but the experience of himself as a sinner made this presence vanish. The mystical night was not only a method, negative or affirmative, of knowing God; it was a live experience of his total being. This happens to every saint to whom God gives the great grace of such a painful and joyful communication.

Speaking to a Carmelite nun at Ripacandida, Sister Maria of Jesus, Gerard shared with her his painful mystical experience: "I feel full of sins. Pray to God to pardon me. Everyone else converts and I continue obstinate... I see myself totally downcast and in a sea of confusion, almost close to desperation. I believe that there is no God for me; his divine mercy has run out for me, and above me only his justice has remained. Look at the miserable state in which I find myself....I beg you, have pity on my soul, because I no longer dare to present myself before creatures."[8]

Any commentary would spoil this vision of Gerard, this page that is one of the most beautiful in all of mystical literature. As he said to the same nun, speaking of God: "His divine will wishes me to make my way beneath water and wind."[9]

It seems opportune to ask here: could this mystical experience of himself as a sinner have been the source of his implacable mortification, which went so far as to make sacrifices that leave us perplexed? Did the radicality of his penance correspond to the mystical experience of God? It could be, although his penance also matched his thirst to become one with the crucified Christ and to expiate the sins of others.

Contemplation of God in the Persons Whom God Loves

We know that Gerard, especially when he became a religious, often read the state of conscience in which people stood before God. Many people who were in a state of sin found themselves reproached by Gerard; with no possibility of contradicting him, they converted. He also recognized the state of innocence and the capacity to come to be a person of high spirituality. In that case, Gerard rejoiced and manifested it externally with words and gestures, motivating these persons to sanctity. But he wasn't always understood.

Once he found himself in Lacedonia, a guest of the family of Constantino and Manuela Capucci, parents of three young ladies, who opened their house to him with complete freedom.

"One day he was conversing familiarly with the three girls from this family. Their mother thought it was improper for Gerard to talk to the girls with such freedom. Then the holy brother, turning to her, said: 'I speak according to the heart of God; but it behooves you, as a prudent mother of a family, to be jealous with your daughters; and I don't fault your thinking.' "[10]

Gerard did not dwell on the physical appearance of the young ladies; he saw their spirit in the presence of God. He contemplated the transparency of God and he knew well that the three sisters were loved by Him, so much so that two of them wound up becoming Redemptoristine nuns in the monastery of the Most Holy Savior in Foggia. He saw and judged things in God; "He spoke according to the heart of God." Gerard's serenity is admirable. It was a serenity that left him free in his actions (perhaps thinking that others were free as he was), a serenity that made him bear witness to his truth. He thought he was defending not his impression, but God who was present and personally active in the three sisters.

As for his praise of the mother's prudence, it has to be said that Gerard considered prudence a virtue of supreme importance. Writing to a Carmelite nun who had recently been elected superior of her monastery, he said: "Mother, be full of infinite prudence." In the same letter he shows a fine awareness of feminine psychology in the relations of the nuns with their superior and among themselves.[11]

Another example of how Gerard saw God through the persons loved by God is found in Pagani. He was under penance because of the calumny against him, and he had been punished by Saint Alphonsus, "even though he gave no credit to the falsehood," as Caione says. And how did Gerard react? With extreme serenity, without defending himself. On the contrary. "I do not know if it was on that occasion or another when upon meeting the Rector [Saint Alphonsus], he told him, 'My father, you have the face of an angel. Every time [that I see it] I feel totally consoled.'"[12]

The Salvific Will of God

Many great mystics who have reached the highest contemplation of God tell us marvelous things about the divine essence and its attributes: immensity, infinity, sanctity, absolute intelligence, omnipotence, and clairvoyance. Some, like the Venerable Celeste Crostarosa, speak not of the divine essence, but of being, which is more than essence or existence, because in the contemplation of the Absolute of being one can avoid certain anthropomorphisms that arise from our mode of conceiving essence. Some theologians, for example, find themselves in difficulties when trying to reconcile God's justice and mercy, God's action in the human being, and human freedom of action.

Gerard submerged himself in the contemplation of the being of God and perceived it as a will to love, which communicates its life as sharing its being with the human race. Thus, becoming one with God means getting on the same wavelength with this divine will on the part of the person who wishes to be holy. In fact, contemplation comes to be in him a unifying tension between one's own will and being on the one hand, and the will and being of God on the other. This is something characteristic of Gerard's spirituality. It could also be called the virtue of obedience, but in him this obedience was far superior to ascetical obedience, because it had the mystical animation of a strong faith-charity-hope.

Conformity With the Will of God

Gerard wrote the following lapidary sentence in a letter to a nun: "The center of true love for God consists in surrendering totally to him, conforming in everything to his divine will and being that way for all eternity."[13] And again: "What a great thing is the will of God. Oh, hidden and priceless treasure. How well I understand that you are worth as much as my dear God. And who can comprehend you except my dear God? ...Continue always in this transformation into perfect unity, in this identification with the will of God. What the angels do in heaven is what we want to do on earth. Will of God in heaven, will of God on earth. That is to say, paradise on earth."[14]

In these words of Gerard, we see clearly the mystical conception of obedience being transformed into the will of God, which is God himself. It is not a question of a simple legal obedience of actions, identified with God's concrete wishes (ascetical obedience), but of the transformation of the origin of actions, that is, of the person. As in paradise, where there is no need for the ascetical obedience that is necessary for us here on earth, but only for obedience or mystical uniformity of the persons transformed by beatific contemplation. The true mysticism here on earth is the beginning of heavenly life, thanks to the Spirit in the sacramental union with the risen Christ. Such was Gerard's life. This was a life open to all Christians who live sincerely in faith-charity-hope, even without the so-called mystical phenomena.

In this transformative and mystical obedience, Gerard saw the union between the one Church of the blessed in heaven and the believers on earth. And this explains how in Gerard's case contemplation came to be action; mysticism expressed itself in asceticism, with no need for external schemes, but by the liberty and spontaneity peculiar to God's children.

Contemplation As Action

Gerard's biographers tell us that during his youth in Muro Lucano he intended to lead an eremitical life, but was dissuaded from this by his confessor. When he entered the Redemptorists in 1749, at the age of twenty-three, perhaps he thought that his dream of contemplative solitude was coming true. But scarcely had he entered the religious community than he was put to the test, to see if he could be "useful" in the hard domestic work assigned to the coadjutor brothers. Then he had to work by traveling all over the region, busy with the economic affairs of the house that was under construction. But the desire for contemplation in solitude was sharp. After communicating, he felt internally drawn to recollect himself in prayer. And the intense thought of God often absorbed him during work. It was then that Father Cafaro, at the chapter of faults in the presence of the community, ordered him not to think of God, as if it were his fault: he had to think about working. And he wrote among his resolutions this truly heroic one: "In order to do what God wants it is necessary not to do what I want. Yes, I want God alone. And for God I do not want God, but only what God wants. And if I want God alone, it is necessary for me to distance myself from all that is not God."[15]

The Redemptorist Francesco Giovenale reports that when Gerard was ordered under holy obedience not to think of God, the poor man went immediately to work after Communion, refusing to think about God, who was attracting him, and as he hastened down the corridors, repeated: "I do not love you, I do not love you."[16]

"For God I do not want God, but only what God wants," or, I leave contemplation behind and I love action, because that is what God loves. But in that way his action wound up revealing his contemplation. He worked, he judged, "he spoke according to the heart of God," who was in his heart. For this reason, obedience wound up being for him spontaneous and free; and he obeyed with complete radicality, to the point of paradox.

"He loved solitude and he was a soul of prayer and sublime contemplation; nevertheless, when his superiors ordered him outside the house, he went joyfully, as if this was his vocation. Later, owing to the praise that he received from all those who saw him on account of the great works that he did, thanks to God, his superiors no longer let him leave the house, and even prohibited him from speaking with strangers. He showed himself joyous and conformed [to the divine will] to the point of doing miracles."[17]

The heroic nature of his obedience to superiors released new energies in his exhausted body, but they ended by bringing him low. This is what happened for the last time in mid 1755. The needs of the construction in Materdomini were great, so much so that the archbishop bade the parish priests from the towns near Caposele receive the Redemptorists when they came to take up a collection. Rector Caione thought of Gerard, who was suffering greatly at that time. When they asked him how he felt, he plainly told them the truth about his condition, but added that he would go "gladly."

"Despite everything, the superior feared that this journey might be harmful to him and even ruin his health [Caione himself tells us]. He placed his hand on Gerard's forehead and ordered him mentally: 'I want you, in the name of the Holy Trinity, to be well.' Then the brother began to smile in front of his superior: he looked at him and smiled. Father Caione, without wishing to make him understand anything shouted at him, asking what that laugh meant. And Gerard told him: 'Yes, sir, I wish to obey, I wish to be well.' The superior stood in astonishment as he saw that Gerard had read his thoughts and had answered appropriately to the command that he had given him in silence. After this, he went out to beg in the diocese, and his entire journey was nothing but a chain of miracles and virtuous acts."[18]

But it was also the beginning of the journey to death, so

that in fact obedience was his martyrdom. He obeyed, literally, to the point of blood. Tuberculosis invaded him and finished him off.

Where did the power come from to obey radically? From the love of God.

"In his rules he had written: 'Love God greatly; be always united to God; do everything for God, love everything for God. Conform to his holy will. Suffer everything for God....' This love of God gave birth to that heroic uniformity with the divine will in all the difficulties of his life. If there was any virtue that he practiced to the point of heroism, it undoubtedly was conformity to the divine will. He spoke of it in an extraordinary manner, he wrote admirably of it, and practiced it most perfectly."[19]

When Caione says that Gerard "spoke about...wrote about...and practiced most perfectly" conformity to the divine will, he was not exaggerating. Here one would have to read in its entirety a letter written to the Carmelite nuns of Ripacandida about obedience to the bishop, in order to conform to God's will. "A letter worthy of eternal memory," Caione says.[20]

From it I take only a few phrases: "When the will of God is at stake, everything else takes second place....I have not been able to understand how a spiritual soul, consecrated to God, can find bitterness on this earth and not wish to please always and in all things the beautiful will of God, since that is the only substance of our souls."

It is necessary to say here that the bishop wanted to soften the nuns' regulations, and they resisted him. Saint Alphonsus himself supported them, but he suggested that they proceed with prudence. The nuns might think that obeying the bishop's will was not the will of God. Gerard intuited this and wrote: "Isn't it the supreme God, who rules all, who permits this? Isn't it his sacrosanct will even when it doesn't seem to be? Is there by chance a different conduct that is capable of bringing us to eternal salvation?...Let us, then, be indifferent in all things, so as to do in all things the will of God, with that supreme purity of intention that God wants from us."

And there follows a true hymn to the will of God, which
we have already read: "What a great thing is God's will, oh
hidden and priceless treasure!"

Note Gerard's expression: "Isn't it the supreme God who
rules all, who permits this? Isn't it his sacrosanct will even
when it doesn't seem to be?" In other words, one has to look
at the universal governance of God, who sometimes wishes
directly, but at other times permits what doesn't seem to be his
will." "Let us be indifferent in all things," he says, and let us
obey with purity of intention. God knows why he permits what
"doesn't seem" to be his will. The only thing that concerns us
is "obeying."[21]

Gerard wrote this for others, but he lived it to the point of
heroism when God allowed him to struggle with what he didn't
directly want, such as being deprived of the Eucharist for a
month, a punishment imposed by Saint Alphonsus, at least for
reasons of community prudence. And Gerard, "prompted by
someone to ask the rector the favor of allowing him to take
communion, started to think a little, near the door of the choir
of Pagani, and then with lively feeling, said: 'No!' gave a powerful blow to the pillar of the staircase and added, 'Let him die
under the pressure of my dear God.'"[22]

It was "my dear God," even though his will crushed him
like a vise. Only the saints understand God and his holy will.

"Incomprehensible" Obedience

There is no denying that some episodes of Gerard's obedience
to the orders of superiors seem to defy rationality and are disconcerting.

Here is one of them. Gerard, still laboring beneath the
weight of the calumny, spent a few weeks in Pagani. The superior of the community told him to go to Castellamare to wind
up some business and to take the donkey. Gerard took the
animal just as a companion for the trip and went and returned
without making use of it. The superior, when he saw Gerard
return, "totally exhausted, with his feet covered with sweat
and dust," realized what had happened and felt compassion

for him. Gerard told him, "Your Reverence ordered me to take the donkey along, not to ride it."[23]

Perhaps alluding to this episode, Caione writes: "Whoever sent him outside the house had to be careful to order him to use an adequate mount; otherwise he was capable of going on foot and leading the beast by the reins, without using it, which happened once or perhaps many times."[24]

At Gerard's beatification trial, the "promoter of the faith," also known as the devil's advocate, said this was ostentatious obedience to the point of "delirium and madness."[25] The episode is frankly troubling, and all the more so because the superior did want Gerard to use the donkey. Father Caione helps us to understand Gerard and the real reason for that method of obeying. He mentions this episode not to show Gerard's obedience, but to demonstrate his heroic vow always to do "what seemed most perfect to him, and to do it with the greatest mortification, as he saw it before God, always assuming that he had permission to do so."[26] This vow, which had been authorized and blessed for him by his spiritual father, was an expression and actualization of love. That love inspired him each time to do what "seemed" to him most perfect and most mortifying. Each time. Only God could intuit the value, not of the act in itself, but which was perhaps objectively irrational, but as Gerard experienced it, that is, as an act of love, shown to be such by the maximum degree of mortification. It was a question of acts that cannot be imitated. They are invented each time by love, with radicality and tension, by a love for which intuiting and doing form a single and instantaneous act. Only God can judge him.

The powerful love of God, therefore, explains the forms that seem paradoxical to us in Gerard's obedience: a love expressed with the greatest possible mortification. And nevertheless the same love for God, when it presented itself to him as love of neighbor, carried him to an opposite paradox: it was transformed into intense prayer so that God would almost conform to Gerard's will. Listen to his words. A nun was very sick and Gerard wrote to another nun about it: "I want you to strive strongly, begging God for a sister who is about to die. I don't want her dead. Tell my dear God that I want her to become more holy and may she die very old, so that she may rejoice at having served God for many years. Courage, strive with the power of God. And this time may God let it be done as we wish. In the name of God, I order you by holy obedience not to let her die. I wish to begin a novena to the power of God for the salvation of this nun."[27]

It is normal to pray intensely to God so that he will heal a beloved person; it is not against the will of God. On the contrary, God wants us to show our mutual brotherly love in this way. But our attention here is piqued by Gerard's almost unusual expressions. Three times he peremptorily says "I want" and at the end he adds: "And this time may God let it be done as we wish." Is that uniformity of God's will with our will? No. Gerard knew well the heart of God, the "philanthropy" of God, because it is He who has placed in us a human heart and the strong desire not to see the person we love die, a person who is still young. The mercy of God consists in this, his "tenderness of heart" toward humanity. The Church tells us that God shows his power in pardoning and taking pity. And so Gerard begs God's power and wants the sister to put pressure on divine omnipotence. In the name of God's power, he worked great prodigies. What is the power of God but his supreme and absolute will, which at times seems to modify the natural course of events, when these too express the ordinary will of the same God? Gerard, as he contemplated God in his immensity, knew well the unfathomable paternal mystery of the will of God. He regulated himself "according to the heart of God."

This was obedience of a mystical nature. Mysticism spontaneously prompted Gerard to do ascetical acts that were at once generous and paradoxical.

Perhaps we might think: we have not conformed ourselves that much to God's will because we are not made for mysticism. No! We have to live this uniformity. Why? Because the vital energy of contemplation and mystical union with God, with Jesus, is Love. Love makes us know God, namely Jesus in us, with profundity; and he causes our entire person, borne by love, to deny nothing to God. Then the ascetical "effort" to perform acts of obedience to God is transformed into a strong spontaneity of love, or, into freedom to love. Everything is done for love, including accepting death. But this love is already mystical, even when it doesn't seem to be, because it is a gift of the Holy Spirit. This is the great spiritual lesson taught by Gerard, the friend of the Holy Spirit.

THE SPIRITUAL PATH IN GERARD'S DAY

The will of God was the "substance" of Gerard's spiritual life. But the Holy Spirit made him realize that this will was expressed primarily and adequately in the "mystery of Christ" and of the crucified Christ, the Redeemer, that is to say, the liberator of the human race in the new life of the resurrected. Thus Jesus crucified comes to be the form and transformative principle of his entire spiritual life.

Christ, Ascetical Model or Internal Principle?

The liturgy tells us that God drew Gerard from his youth on, so as to make of him a living image of Christ. Gerard's affirmative response entails the wish to become a saint according to the form of Christ. This decision, taken from boyhood, was one he would later intensify as a religious: "If once I have the opportunity to become a saint, then what is stopping me from being a saint? Forward: I want to become a saint. Oh how important it is to become a saint....Brother Gerard, resolve to give yourself entirely to God."[28]

This decision to become a saint was sustained by the continuous presence of Christ, whom he loved to the point of madness. But here is where the crucial question arises. How did Jesus become present to him? Was it as a model of holiness that he had to copy, until he reached perfection with virtuous acts that were always more perfect? Or did the risen Christ become present within him as a principle of life through the Holy Spirit, so that spirituality as the "substance" of his person was expressed in virtuous acts? In other words, was this sanctity a perfection of actions (the ascetical way) or holiness through the living spiritual-sacramental-ecclesial contact with the person of Christ, "holy by the generation of the Father"?

It is always said that Christian life is an "imitation of Christ." What is the nature of this imitation? Is it mainly ascetical, by which his acts are taken as the norm for our acts; and Christ with his personal and sacramental reality "helps" us to copy his acts and norms? Or else, without denying this ascetical and pedagogically necessary aspect, does the imitation of Christ consist in letting oneself be baptized internally by his Spirit, ever more intensely, by sacramental life and by the path of incessant prayer? Note that the Spirit always draws upon the risen Jesus (see Jn 16:14–15). It is a continuous transforming communication, which has its maximum expression on the part of Christ in his coming to us in "eucharistic communion," which is not simply a "help," an "ascetical means," but the principle that transforms us into a new life, above all if the Eucharist is lived out in its "sacrificial tension," as a living memory of Christ, the crucified liberator. The mystical thirst for communion in Gerard, even though he was not a priest, possessed this sacrificial tension toward the crucified Christ. Meanwhile we, unfortunately, often reduce communion to a simple "devout act." What an impoverishment! Eucharistic-sacrificial communion is in itself an act of mystical life in Christ.

Thus another fundamental truth becomes evident: the Christian life of the virtues is a mystical life before being an ascetical life. The fundamental truth is that the Holy Spirit, transforming us into the humanity of the risen Christ, pours out charity in our heart (Rom 5:5), that is, in our innermost being. And charity, on our earth, becomes the operative energy of faith (Gal 5:1) and a hope-filled straining toward the "blessed hope," of which we already have, through Christ, the "first fruits of the Spirit" (Rom 8:23; Eph 1:13–14). This means that the three great theological virtues, before being ascetical norms for moral acts, are constitutive ("substantial," Gerard would say) energies of our new person in Christ. And so all the other virtues that the ascetical experts and moral theologians speak of have to be informed and substantiated by this faith-love-hope, if they want to be authentically Christian virtues. And as continual prayer is the constant expression of this faith-love-hope, we can see how prayer is the culmination of the spiritual life. By its very nature, prayer tends to be mystical invocation and contemplation. This is what the true path of sanctity consists in: a sanctity offered to everyone; and hence it is not difficult, as it might seem, were it to be considered only as an ascetical path. When Gerard entered the Congregation of Saint Alphonsus, which takes the love of Christ and prayer for the foundation of its spirituality, he realized that he found himself in what had been his very own home since his earliest childhood.

Ascetical Way Or Mystical Way?

In the seventeenth and eighteenth century, spiritual directors insisted on the ascetical way and distrusted mysticism. In a word, the suspicion of the mystical way as a normal path of holiness was determined by historical events; but historical reasons, as often happened in those days, came to be taken by many people as doctrinal reasons.

The separatist movement of Luther had raised to the doctrinal level the devaluation of works and virtuous acts as meritorious deeds on the path to salvation. It was thought that to attribute salvific merit to acts of virtue was to offend the passion and death of Christ, which with its superabundance had merited eternal life for us. As a result, the merits of Christ, which covered our inevitable sins, opened to us, all by themselves, the possibility of eternal life. For our part, it was enough to have an intense trusting faith in the salvific action of Christ. This was not to deny the value of virtuous acts, but they were reduced to the exigencies of an ethical and social life, that is to say, a simply secular and cultural morality.

The notion that sins were absolutely inevitable led to the theory, and the practice as well, of uniting reprehensible morality and blind faith in God through the merits of Christ. The combination of those two was called the mystical life, the inner life, or Christ-centered life. Faith was enough, pure love was enough.

Clearly this type of interiority, labeled mysticism, was unacceptable. And it frequently led to the opposite extreme: every call to interior charity, every motivation to abandon oneself with faith-love in Christ, was viewed with suspicion. In this contest, the winner was life according to ascetical guidance, by which the interior perfection of the virtues came almost entirely from the effort to work according to precise norms. The point of departure was a very pessimistic concept of natural human inclinations. It was always necessary to act against them. The sacraments, prayer, and, above all, meditation on one's motives for virtuous conduct, "devotion" to Christ, the Virgin, and the saints were "helps" in performing virtuous acts. Christ was the perfectly virtuous man. The first place was occupied by the "ascetical director," and the basic virtue was absolute, unreflecting obedience, with no suggestion of "one's own judgment." Asceticism evolved into a technique; hence the importance of the "director."

It must be acknowledged that, in concrete history, the spiritual life of the faithful, always animated by the presence and action of the Holy Spirit, had largely avoided these two extremes. But it was a common doctrine among theologians that lay people could not become saints because, by reason of their state of life, they lacked the necessary ascetical means, and because the mystical life was reserved to a privileged few, that is, to those who had consecrated themselves in the states of perfection. In practice, this doctrine affirmed that normal Christian life, by its very nature, is primarily ascetical. The gospel, therefore, without an ascetical director, would have only an exhortative and formal value for the life of holiness.

The Second Vatican Council, in the fifth chapter of *Lumen Gentium,* corrected this teaching: by baptism we remain incorporated into the risen Christ, who is "the holy one" and who makes us a "holy Church."[29] Baptism and membership in the Church are the beginning of the mystical life, which has its culmination in the "eucharistic communion" with Christ. Gerard Majella, from his infancy, was taken up and directed by God on this mystical path: a mysticism that does not deny, but assumes and elevates, the mystical life.

The Spiritual Path According to Alfonso Rodríguez

As a young lay person in Mura Lucano, Gerard had read a book that spoke of Christ: "The Painful Year, or Meditations on the Dolorous life of Jesus Christ Our Lord for All the Days of the Year," a work composed by the Capuchin friar Antonio Da'Olivadi. The first imprimatur was given in 1693, the second in 1709. It's very likely that Gerard got it from an uncle on his mother's side, the Capuchin Bonaventura de Muro, superior of the convent of Muro Lucano. The book laid out, for each day of the year, meditations on Jesus crucified, who suffers and sheds blood, beginning with the circumcision. At the beginning of each month, there is an illustration vividly depicting a scene in which Jesus suffers.

It was a book not of spiritual doctrine, but of simple descriptions of the sufferings of the Lord, often arbitrarily imagined, as preachers did, with unjustified exaggerations. For example, the picture for the month of October presents the crucifixion, in which the men crucifying him stretch the arms of Jesus with ropes to make his hands fit the nail holes already cut out of the wood. This is an arbitrary fantasy, but it vividly struck Gerard's imagination, so much so that at the beginning of his religious life, in a grotto at Deliceto, he had himself tied to the cross with his "arms and hands stretched out very tightly...amid great pain." Father Giovenale told this to Caione, and Tannoia confirms it, evoking the passage that Gerard read in the "Dolorous Year."[30] The lesson that he took from that book was to transform himself, even visibly, into the person of Jesus crucified.

But reading the works of Father Rodríguez (which were

the daily bread of Redemptorist seminarians, both in the novitiate and in the weekly ascetical conferences), Gerard could
come to know the teaching of this seventeenth-century Jesuit,
which we shall now present in three points.

Fruits of Meditating on the Passion

After a masterly treatment of the treasures that we have in
Jesus Christ, Rodríguez discusses "the imitation of Christ that
we have to achieve in meditating on his sufferings." He writes:

> The seventh thing that we must extract from medita-
> tion and prayer about the Passion, in which we must
> exercise ourselves, is the imitation of the virtues that
> shine out here in Christ. There are two principal causes,
> the saints say, why the Son of God came into the world,
> becoming man and realizing these sacred mysteries.
> The first and principal one was in order to redeem
> man with his passion and death. The second was to
> give to men the most perfect example of all the virtues
> and in that way to persuade them to imitate him and
> follow him in them. [...]
>
> The Cross is not only the bed in which Jesus dies; it
> is also the chair from which he teaches us with his
> example what we have to do and imitate. And if all
> the life of Christ was a display of exemplary virtue, it
> seems no less true that in his passion he wishes to reca-
> pitulate what he had taught us in all his life, by word
> and example, making all the virtues shine forth, to the
> ultimate degree, on the cross. [...]
>
> This has to be our ordinary occupation in prayer
> about the Passion of Christ and his most holy life and
> the principle fruit that we must take from it. Let eve-
> ryone persist in the imitation of the virtue he needs
> most, dedicating himself, digging, making deeper, and
> placing himself within it, till he is saturated and pen-
> etrated by it in his heart and thus calming the passion
> and contrary vice. Afterwards, one passes from this

virtue to another and another. This is better and more useful than pecking away at prayer in many things and passing lightly over the virtues.[31]

All this is true and spiritually valid. But it is also possible and necessary to consider and live other depths in meditating on the passion and death of Christ on the cross. The "principal fruit that we have to extract" from meditation is of a higher order and greatly increases the value of what Rodríguez says. The latter, even as he makes his case, runs the risk of leading us only to a personal perfection of the virtues considered in Christ crucified.

The cross is the university chair of virtues that we have to imitate, copying Jesus who is "virtuous to the point of perfection," but the cross of Christ is also and above all a baptism of blood in which Christ baptizes humanity. And this baptism, apart from the redemptive expiation of our sins, is the altar on which Christ assumes all of humanity, sanctifies it as a new people and, offering himself to himself, offers in himself all of humanity to the Father as a sacrifice of praise. He sanctifies not only every human being one by one, but all of them, making them into a new priestly people, a Church, his spouse (see Eph 5:25–27). Redemption, beyond making a reality of the justice for which Jesus pays for our sins, is a work of love. This is the love of Christ, not merely as the motivation that makes him accept the cross and death, but as a communication of his love, of his Holy Spirit, who comes to be the substance of our new life. It is necessary before all else to meditate on and live in Jesus crucified, transforming ourselves into him.

Luther's teaching does not admit this substantial transformation by which we come to be a new creation, a new priestly people, in Christ, the crucified priest. In his approach, the human being remains in sin, and nature continues to be intrinsically sinful. Likewise, the juridical doctrine of "satisfaction for sin," by which the death of Jesus is intrinsically a work whose only value is our expiation, is, at the very least, imperfect.

Thus, we can understand why it is affirmed that the virtu-

ous life is a new life, generated only by ascetically imitating
the moral goodness of Christ. Rodríguez proposed this, and it
was a common doctrine in the past, until a full biblical-theo-
logical reflection on the constantly growing development of
liturgical life and the life of the saints led finally to the understanding of the mystery of the Crucified as a paschal mystery
of the people of God, who live in Christ and offer themselves
to the Father, thereby making a holy Church in the eucharistic
sacrifice, which is a "living memory of the Crucified."

For all these reasons, the cross is not only a place of expiation, not only a school to teach the imitation of the virtues of
Christ, a virtuous man; it is also the priestly altar on which
Christ genuinely takes on humanity, animates it with his charity, and offers it to God as a new priestly people making its
way toward the day of the Lord. This makes apparent the intimate link that grounds the transforming meditation of the
cross and the life of the eucharistic sacrifice. That is, the cross,
before appearing as the school of ascetical imitation, finds its
place as an altar of mystical life. In exchange, asceticism presents the Eucharist and the sacraments as means for copying
the virtues of Christ and thus coming to be spiritually perfect
individuals.

Gerard's spirituality lives on the Crucified and on the Eucharist, so that imitation is, before anything else, a transformation from within into a living image of the crucified Christ.

Fruits of Eucharistic Communion

Rodríguez explains at length what the believer's preparation
should be for receiving communion and what the fruits are
that it produces in us. One chapter announces the teaching
this way: "Another principal fruit that we must derive from
holy Communion is uniting and transforming ourselves into
Christ." He explains it this way: "One of the principal ends
and effects for which Christ, our Redeemer, instituted this divine sacrament—or actually *the* principal one, the saints say,
was to unite us, incorporate us, and make us the same thing
with him. Just as that which was bread is changed into the

body of Christ by virtue of the words of consecration, so, by virtue of this sacred Communion, that which was human comes to be admirably transformed into God. And this is what Christ himself tells us: "My flesh is food indeed and my blood is drink indeed; whoever eats my flesh and drinks my blood abides in me, and I in him" (Jn 6:55–56). So that just as food, by virtue of natural heat, is converted into the substance of the one who eats it and becomes one with him, so he who eats this bread of the angels is united and comes to be one with Christ. Christ is not converted into the one who takes nourishment, but he transforms and converts into his person the one who receives him." Thus, for Rodríguez, who declares that "the saints say" this, this doctrine is perfect: it expresses the mystical transformation that occurs with Communion, if the faithful open themselves to Christ with true charity.

But next, having expounded this doctrine, as if wishing to correct or qualify this mystical version of communion, he adds: "But, leaving aside the true union of Christ with him who receives him, which he expresses when he says, 'he is in me and I in him,' and which the saints express by with some highly exaggerated comparisons, let us come to the most particular practice. The fruit that we must acquire in holy communion is the uniting and transforming of ourselves spiritually into Christ, which signifies becoming like him in life and in behavior: humble like Christ, patient like Christ, obedient like Christ, chaste and poor like Christ."

Rodríguez's language makes us understand how, at least in practice, eucharistic union ought to be presented; or one might say that there has to be an ascetical transformation where the initiative passes to the believer, while mysticism starts from Christ. It's quite painful to see how many people nowadays receive the Eucharist as if it were a simple act of a social-communal cult. But might not the problem lie in the fact that no one explains to the people the transforming mystical energy that there is in this sacrament? Unfortunately, in the past, asceticism was very much separated from dogmatic theology; this has led to its being rather technical, moralistic, and casuistic. And communion has been considered as an "ascetical aid" for performing acts of virtue that lead to perfection. To be sure, communion is also medicine for those who are sick in spirit. The cure is in the transforming contact with the love of Christ. In this contact, the sick come to know Christ, they love him and surrender to him, and make of him the only motive of their lives and intense prayer.

"In the consecration the substance of bread is converted into the substance of the body of Christ, while the accidents remain intact. In Communion the opposite takes place, that is, the substance of the human being remains, and the accidents change, because a person changes from proud to humble, from unrestrained to chaste, from irascible to patient, and in this manner is transformed into Christ."[32]

This is what Rodríguez's book says. But in the spiritual person the heart, as Jesus says, is the source of good acts and bad acts (Mt 15:18–19). The heart, therefore, constitutes the center of the spiritual person. That is why we read in the prophet Ezekiel: "And I will give them a new heart, and put a new spirit within them; I will take the stony heart out of their flesh and give them a heart of flesh, that they may walk in my statutes and keep my ordinances and obey them; and they shall be my people, and I will be their God" (Ezek 11:19–20). With the Eucharist, Jesus and the Holy Spirit renew the intimate substance of the human being in sacramental-mystical-eucharistic transformation; which leads to the transformation of the accidents, that is, the acts, which will be good thoughts and actions in keeping with the norms of God. Guidance from spiritual directors with their ascetical norms helps, and is pedagogically necessary, but the transformation that counts is that of the person in his or her heart, in his or her fundamental conscience; and this is the work of the Holy Spirit. True prayer and charity are placed in our hearts by the Holy Spirit: "For we do not know how to pray as we ought, but the Spirit himself intercedes for us with sighs too deep for words" (Rom 8:26). "God's love has been poured into our hearts through the Holy Spirit which has been given to us" (Rom 5:5). Because true prayer is by nature mystical, or made from the heart in harmony with God. The same is true of the three theological virtues.

The comparisons that the saints make to indicate the fusion with Christ in the Eucharist, as in the words of Jesus, "Abide in me and I in you," are not exaggerated: only those who are in Jesus, like a branch of a vine, bear much fruit (Jn 15:1–7). In the spiritual life of Gerard Majella, the fact of his first communion is symptomatic: when the priest refused to give it to him, because he was too young, the angel brought it to him, and so began his life of both lofty mysticism and harsh asceticism.

Consecration and Communion

After having said, with theological rigor, that the Mass is a "living memory" which represents the sacrifice of Jesus on Calvary, Rodríguez divides the participation of the faithful at Mass into three parts: from the beginning to the Credo, the Mass of the catechumens; from the offertory to the Our Father, the Mass of sacrifice; from the Our Father to the end, the Mass of the consumption of species [of bread and wine] and thanksgiving. He stresses that in the consecration lies the essence of the eucharistic sacrifice, insofar as "in the consecration of the blood, which is carried out after the consecration of the body, the shedding of the blood of Christ is vividly represented and hence the separation of the soul from the body. So that with the words of consecration the sacrifice is produced that is offered, and the oblation is made."[33]

In this reading, the Mass, as a sacrifice offered to God, would consist formally and solely in the immolation and death of Christ, represented in a vivid and real form by the separate-and-separating consecration of the wine with respect to the bread, of the blood with respect to the body. Once the solemn offering to the Trinity has been made, with the body and blood separate, by Christ, with Christ, and in Christ, the Mass as a sacrifice would be finished. What follows would serve merely to consume the species and thank God for everything. The communion, both of the priest and the faithful, would be part of the Eucharist as a sacrament, but not as a sacrifice.

Saint Alphonsus thought differently: communion is a constitutive part of the Mass as a sacrifice.[34] The consecration and communion are inseparable acts in this "sacrifice of praise" to the Father, which is the same sacrifice of the Crucified on Calvary. There Jesus offered his life to the Father in order to communicate to humanity this love made flesh and blood of Christ.

At the Last Supper, Jesus presents the sacrifice of the cross in such a manner that the cross and the Eucharist turn out to be inseparable. That is why the communion of the priest is neither a simple sacramental act nor a sacrificial act in Rodríguez's sense.

It is a sacrificial act not only in the destructive aspect, as stressed by Saint Alphonsus but also surely in its aspect as an offering to the father of new life communicated to all of humanity. We also understand that the communion of the faithful acquires an extraordinary value. It is priestly, not of the priesthood that consecrates, but of the priesthood of Christ who comes eucharistically to the faithful, transforms them and offers them with himself to the father. That is, the ecclesial transformation occurs that Jesus spoke of throughout his discourse at the Last Supper. Spiritual life consists precisely in becoming aware of this transformation, which is initiated with baptism, and in living it in prayer, in faith-love-hope and in works.

Speaking of the communion of the faithful, Rodríguez observes:

> We cannot communicate sacramentally but spiritually.
> …This, then, is the third devotion of the Mass, and it is very good and very useful: that when the priest takes communion sacramentally, those who are present should also communicate spiritually.[35]

By contrast, Saint Alphonsus's whole pastoral preoccupation was to lead the people to frequent sacramental communion. Historical reasons caused daily communion to be thought of as unusual and rare; but one might also think that this infrequency was favored because communion had been reduced to an appendix of the Mass-as-sacrifice.

Gerard had understood very well what it meant to communicate and that receiving it while the priest partook of the body and blood of Christ was to participate more fully in the sacrifice of Christ. Father Francesco Giovenale reports: "I asked him to serve my Mass, and as I knew well that after Communion he 'took leave' of his senses, I told him to communicate before Mass; and then the Mass would serve as a thanksgiving, so that then he could move on quickly to his occupations. He answered: "Father..." I cut him short: 'What do you mean, "Father"? Don't you wish to obey?' "'Fine,' he said, 'I will take communion before Mass!' And he was trembling. When the Mass ended, he withdrew behind the altar and stayed there a long time."[36]

How eloquent this "trembling" of Gerard's is. And the invocation, "Father," broken off on his lips. He was caught between two opposing fires: his eucharistic experience with the intimate thanksgiving and obedience. Nowadays we speak of the Eucharist with a more or less adequate theology, but Gerard lived it in the sacerdotal truth of Christ, in the unity of the Last Supper and Calvary.

THE SPIRITUALITY OF GERARD AS A LAYMAN

During Childhood and Youth

The Eucharistic Jesus of His Childhood

We know that as a boy Gerard did "church things" at home, putting up many pictures of the saints and imitating the priest celebrating Mass. He had not made his first Communion and he approached the altar to do so, but the priest passed him by.

"Master Alessandro del Piccolo and Catalina de Dionisio

Zaccardi declare that they listened to Gerard tell how when he was seven or eight he approached the sanctuary as the priest distributed Communion to the others, but he was rejected. Nevertheless, that night he took Communion from the hands of the Archangel Saint Michael."[37]

Gerard was discovering a different dimension of the reality surrounding him, from which the eucharistic Jesus came to him. "At the age of seven years, when his family was very poor, he went out at breakfast time toward a place called 'over La Raia,' and then returned home with a loaf of bread in his hands. When he was asked who had given it to him, he answered that it was a certain boy. It went on like that for a long time."[38]

The fields of Muro likewise invited him to discover God as immensity, in which God became present to him. "Other times he met the same boy on the lap of a lady, in the little church of Capodigiano, who came to play with him and always gave him the same loaf of white bread."[39]

Thus, there emerges a distinct reality, from which a person comes down to dialogue with him and gives him a loaf of white bread—a real, concrete loaf. This is much more than the words that he hears in the house or the parish, speaking to him of Jesus. He now meets that boy on the altar, when the priest celebrates Mass, and he sees him disappear when the priest takes communion.[40] And when he reaches the age of ten years, he receives that boy by means of his first public Communion.[41] From then on, Jesus in the Eucharist was the center of his spiritual life, not in the Communion he took every other day (at that time daily communion was practically forbidden), but also by going often to the church and remaining there for long stretches.

"When he got bigger, he began to frequent a church outside the village, where he spent almost the entire day, using the time before breakfast to serve and listen to the Masses being celebrated there, and in the afternoon praying and doing other works of piety."

Caione adds that at times he would remain in the church

for three or four days, without returning home. At night he slept right there for a few hours sprawled on the ground.[42]

We recall that the sacristan, who was a relative of Gerard, had given him the key, so that "early in the morning, before dawn he went to the church and stayed there, absorbed in prayer in front of the Most Blessed Sacrament."[43]

The Lord, who is alive and present in a particular form in the tabernacle, established a special dialogue with Gerard. Many people testified at the beatification trial that the Lord had called him "little madman, little madman." The canon penitentiary of the cathedral of Muro, Michelangelo Marolda, stated in the trial: "I know by tradition that brother Gerard, when he came into our cathedral and passed beneath the pulpit in front of the sanctuary, heard a voice saying to him: 'You are a madman!' And he answered: 'You're even more insane, because you deliberately imprisoned yourself.'"[44]

The Crucified Jesus of His Youth

The other characteristic of his spirituality is his love for Jesus in the mystery of the cross. When Gerard had learned to read, he received the book *The Painful Year*. "He always had it in his hands," said the postulator Giuseppe Mutone," adding, "it made a great impression on him to read that Jesus had been declared insane," and "madness" for Jesus entered his heart, in an ardent desire to be treated as a madman by others and thus to suffer in order to become like Jesus.[45] That was why in his boyhood and adolescence in Muro Lucano he would seek out sufferings and scorn in many forms that he himself invented.

The love for Jesus in the Eucharist now also expressed itself as love and sensitive transformation in his sufferings. Gerard's two sisters, Brigitta and Anna, affirmed that "while he was still a boy, he went to confession and communicated every two days and he whipped himself a number of times a day."[46]

His inherent spiritual identification with the Eucharist came to be spontaneity with the passion of Jesus. Caione says that Gerard had a "natural inclination to sufferings and the cross."

Here we can clearly see that his wish to suffer, which at times frightens us, was not driven by eagerness for ascetical self-punishment, but was a form of transformation, including the body, into the crucified Christ. It's inappropriate to speak here about self-punishment; only those who are totally ignorant of the life of the spirit can argue that way. Nor should we even speak in Gerard's case of a punishing of the body, as if it were to blame for the falls of the spirit. This dualistic Manicheism does not apply to anyone, and least of all to Gerard.

What does fit Gerard is what Saint Paul says of himself: "[We are] always carrying in the body the death of Jesus, so that the life of Jesus may also be manifested in our bodies" (2 Cor 4:10). The term "body" does not mean the body as distinct from the soul, but the total human condition in its concrete existence, exposed to adversity, sufferings, and temptations. And the expression "death" loses its loftiness if it is translated as "mortification" in the ascetical sense, burdening it with all sorts of afflictive conceptions, with disciplines and fasts. As if anyone who doesn't perform such penitential acts is not like the "mortified" Jesus. Such mortifications are useful; for some persons they are necessary, and no one should make fun of them. But what Paul wishes to stress is the afflicted life of Jesus present in him. Gerard wanted to experience the suffering condition of Jesus. Even if the external forms seemed ascetical, in his case they were not "ascetically punitive," but "mystically unitive," because they made him like to Jesus. As a religious, he would also take on the suffering dimension, but in order to expiate the sins of others.

This internal assimilation to the eucharistic and crucified Jesus had as its only reason an immense love for Jesus. That is, it was the work of the Holy Spirit in him. When Gerard was fourteen years old, on June 15, 1740, the bishop of Lacedonia, Monsignor Claudio Albini, administered to him the sacrament of confirmation. The date was a very important one for Gerard. As a religious, he would later speak of "my Holy Spirit" or "the Holy Spirit, our loving Lord."[47]

Episodes From 1747–1749

There is an episode in the life of Gerard that, when read in a succession of facts, clearly shows his spiritual life striking outward and upward to new horizons, but always in line with God's unchanging plan for him.

In January 1747, Gerard went for a month to San Fele as the caretaker of a school. Both the students and the teachers amused themselves by crucifying him, making fun of him. In February, he returned to Muro and opened a tailor's shop. During Lent, he intensified his penances and nightly prayers before the Blessed Sacrament. That was how he lived the liturgical cycle of the year "ecclesially." During the day, he worked and he shared the little money that he earned with the poor. "On Sunday he passed out all the fruit of his labors to the poor, without leaving himself even a coin for himself, thanks to which he wound up being the poorest of all."[48]

It seemed that with the tailor's work that he did and with his duty to help his mother, who was old by now, he would have chosen to be a layman in the world. The only thing preventing this from becoming definitive was marriage. He didn't lack opportunities, which also would have meant being able to provide better care for his mother. But then, as Tannoia tells us, the first obstacle appeared: "In Muro a feast of the Virgin (I don't know which one) was being celebrated, and her statue was displayed in public, [Gerard], in front of many people, after kneeling for quite a while before it, stood up transformed and placed a ring on the finger [of the statue]. In this way he wished, as he said, to contract matrimony between his purity and the purity of Mary."[49]

Mutone says that the feast was the third Sunday of May and Dilgskron places this episode on the third Sunday of May in 1747.[50] To us the date is as interesting as the episode itself. History shows us that this act was not something isolated. Rather it had a prophetic value: it was the first step to a new path that Gerard scarcely glimpsed.

He got the idea of leaving secular life. As his Capuchin uncle had dissuaded him from becoming a Capuchin, he proposed to lead an eremitic life in a solitary place. He began along with a companion, but a few days later he had to desist because he lacked the physical strength for it. He intensified his life of penance and prayer in the churches, especially during Lent. In August 1748, he met his first Redemptorist, Brother Onofrio. In that way he came to know a life of recollection and mortification, and decided to enter. But he had to wait for eight months, until God himself opened the doors.

During Lent of 1749 an episode took place that, if properly dated,[51] could be considered the symbolic announcement of a profound change in Gerard's life. Tannoia reports: "On the occasion of a tragedy being put on in Muro about the passion and death of Jesus, Gerard was chosen to play the protagonist. When the cathedral opened, he was seen on the cross, agonizing and dead. This spectacle, while it was merely a staged scene, moved the town. His mother was there too; and, upon seeing him pierced with the lance, without paying any further attention to what happened, fainted away and almost didn't recover."

Tannoia tells us that his mother's pain was so great that some time later when Gerard was about to leave his father's house to join the Redemptorists, she knelt down in front of him and said: "Son, don't make me suffer the way I did when I saw you pierced on the cross." Gerard himself recounted this to his Redemptorist confreres.[52]

If this representation of the mystery of the crucifixion and death of Jesus in the person of Gerard took place, which is highly probable, on Good Friday, it is necessary to add that nine days later, on April 13, 1749, Father Cafaro and other Redemptorist missionaries came to the same cathedral to launch a large-scale mission. God responded to what Gerard was waiting for, and in such a way that he decided to flee from his house and leave with the missionaries. The Redemptorists rejected him; he ran back to be accepted. He said: "If they don't want me, I'll be content to receive the bread of the poor at the door of the house."[53]

That was how men treated him. But before God, in the story that he was weaving with Gerard, things were very different. Gerard would now be really crucified in his inner self, in such a fashion that external reality would become a symbol of divine action.

Gerard As a Layman and the Values of Nature

It could be said that Gerard, who till the age of twenty-three lived the familiar life in a world of peasants and artisans, experienced the discrimination imposed by the aristocratic and feudal culture, but he also kept the most simple and genuine values. The first spontaneous value of poor people is having compassion for the poor. In Gerard this compassion was extraordinary. But here we are interested in certain values that are crystal clear in the natural state and that can be abused. And that abuse can give rise to a doubt about them; and it may establish restrictive moral norms, as if all those values were suspicious, insofar as they are derived from the first of them, which is the body.

True, Gerard was rather severe in chastising his own body with mortifications, fasts, and vigils. Still, he did not consider this to be punishing the body, but a means of uniting himself with the sufferings of Christ on the cross. Just as Christ on the cross did not punish his body, but offered it for us so as to make it a sacrament of salvation, and to glorify our own bodies, according to the splendor of his resurrected body (Phil 3:21).

Some episodes of his religious life allow us to intuit what was, until he turned twenty-three, his way of looking at and judging certain behaviors in communicating with others.

Among the Redemptorists who gave him spiritual guidance as a religious, Father Francesco Giovenale was active for some time. And we owe to Giovenale part of the reports about Gerard that Caione collected. He tells us: "[Gerard] had received a special grace from God: to be free of temptations against purity. He did not even know what they meant. For example, he let his eyes roam freely. Noting this, I called him

over and told him: Why are you immodest with your eyes instead of keeping them lowered? He answered me: Why do I
have to keep them that way? Knowing his simplicity, so as not
to awaken wickedness in him, I told him: Because I want it
that way. From then on he no longer raised his eyes, not, certainly, out of fear of temptations, which he did not have, but
out of obedience."[54]

Obviously the issue here is looking at women's faces when
speaking with them, something that back then was considered
to lack modesty. Asceticism had identified a "free glance" with
"immodest eyes." We believe it would be hard to find anyone
today who thinks this way. It is one thing to observe with desire something that is inappropriate, and another thing altogether to look at others as part of communication, with eyes
that animate the conversation and show appreciation for the
other person. Until he was twenty-three, Gerard had in all simplicity conversed with men and women. His freedom was of
the sort that God has given by creating us as persons in dialogue, something quite different from libertinism, which does
not dialogue, but deceives and seduces. Gerard came from a
family of simple people, who saw things as God made them.
By contrast, those who have had the bad experience of a culture that makes women an object of seduction and in so doing
offends them, may need some restrictive asceticism here.

Another sign of Gerard's courtesy in treating men and
women is the episode from July 1750 when he was accompanying a novice from Deliceto to Ciorani. At a pensione, the
daughter of the landlord felt attracted to him and, thinking he
would make an ideal husband for her, proposed marriage.
Gerard did not become indignant, as if she were trying to pro-
voke him. Father Caione says that this happened because of
"the arrangements of the devil." But Gerard, who knew the
devil very well, did not react against either Satan or the woman,
but "with admirable gentleness," hid his feelings and told her
that he was already married to the Virgin.[55]

Let us also recall the "familiarity" with which he treated
the daughters of the Cappucci family in Lacedonia. Gerard

was not naive. He knew how many people act, abusing natural values. But *he* acted with the freedom of the children of God and saw things "according to the heart of God," that is, as God created them. For twenty-three years he behaved this way among the good people of Muro and so he grew in humanity and holiness.

THE SPIRITUALITY OF THE YOUNG RELIGIOUS

In mid May 1749, Gerard entered the Redemptorist house, sent there from Rionero by Father Cafaro and his missionary companions. It was simply a test. It had not seemed opportune to accept him immediately, without requesting the authorization of Saint Alphonsus, even though Cafaro *had* directly accepted the cook of Monsignore Vito Moio, the bishop of Muro. Gerard, who saw the things of God, gave himself to the congregation not on a trial basis, but totally. "He was received by 'Ours' in the house of Santa Maria della Consolazione [Deliceto]. We all know how he lived: humble, patient, mortified, recollected, dedicated to prayer, exemplary in everything."[56]

God had brought him to the congregation of Saint Alphonsus, which had won the approval of Pope Benedict XIV only three months before, in order to take on the missionary charism in favor of people who were spiritually and objectively abandoned, in order to change himself into a living "memory," a "living, animated portrait" of Jesus crucified, and thus to be, although not a priest, a great Redemptorist missionary. As a layman he had been transformed by the Holy Spirit into a living memory of the crucified Jesus by the path of compassion with Jesus on the cross. On the Holy Friday when he took up the cross and appeared before the people in the cathedral of Muro, it can be said that God showed him so as to point out how Gerard, until that day, had identified with his suffering Son. Later on, not only in Muro and in its cathedral, but in the Church as a whole, starting with the Redemptorist Congregation, his compassion would come to be co-re-demption. With total dedication he would surrender himself to be transformed into Christ according to the special charism of the Redemptorists. Very soon, by a divine design, he would be in Foggia with a nun who would come to be his spiritual sister: Mother Celeste Crostarosa. In 1725 she had written an inspiring page on this charism into the Rules of Alphonsus's Congregation.

Gerard As a Redemptorist Brother

It has to be said that the spiritual charism of the Redemptorists, as Saint Alphonsus lived it, beginning with his first apostolic experience among the poor of Naples, and as he later inspired his Redemptorist Congregation, was centered in Christ, sent by the Father as a missionary to save human beings, especially sinners and the poor. The charism was confirmed from on high for Alphonsus, as he himself describes it, when in 1731 he approved a Rule based on the mystery of Christ the Savior, according to which the nuns were called to be a "living memory" of Christ in saving souls with a life of testimony entirely centered in Christ. The testimony of Alphonsus and of his missionaries had to be a "living memory" of Christ, who still goes through the world today as Savior. Redemptorists were to imitate him by means of the transformation into Christ the missionary of the Father, taking up the living Gospel as the norm of spiritual life.

Action and contemplation, asceticism and mysticism, were thus brought back to the norm that animated the apostles: receiving in prayer the Spirit of Christ and becoming a Church by announcing Christ, the Savior of the world. This was apostolic spirituality in the strict sense, rather than ascetical or mystical spirituality; it was of a kind that must be called "Christic," that is, the type that sees in Christ the plenitude of the life of God and of the life of the human being, from which it takes in order to give it to the world. It was faith-love-hope and continuous prayer, with a clear separation from everything that is anti-Christ and that wants the world lost. The concrete ascetical norms must suppose this basic baptismal option, this radical choice that is Christic and ecclesial.

This decision constitutes the heart of the Redemptorist charism; and it can be lived by a priest or a lay brother. It has been that way from 1732 until now. There is nothing to prevent the adding of other concrete norms to these, but the inspiration always has to be the same, that is, to be a living memory of the Savior, responding to the crucial moments of redemption in Christ that the history of salvation causes to emerge.

When we say that Gerard made his own the spiritual model of the Redemptorist lay brother, we wish to stress this special charism. Work, too, would be in his case a testimony of prayer and an apostolate.

After this premise, we should note that until now Gerard had had the Holy Spirit, that is, the love of Christ, as his spiritual director. Upon becoming a religious, he had to choose a spiritual director. "He chose as his spiritual director Father Paul Cafaro...and he continued with him until the father died, on August 13, 1754, obeying him in everything with absolute perfection."[57]

Father Cafaro was an austere man, who emulated the ancient ascetics of the desert, from the first centuries. A great preacher, he attracted people from the pulpit; but he inspired terror when he spoke of eternity and the majesty of God. He was demanding in the government of the religious community, so much so that in June 1751 Saint Alphonsus had to send a canonical visitor to the community of Deliceto, Father Giovanni Mazzini, to investigate the severity of the superior. At the thought of another visit like that one, Cafaro felt "chills and a fever"[58] come over him. But we must not exaggerate; perhaps the fear was produced more by the laments of his confreres than by visitator Mazzini, who was himself under Father Cafaro's direction. Whatever the rigor of Father Cafaro may have been, Gerard had a high opinion of him, and when he died, he had a vision of him in heavenly glory.

In October 1749, Cafaro became aware of Gerard's spiritual greatness, and thought that it had to be protected and amplified by means of total separation from the world in the solitude of Deliceto. He treated him with a "harsh hand" and opposed "any contact with the public and any leaving of the house." These are the words of Father Caione.[59]

In this solitude he would acquire the forms and the language of normative asceticism. For this reason he would write in his resolutions: "Before all else I shall have to cling, in my mind and in my heart, to the resolution that I made during the exercises in Deliceto, that is, to be minutely observant of every part of the rule, to persevere and grow in perfection, to strive to acquire silence, patience, and, especially, union with God. To do the contrary would be to receive my punishment, according as the Lord spoke to my heart; it would mean being outside the congregation, and, as a result, condemned."[60]

The new language is noticeable. Earlier, his norm had been Christ as a person in the Eucharist and on the crucifix, who transforms him into his likeness. Now he speaks of conquering perfection and achieving silence, patience, the detailed fulfillment of the rule. This is the language that was and is used in ascetical conferences and in spiritual direction. The inspiration of the Lord passes into ascetical direction, which avails itself of the fear of remaining outside the congregation and being condemned. The language is correct, but it accents the model of spirituality that is ascetically motivated toward a virtuous perfection, which has to be achieved. Gerard, who was already living immersed in the immensity of God and was drawing upon the "plenitude" of Christ, made this model his own with great docility, but he gave it a nuance that proceeded totally from the Holy Spirit.

With this tension, he gave himself to heavy work, which was normal back then for Redemptorist lay brothers. Brother Nicola testified: "He was especially fond of physical labor, so that he never wasted time. When he didn't have something to do, he tried to help others in their occupations; and when the others didn't need him he set himself to pulling down some old wall and prepared the material to rebuild it, and all this with supreme energy."

And similarly: "When the bread was being baked for the community, he worked as much as four men; he took the initiative and told the other brothers: 'Let me do it, you rest' and worked alone. Nevertheless, in the midst of manual tasks he was always recollected and united with God; he was always seen with his eyes lifted to heaven, as if he were in ecstasy."[61]

His hands kneaded the dough for the bread, and his mind dove into the mystical union with God. Action became contemplation. The ascetical sacrifice turned into mystical elevation.

His macerations of the flesh continued. Father Cafaro had an advantage on him there, because for him flagellation had the power to repress temptations. Gerard followed him with his whole spirit; not, however, to repress temptations, but to become one with Christ crucified. The mortifications he inflicted on himself in eating and sleeping were also harsh. "His bed," Caione tells us, "was made of boards and a sort of paillasse with a little straw in the ends, but in the middle, the part he slept on, it was full of stones, and the pillow was a larger stone."[62] Needless to say, it wasn't always that way, because Caione himself tells us that his bed was at the disposition of the community. "When some guest arrived in the house and there was no place to put him, Gerard's bed was always available for the others; and he went to sleep in the church behind the main altar. He placed himself there for the great love that he had for Jesus in the sacrament."[63]

For meals he adjusted to the community's standards; but, as he says in his Rules, he fasted Saturdays on bread and water, and the rest of the week he ate somewhat less than the others. What he did eat he made so bitter that it was painful to the taste. His lungs had already begun to bleed, but he continued doing the work of four men.

God Continues His Mystical Action in Gerard

The following episode, narrated by Caione, strikes us as symptomatic: "One time, during the retreat [for priests] he had been assigned to the dining room. He wished to do even more and set himself to helping the others in their chores. Upon entering the refectory to begin to prepare the necessities, he happened to glance at the picture of 'Ecce Homo' that hung there; and such was his ardor in looking at it that he remained on his knees, beside himself, looking at the painting. The other brothers came in, and upon seeing that nothing had been prepared, and that he was in ecstasy, began to shout at him. As he didn't react, they called Father Paul, who shook him by the arm, ordered him to get up, and gave him a severe chiding. Then he set about attending to his duties."[64]

Here work and ecstasy intertwine. At work Gerard gave himself completely to action and to the community in doing domestic chores, but God swept him away to himself. In the end, obedience caused him to make the ascetical effort, although it wasn't his fault that the Holy Spirit drew him to mystical contemplation. The inspiration for mysticism and asceticism was one and the same: to be transformed into Christ.

And along with Christ there was also his mother, Caione tells us, speaking of himself in the third person: "This prodigious life [of Gerard] was favored by the Lord with many supernatural graces, such as ecstasy, raptures, and others. Gerard himself commented on these things to Father Caione, although he didn't want to make much of himself in all this. Unless I am mistaken, in the church of Deliceto he was blessed by the presence of Mary Most Holy, and he [Caione] heard this too from his own [Gerard's] mouth when he was in Materdomini. These ecstasies and others ceased, owing to the obedience that he imposed on himself, as Father Giovenale attests and as Gerard himself told Father Caione.[65]

Here, too, the ascetical obedience to Father Caione moderated Gerard's mystical life, so that it put an end to those

ecstasies in the church of the Virgin of Consolation and elsewhere. The Holy Spirit illuminated Gerard, not only by making him understand and experience the immensity of God, the
profundities of the crucifix, of the Eucharist, or the goodness
of Mary, but also in the truth that the theologians were trying
to intuit, reasoning on the basis of facts revealed and believed
by faith. Gerard could see where the theologians faltered. That
was what happened during this period of the novitiate in
Deliceto, with Father Cafaro as spiritual director and rector of
the community.

Tannoia reports: "Father Cafaro realized that [Gerard] was
being led by God in an extraordinary manner. When they discussed ascetical and theological matters, he spoke like a master, to the admiration of everyone. The most obscure mysteries
were clear to him. On one occasion when Father Cafaro posed
various questions to the brothers, and they did not know what
to answer, Gerard explained things like a theologian. In that
way, everyone acquired an adequate judgment and estimation
of him." And Father Cafaro understood that Gerard was not
the stupid young man he had taken him for when he met him
in Muro and Rionero in April–May 1749.[66]

Gerard saw clearly, in the light of the Holy Spirit, into the
state of conscience of the priests and lay people who came to
Deliceto to make their confessions. His biographer Carl
Dilgskron places the following episode, narrated by Caione,
in this period when he was staying in Deliceto: "A bishop had
sent a notorious public sinner to make a retreat. He seemed to
be making it with devotion and to have gone to confession.
Gerard met him and asked: 'Where are you going?' 'To take
communion,' the man said. Then Gerard, full of apostolic zeal,
began to speak to him as he was accustomed to: 'What? To
take communion? And those sins?'—and he named them. 'Why
didn't you confess them? Go, go, confess properly. Otherwise,
and so on.' The man, seeing his inner self laid bare, terror-
stricken and weeping, confessed the truth, went to make a good
confession and came out of the retreat sanctified and fervent.
But once he got back to his city, he returned to his old life. He

later returned to Deliceto, and Gerard asked him how he was. Blushing, he replied, 'Well.' Gerard took the crucifix from the house, went to the sinner's room, closed the door and the window and told him. 'Ah, ingrate! Ah, liar, how could you? You haven't done anything. How did you fall again? And these wounds of Jesus Christ that he gave himself? And this blood: who made it spout?' And then the crucifix began to drip real blood. Gerard insisted: 'And what harm did this God do you, what harm? He wished to be born as a poor child on straw in a stable for you?' Christ appeared like a baby in the arms of Brother Gerard. Finally Gerard told him: 'If you do not change, don't you see what is awaiting you?' And as he said this, the man saw a most ugly devil trying to seize him and carry him off to hell, at which he practically died of fear. At the words of Gerard, 'Be gone from here, horrible beast,' the demon disappeared. The sinner, trembling and full of compunction, went to the feet of Father Petrella and told him everything that had happened. He made a painful confession and gave [the confessor] full permission to talk about the whole episode. Upon returning to his town, he went on to lead a holy life and served as an example for all the people."[67]

What must leave the strongest impression on us in this story is not the bleeding crucifix nor the little baby in the hands of Gerard nor the devil causing terror and then being "expelled," but the conversion of the "notorious" sinner. Gerard wished to give him strength by means of harsh words, making an impression on him so as to wipe out the powerful custom of sinning, which had already come to be practically second nature. But what we wish to stress here is how God continues acting in a physically perceptible way in Gerard, and how mysticism is converted into uncontainable apostolic zeal.

Gerard's Resolutions and Feelings

Between the end of June and the first days of July 1754, Gerard was still under the regimen of separation and penance because of the calumny circulating against him; and he was sent to

Materdomini under the careful eye of Father Giovenale. That priest never believed the calumny. And he had an idea for which we will always have to be grateful: to know and make known the spirituality of Gerard as an observant religious and a saint. He told him that to guide him better and thus to help him on his path toward union with God, he had to provide a complete report on his interior life: desires, feelings, resolutions, and explanations of the special vow he had made. Gerard, simple and obedient, wrote a long account; and it is admirable that it contains no reaction to the violence of the calumny and the ban on his taking communion. Let us comment on some sections of this report or Rules [the complete text can be read in the previous chapter of this book].

It might seem that, speaking of the period in Gerard's life between 1749 and 1754, it could be inappropriate to comment on a series of rules written in the summer of 1754. But Gerard himself, when he enumerates his "resolutions-memories," says that he had made them before, and all the "rules" have the character of an ascetical-spiritual program for the whole of life. It is clear, then, that it could not have been drawn up in the last six years of his religious life, but at the beginning, in the period of which we are speaking.

To Unite Myself More With God

The goal was greater union with God, something which had been mystical in nature since childhood. This is source of the most secure ascetical path to salvation, the mortifications and the concrete resolutions. But the heart would always live "on desires, on feelings," on an all-encompassing vow.

Everyday Mortifications

It was a common practice among the Redemptorists to mortify themselves at their meals on Wednesdays, Fridays, and Saturdays. They also whipped themselves communally on Wednesday and Friday; they placed iron chains on their arms or legs. The use of bitter herbs in food was frequent. All this was practiced until the middle of the twentieth century, with the goal of maintaining a "spirit of sacrifice," getting used to what was difficult, to suffering. Gerard was accustomed to saying: "The love of God does not enter the soul if one is filled up to the throat."[68]

The spiritual father who had to give permission for these and other penances was Father Giovenale, who "watched over" Gerard only for a few weeks. His spiritual directors were Father Paul Cafaro from October 1749 to August 1753 and, after that, Father Francesco Margotta. Father Cafaro could readily approve these penances, which we find frightening, because he practiced them just as much as Gerard. Nowadays we don't understand such exaggerated mortification, but we cannot judge Gerard negatively, since he only wanted to reproduce in himself the sufferings of Jesus on the cross for us.

Desires

"Love God greatly. Do everything for God. Love everything for God. Suffer greatly for God." For Gerard, the desire to suffer greatly for God was the desire to love him greatly. This was the mystical motivation for all his ascetical mortifications.

Feelings of the Heart

"Once I have the excellent opportunity of becoming a saint and lose it, I lose it for ever. And if once I have the good fortune of sanctifying myself, what do I lack then for becoming a saint?"

And so his maxims continue, every one of which has to be meditated upon at length because they have an unusual profundity. Some of these maxims may have been written in different periods. But what did he mean when he wrote at the end: "Many people tell me that I am making fun of the world"? Was he alluding to the gossip that since 1742 he didn't like his apostolate? Is there a veiled allusion here to his situation of being under accusation, as if he belonged only to God?

Reflection

"Lord, make my faith in the Most Blessed Sacrament of the altar especially alive." We know that in his time of trial, the hardest punishment was being deprived of holy communion. Perhaps for this reason he asked God to arouse his faith in the Eucharist.

Resolutions

Examining the structure of these regulations, it seems to us that the paragraphs that follow form a central body, perhaps the principal part of a small book that came to be traditional among the Redemptorist novices and that had as its general title: "Notebook of Resolutions."

To this general title Gerard added a lovely little prayer, most likely touched up by Father Giovenale: "My Lord Jesus Christ, I am here, with paper and pencil in hand, to write and promise to Your Divine Majesty the following resolutions, which had already been made by virtue of holy obedience and which I now confirm."

Examination of My Hidden Interior

This paragraph is divided into two parts: in the first, Gerard asks for help from his guardian saints so as to be able to keep what he promises; in the second, he turns to his conscience in order to make a commitment with it, in an act of humble but self-confident responsibility.

He begins by invoking the One from whom comes all good thoughts and the strength to live them: the Holy Spirit. "I choose the Holy Spirit as my only consoler and protector in all things. May he be my defender and conqueror in all my struggles. Amen." He then turns to the woman he has consecrated himself to: "You, my only joy, Immaculate Virgin Mary, you are unique, the second protectress and consolatrix in everything that will happen to me." His only joy, he says, precisely when he was making his way "beneath water and wind," struck by the calumny and deprived of the Eucharist. There follows a touching invitation to the blessed in heaven, to whom he turns with a surprising familiarity. He had a sure sense of the Church as a "circulation of charity."

The second part is aimed at his conscience, so that it may be responsible. "Ah me, Gerard, what are you doing? Do you know that some day this writing is going to be thrown in your face? So be sure to observe all of it." But he, with spiritual refinement, tells his conscience to understand that it does not have the strength on its own to carry out what it promises; and hence it must always be in a state of abandonment, trusting in God, who must be the life of his life. Here it seems to us that we see the typical transition from asceticism to mysticism, where he lives, but without life, because his proper life is God. "Let him make of my life what it pleases him. I live but I do not live, because my proper life is God. In him alone do I trust, and from him alone do I hope for help, in order to execute all that I have promised him on this point." The term "execute" comes from classical asceticism, and Gerard accepts it; but this execution comes to him from the fact that he lives without living, because his life is God. Asceticism, animated in this way by mysticism, comes to be mystical and renders superfluous the reproach or exhortation that is based only on punishing failures of observance. In this way, Gerard highlights "his truth."

Memories

With this term, Gerard indicates the resolutions or concrete norms for acting in daily life. Memories, meaning: remember, you promised it.

The first resolution is fundamental for the whole of life: to see in the events of each day, however they may play out, the will of God. All the situations of life are "precious gems of your divine wishing." It is enough "to raise one's eyes to heaven" to grasp God, his providence, or, as Gerard puts it, "his divine hands."

The three resolutions that follow touch upon the obligations of the religious vows: obedience, poverty, purity, and clarity in God. "My God, for love of you, I will obey my superiors as if I were looking at and obeying your divine person...I will be most poor in all pleasure, in my own will, and rich in all miseries. Among all the virtues that please you, my God, the one that I like most is purity and transparency in God...." From chastity he moved up to purity and clarity in God, because he knew the pure and clear being of God, who opposes any narcissistic self-involvement. This was the concept shared by his other spiritual sister, Maria Celeste Crostarosa, for whom chastity meant having pure eyes so as to rivet them, as the eagle does, on the pure being of God and thus fly to him.

The other five resolutions that follow tend to moderate his "talking" in communication with others. Here is the sixth resolution: "I will not speak except under these three conditions: (1) that what I must say may be to the true glory of God; (2) for the good of my neighbor; (3) in some necessity." The tenth resolution is one he was living with heroic energy at that very moment: "I will never excuse myself, even when I have every possible reason for it: it is enough that in what they tell me there is no offense to God or damage to my neighbor."

There follows a brief resolution that demonstrates Gerard's great sensitivity about not giving occasion to faults against common life: "I will be the enemy of any particular friendship." Then come three resolutions that show the reach of true community brotherhood: "I will never accuse or speak about the defects of the others, not even in jest. I will always excuse my neighbor and I will see in him the person of Jesus Christ himself when he was unjustly accused....I will admonish anyone who speaks ill of his neighbor, even if it were Father Rector." Brotherly charity easily overcomes the deference that is due, even externally, to superiors. The refinement of his charity makes him attentive to the reactions of others: "I will strive to avoid any occasion of making my neighbor lose patience." When we realize that in order to be a saint one always ends up irritating those who follow a life opposed to sanctity, we can imagine how far Gerard's "diligence" went in this area. It is well known that Gerard's company brought joy to the brothers.

According to the Gospel, fraternal charity also demands that one help another to become aware of any defects and to correct them, but without running the risk of ruining the brother's reputation. "When I become conscious of some defect committed by my neighbor, I will be attentive not to tell him about it in the presence of the others, but between him and myself with total charity and in a low voice." A low voice, so as not to sound like a reproach. This is demanded by the delicacy of charity, as Christ says in the Gospel (Mt 18:15). Fraternal charity goes out to meet the material needs of the other: "When I see any father or brother in great necessity, I will leave everything to help him, unless there is a contrary order." "I will visit the sick every time I am allowed to."

There are seven resolutions referring to fraternal charity, while there are only three that deal with the vows. We emphasize this, because many times religious rules are stretched out and almost become a casuistic system of precepts and prohibitions about the three vows, while that is not the case with fraternal charity. Nevertheless, this is the fundamental virtue of all religious communities that embody the true charity of God.

Gerard was a lay brother, and as such he was busied with domestic matters. Fraternal charity and peace demanded generosity in this area, but any shade of bossiness had to be avoided: the know-it-all, busybody attitude: "I will not volunteer on my account for a job or any other thing unless I am first sent there." He did not volunteer in order to get assignments; rather he was the first to take on a job, as when the flour was being prepared to make the bread. He told the others to rest while he took over the kneading, putting the loaves in the oven, with the terrible heat at the oven door. That was how he became a saint.

Another delicate touch, which can be appreciated only by those who live and eat in a group: "At table I will not look this way or that, but only for my neighbor's good or to do my job....I will take the plate that is closest to me, without looking at the others." No commentary is needed; in Gerard virtue and good manners were one and the same thing.

The seven resolutions that follow refer to the interior life. The first of these is psychological in nature: Gerard "did not have water in his veins": whenever someone chided or accused him, he reacted. What to do? Here is his resolution: "In all the internal movements of rebellion I will be careful not to respond immediately…allowing the bitterness to pass until the sweetness comes later." For the resentment to pass and the sweetness to come, Gerard had to make a basic decision. "Ultimate resolution, to give myself wholly to God. For this reason I have to hold before my eyes these three words: deaf, dumb, and blind." Without this ultimate, fundamental vision, Gerard would not have been able to overcome the bitterness from the false charges against him.

"Let these words not exist for me: I want, I don't want; I would like, I would not like. I want only what God wants." That is, the only thoughts and desires in him should be of God. Thus, transformed in God, nature would let the bitterness pass, and the love of God presented itself as sweetness. That is why Gerard was always serene, joyful, and affable with everyone.

In the same resolution, there is a radical proposition to which we referred when we said that when he took up the daily services of the community, despite being made for mystical contemplation, he had to get involved in action that gave the first place to ascetical effort. "To do what God wants, it is necessary not to do what I want….For God I do not want God, but only what God wants. And if I want only God, it is necessary for me to separate myself from everything that is not God." We commented on this when we spoke of the will of God as the foundation of all Gerard's spirituality. The lapidary expression: "For God I do not want God, but only what God wants." Unless I am mistaken, here action comes to be the highest contemplation.

There follows a brief resolution that would appear to be ascetical: "I will forget to seek anything for my own comfort." Thinking about the way that Gerard lived out this resolution, we see that it was a radical expression of his vow to always do what seemed to him the most perfect and mortifying thing as an expression of radical love. It might be a good idea to give an example of just how radical this love was, which in the state of extreme self-giving fused asceticism and mysticism. Thus Caione reports: "Upon finishing the house chores, he sought for nothing, neither food nor drink nor a room nor a change of clothing. Many times he finished his work sweaty and soaking wet, and since no one gave him anything to change into, or because his room was occupied by some guest, he remained stretched out on the ground, the whole night, dying of cold. And this occurred a number of times."[69] Thus, while on the "naked earth," he felt himself passing out. God joined him with himself in the fire of love. Those who lack faith cannot understand the "superior rationality" of this way of acting.

Further on there are two resolutions that refer to the traditional custom of religious at the end of the day: all asked the superior for his blessing, and the brother coadjutors asked for permission to take communion the next day. Then Caione says: "The thanksgiving has to be from the moment in which the priest communicates until noon and from then to nightfall," indicating that the whole day is animated by the thought of Jesus in the Eucharist. In the resolution about visits to the Blessed Sacrament, Gerard expresses himself in part with the words of Saint Alphonsus in the daily prayer for visiting the Blessed Sacrament.

The next resolution is like an explosion of Gerard's heartfelt love for the good Lord: he makes his own all the acts of love by Jesus, Mary, and the saints: "My God, I wish to love you with all the acts of love made by the Most Holy Virgin Mary, and all the blessed spirits from the beginning and with all the faithful of this earth, and with the same love of Jesus Christ for himself and for all his chosen ones." Gerard wanted to love God with the same act of God by which Jesus loved himself and his elect. This is the act of love within the Trinity and the love in the Church, that is, the Holy Spirit continually given by Christ. Such was the depth of the of Gerard's love. Mysticism in Christ!

Vow to Do What Is Most Perfect

"He sought and obtained from his director the obligation to always do what seemed to him the most perfect thing, and he kept this vow till his death."[70] The director who authorized Gerard to make this great vow could be none other than Father Cafaro. With it, he showed in what high esteem he held Gerard, if he found him capable of observing such a difficult vow. How far did this vow extend? Here is Gerard's explanation, which is connected to the act of making the vow: "Explanation of the already mentioned vow to what is most perfect. …Take on all tasks, even the little ones, that I will be obliged to do with the greatest mortification and perfection, as I see it in God's presence." How many doubts could arise, how many scruples or how many excesses? Is it prudent to express any reservation? Gerard writes: "Reservations about the aforesaid vow: (1) All things and actions carried out without paying attention…are not subject to the same vow; (2) seeking is not against the vow; being able to ask permission from whomever so as to avoid confusion or scruples that would prevent me from acting."

The spiritual father (Margotta or Giovenale?), who wanted such limitations, evidently sought to eliminate the state of tension in Gerard's conscience, for which every action, however minimal, had to be sifted and scrutinized as more or less perfect. Furthermore, the heroic interpretation of the vow was corrected, since it might make seeking *anything* contrary to the vow, something that Gerard had perhaps done at other times. But the criterion of the "greatest possible mortification" remained, a criterion that within Gerard's intense love for God led him to live in a continual heroism. This demanding love, however, was a source of an intimate and profound joy. Gerard was always happy, joyful, and free, without the scruples of small minds.

Devotions

Piety is also expressed in particular acts of devotion. Gerard placed the Holy Trinity in the first place: "I commit myself with you to always do this small devotion, that is, to pray a 'Glory be' as often as I look at a cross or pictures representing any of your three divine persons, or hearing your names mentioned, and at the beginning and end of every action." After the Trinity, the Most Holy Virgin: "In the same manner I wish to proceed with Mary Most Holy, and I will say a Hail Mary in honor of her purity every time that I see a woman." For Gerard, purity was "clarity" in God; he looked upon every woman from the vantage point of that light. The Hail Mary was praise and not ascetical invocation. This is followed by the devotion to the advocate-saints.

Affections

One might think that these "rules" are the expression of Gerard's spirituality as a religious who strives for personal perfection by professing the religious vows, by penances, meditation, and the practice of virtue. For all this, the solitude of Deliceto was favorable, in the hermitage of Santa Maria della Consolazione. Gerard's master of novices, Father Cafaro exclaimed: "In this house of the Virgin of Consolation in Deliceto I seem to enjoy the solitude that the anchorites of Egypt had. Here, retired after the missions given in winter and spring, we are tranquil and alone, absent from the tumult of the world, without knowing what is going on outside. We are far from contact with people, within a forest with good air and a fine panorama, competing with Saint Peter of Alcántara in austerity. Blessed be God who has led me here."[71]

Everything made it look as if God had brought Gerard to Deliceto to satisfy his desire of being a hermit. This seems confirmed by the fact that Father Cafaro was his spiritual director; and, as Father Caione says, Cafaro was opposed to letting Gerard go outside. But do we have regulations made for the eremitic life, remote from human affairs? Surely not. The regulations close with the "affections," which are like a great venting of the heart by a zealous missionary. A great missionary who was not distanced from the world, because it inconvenienced his life in Christ, but who, on the contrary, enclosed the world in his heart and wished to immerse it in the love of God and thus set it free, to convert it from the vanity of sin that makes human beings unhappy. Gerard exclaimed: "Oh my God, if I could convert as many sinners as there are grains of sand in the sea or on earth, as there are leaves in the trees, flowers in the field, atoms in the air, stars in the sky."

The regulations were not dedicated to the cult of singular perfection as an end in itself: they were a way to recollect oneself in Christ crucified, Christ risen, and Christ Redeemer, and to go with him to people who were spiritually poorer in order to announce the Gospel and save the world. One day, as Tannoia informs us, he would say to his physician and friend Nicholas Santorelli: "If I were on top of a mountain, I would like to set the whole world on fire with my sighs," and his heart pounded in his chest.[72] Very soon God would make him descend from the mountain to go through the fields as a great missionary. The regulations end almost silently, telling us how Gerard's day opened and closed.

GERARD'S MISSIONARY SPIRITUALITY

Of course, anyone reading this study of Gerard's spirituality will wish to follow Gerard as he goes down from the solitude of Deliceto and travels through Apulia, Lucania, Irpinia, and the Campagna, and how, as a great missionary, he converted individuals and whole towns and led many of them to the sacrament of penance. But this is the job of Gerard's biographers, and here we do not wish to do a biography; we take it for granted. But there is another dimension of the missionary's greatness, a dimension that lies in the origin of his external action, which constitutes the spiritual energy and intensity for converting people. In other words, a person is a real missionary if he lets himself be inhabited by the missionary sent by God the Father to convert the world—Jesus Christ—and lets himself be transformed by the Holy Spirit, the only one who can animate the words and action of the missionary. It is true that the Word of God and the faith of the simple, sincere people can produce tumultuous results with rather mediocre and, at times, even barely worthy missionaries. But it is also certain that if Christ finds a missionary who lets himself be transformed into him, the missionary action comes to be great and produces not ten but one hundred percent.

Gerard's first biographer, Gaspare Caione, following a narrative method, describes for us the spirituality of the saint upon his return to Muro Lucano, on his trip to Corato, to Castelgrande, Ripacandida, Foggia, Caposele, Naples, Calitri, Oliveto, Auletta, Vietri di Potenza, and so on. But what was the energy that made him so powerful? He was not a captivating orator nor did he give great sermons. Was it the power of his miracles? That may have drawn the crowds, and it filled them with wonder. But the truth, what he called "his truth," was something different; it was totally interior: the truth of God who attracted him to Jesus crucified, a truth that he made his own responsibly, suffering unspeakably and coming to be a "living memory" of Christ the evangelist with the light and power of the Holy Spirit. Let us reflect on this truth that makes him a missionary.

The Redemptive Love of Christ

Let us turn to the theme of redemption in Jesus Christ, already pointed out while we were speaking of the great master of asceticism, Alfonso Rodríguez. From the sixteenth to the eighteenth century dogmatic theologians stressed that the crucified Christ redeemed the world by means of satisfaction for the offense to God through sin. The justice of God demanded reparation down to the very last sin. By dying on the cross Jesus satisfies "in strict justice," as the juridically minded theologians said. Others, not just Jansenists but Catholics as well, said that the glory of God, which they understood as power and dominion of the universe, demanded the destruction of Christ as victim on the cross, because only in this way would the dominion and eminence of God be adequately recognized and affirmed. Others, finally, saw in Christ crucified the model of virtue to be copied in ourselves, a point already mentioned.

Much of this was true, especially if redemption is understood as "satisfaction of divine justice" for our sins, but of justice as love of God the Father for us. This fatherly image of God had been the great truth revealed by Christ to humanity, in place of the "God of the exterminating armies." God the Father had sent his Son to the world not so that they might assassinate him, but to lead the human race to the life of adoption, of being a true people of God. The Father accepted the death of the Son in order to be faithful to the promise of establishing a new alliance, despite the perversity of the human race. A new people, the Church, in which those baptized in the blood of Christ rise to the life of the new humanity, under a new law according to the Spirit of God and the risen Christ. Thus, the crucifixion and death, which the enemies of God wanted in order to annihilate Christ, turned out to be, by means of the Father's love, the destruction of hatred, of the death that brings despair, and the triumph of the glory of God-as-Love.

It is necessary to understand the depth of the mystery of the cross as a triumph of love. Love was the motivation of all the redemptive action of Christ, above all, his accepting of the cross. The Church and popular piety are aware of this love and so they repeat with Saint Paul: "[He] loved me and gave himself for me" (Gal 2:20). But the love of Christ and of God the Father for us has another depth, in which the ultimate truth of the Crucified consists. Love is not only motivation; it is also the substance of redemption as communication of new life. The new life is precisely God as love, Christ as love, the Holy Spirit as love. "As the father has loved me, so have I loved you, abide in my love" (Jn 15:9). In dying, Christ gives his Spirit, or his entire life, into the hands of the Father (Lk 23:46); and the Father receives it as ransom and price paid to his justice, but much more as a new spirit, the new life of humanity. In renewed humanity there circulates the charity of Christ who, dying and rising in God, resurrects all of us. For this reason he could say to the repentant thief: "This day you will be with me in paradise" (Lk 23:43).

We love God and we love one another with the same love of Christ, which is the love of the Father, a love made our "substance."[73] By baptism in the blood of Christ we were submerged in this love, that is to say, in the life of God the Father, the Word, and the Holy Spirit. And all humanity comes to be, by baptism in Christ, the people of God, the Church, on the path toward the final resurrection. The new Law will be love, but love understood as "substance," uniformity with the will of God who has loved us until the end, all the way to the death of Christ on the cross. A simple act of affective love by us is the love of Christ in us, however small an act it may be. Our life is "Christic" life; here is true "mysticism." Such was the life of Gerard, lived with maximum intensity. It can be the life of every one of us by the work of the Holy Spirit.

What happens with sin? Shouldn't the Crucified conquer it? Let us see how the Word of God speaks to us about this victory. In the Letter to the Romans, Paul says that God the Father "sending his own Son in the likeness of sinful flesh [that is, in our existential reality] and for sin [as the culture of evil], he condemned sin in the flesh, in order that the just requirement of the law might be fulfilled in us, who walk not according to the flesh but according to the Spirit" (Rom 8:3–4). That is, Jesus is our Redeemer with all his life, but especially on the cross, where with one supreme and definitive act he stripped sin as an adverse power, made anti-Christ, the culture of hatred and death. Thus we, as we make our way now according to the Spirit, fulfill the new law, the law of the spirit of life that is in Christ Jesus (see Rom 8:2).

Personal sins are the material on which sin lives as the power of the anti-Christ. Satan lives on our sins. Our sins end up being a culture of sin that blocks the river of life and love pouring from the Crucified. Sin is, for this reason, violence to the love of God in Christ and in the Holy Spirit. The history of the world develops spiritually between these two powers, the Crucified and the anti-Christ. But the Crucified will conquer, because in him hatred will be definitively overthrown. Now, too, the resurrection and life always win, even if most of the time this is realized in the silent awareness of those who no longer live according to the flesh, but according to the spirit, in the Holy Spirit of Christ.

If one thinks about the way Christ conquered sin, another profound truth is revealed to us. Saint Paul says, "In Christ, God was reconciling the world to himself....For our sake he made him to be sin who knew no sin, so that in him we might become the [holiness] righteousness of God" (2 Cor 5:19–21). Jesus accepted being considered "a curse," because "Cursed be every one who hangs upon a tree" (Gal 3:13). "He committed no sin; no guile was found on his lips....He himself bore our sins in his body on the tree, that we might die to sin and live to righteousness" (1 Pet 2:22–24).

What happened in the three hours of agony on the cross? The soldiers, the Jewish priests, the scribes, the Pharisees, by hanging Jesus on the cross wished to tell the people that Jesus was an impious man, a sinner, who in proclaiming himself the true Son of God had blasphemed against him. And with this they affirmed that they were the true just, the defenders of the honor of God. By contrast, God in accepting the crucifixion of the Son, by considering him almost "sin," was not punishing Christ, but in Christ he was judging and making justice, or the love of Christ, judge and kill sin. And the Pharisees and the scribes wished to defend the law of Moses, falsified by them and made into the power of the rulers of the world, or the principles and powers of the culture of evil. Jesus, "canceled the bond which stood against us with its legal demands"; this he set aside, nailing it to the cross" (Col 2:14–15).

But this triumph of the crucified Christ occurred in humiliation and in the immense sorrow of the body and the spirit. The body was nailed down and poured out blood. The spirit felt the malice of sin in the hatred, in the hypocrisy of the priests and of the Pharisees and in the madness of the Roman soldiers. Their sins, and with them the sins of the whole world, were felt by Jesus as his, because he was everyone's brother. Thus, not by legal substitution but by assuming us into his love, he communicated new life to us at the same time that sin was hung on the cross. The destroyed body and the poured-out blood were "granted" as a sacrament of love in a perennial Eucharist.

In this sense, resolution #31 of Gerard's Regulations is clear: "During the time of silence, I will strive to consider the passion and the death of Jesus and the sufferings of Mary Most Holy." And he adds: "My continual prayers, communions, and so on, are always on behalf of the poor sinners, offering them to God in the precious blood of Christ." His religious life came to be a continuous "Mass": offering himself entirely to Jesus, who gives his blood to renew humanity and thus offer it to the Father. But sinners are not the only ones who need help; those who are going along the path of holiness and have to constantly resist their weakness, by which they find themselves tempted to stop. "When they tell me that a person lives according to the will of God and that in one moment he believes he can no longer bear up and seeks help, I will pray to God for him...so that thus I may obtain from the Lord the holy conformity with his divine will." Note how Gerard unites himself to the person who is in trouble, offering him or her his prayers, sacrifices, and so on, so that in the communion of charity he or she may rise up to God and implore the grace to be able to go on.

Episodes From 1751–1752

Gerard's spirituality cannot be analyzed or described according to schemas of a progressive and well-directed path toward perfection, but it can be narrated. By always doing what seemed to him the most perfect and mortifying thing possible, Gerard made his own path and followed it constantly to the God who was drawing him closer through different situations. We know that Father Cafaro, Gerard's companion on his personal interior path and his religious superior, did not want Gerard to leave the house, except when it was strictly necessary for the community. For example, in July 1750, he sent him to accompany the novice Sebastiano Ricciardi from Deliceto to the novitiate house in distant Ciorani. But in October 1751, Father Cafaro was sent from Deliceto to Materdomini as rector. With his departure, a new period in Gerard's life would begin.

This new period, which went until his death in October, 1755, would find him busy with domestic chores, but also with an intense missionary activity, in the house and outside it. At first, he was subject to the provisional superior, who was Father Francesco Giovenale.[74] In February 1752, the new permanent superior arrived, Father Carmelo Fiocchi, the consultor general, only thirty-one years old at the time. Following the suggestion of Fathers Fiocchi and Mazzini, Saint Alphonsus allowed Gerard to make his novitiate in six months, as immediate preparation for taking his vows as a religious. He did so in July 16, 1752, three years after having arrived "on a trial basis" in Deliceto. Three years later Gerard would be admitted into paradise by God, as a "most useful" saint for the whole Church.

In December 1751, after the departure of Father Cafaro, Gerard was sent on a trip; and thus began his apostolate outside the house. God opened to him the doors of a place with an intense mystical life, the monastery of the Carmelite nuns at Ripacandida. Saint Alphonsus, who had preached a retreat there the year before, in 1750, acknowledged that "I would never have thought I would find a carnation like this on a rock."[75] Gerard would come to be a spiritual brother and counselor to the superior of this convent, Mother Maria of Jesus, as he would to all the other nuns.

His first letter to Mother Maria gives us notice of the quality of this new apostolate: "Oh you, my divine Love, make yourself always present in the heart of this your chosen and beloved spouse." It is the first of the letters that have been preserved. From it, we can deduce that Gerard had been in Ripacandida for more than one day. The letter ends in this way: "I remain embracing you within the sacred side of Jesus Christ."[76]

Thanks to a letter from Gerard to Father Mazzini, dated July 26, 1752, we know that both of them were in touch with Mother Celeste Crostarosa, the foundress of the monastery of Foggia. Speaking of Gerard's apostolate in Mother Celeste's monastery, Caione writes:

"Another place that Gerard liked very much, apart from Ripacandida, was the monastery of the Most Holy Savior in the city of Foggia; since it belonged to our institute [let the historians note this] and the rule was observed exactly there and the nuns lived in the most exemplary manner, Gerard, so to speak, kept his heart there constantly; and with the superior's permission, he visited them frequently, encouraging them with his fervent discourses to acquire the most solid virtues and regular observance. Still more, with the permission of his superiors, he spent a good part of Holy Week in continual prayers and recollection in the friendly church of this monastery, with infinite consolation for his spirit, as he himself wrote to a nun from the monastery of Ripacandida."[77]

Unfortunately, that letter has been lost. The Holy Week that Caione alludes to must have been that of 1754, from April 7–14.

Besides the Redemptoristine nuns at Foggia and the Carmelites at Ripacandida, there were the Poor Clares of Muro Lucano. In September 1752, when they asked the bishop, Monsignore Vito Moio, for permission for Gerard to come talk to them, he answered: "A conversation with Brother Gerard is worth more than an entire Lent with the fathers of his Congregation."[78]

But his missionary activity was perhaps aimed more at sinners than at persons who were God's friends. This, Caione says, stirred up against him the violent hatred of the demons: "This hatred of the demons against the brother probably originated not so much because of the virtuous and holy life that he led as because of the effort and inexplicable fervor that he had for the salvation of souls and the conversion of sinners, to which he dedicated all his prayers and mortifications. The Lord comforted him marvelously in this with the consolation of seeing the conversion of sinners who had grown old through years in the mire of guilt. God gave such efficacy to his words that for a sinner talking with Gerard was the same as converting. Many people in various occupations asked the local superior to send Brother Gerard to them in order to help some soul in need; and the Lord blessed his journeys in a special way. Still more, when he was sent outside the house for other matters, he almost never returned without a prey snatched from the claws of hell."[79]

He not only converted individual persons, but whole towns. On April 24, 1753, Signore Zaverio Scozzo writes as follows to the superior of the Deliceto house: "Divine Providence has caused Brother Gerard to come unexpectedly, miraculously, to Corato so as to win the salvation of his beloved creatures, since with his coming and with his good example he has drawn the entire town to devotion and has brought about stupendous conversions."[80]

TO DIE CRUCIFIED WITH CHRIST

The Time of Trial

We have already considered how God the Father and the Holy Spirit transformed Gerard, from his youth on, into an image of Jesus crucified. Gerard's love moved him to make his own "the condition of death" that characterized the whole life of Jesus. He did not think about the reasons why he was suffering, only about living in Jesus crucified. Love led him to compassion, to suffer with Christ. This was his truth from an early age. Now, after the silence from 1749 to 1751, this truth would come to be a co-redemption. But that co-redemption had to spring from a still more profound and painful participation in Jesus' condition of death: feeling himself to be sin before God. And the mystical trial of feeling oneself to be almost darkness before the luminosity and holiness of the being of God became more acute and existential, given his total love, which he could also feel, for Christ the Redeemer.

We can intuit this personal experience by looking at Gerard's feelings, as he confided them to sister Maria of Jesus. His letters are the principal, if not the only, source for knowing this "truth."

It is necessary to say a word about this nun, so we can understand that his dialogue with her, as with Mother Celeste Crostarosa, was not simply a question of friendship: "Let us see ourselves in God, in whom we are and live, and together let us love our sole Good, Jesus, who loves us so much." That was how Mother Celeste had spoken to him in the period of the calumny; and so it had also happened between Sister Maria of Jesus and Gerard. As she told him, and as we know from Gerard himself:

> Surely it consoled me greatly to learn [from the letter] that you are strongly engaged in my behalf before your divine Spouse. You tell me that you didn't have any other way of speaking to me privately except within his most sacred side. Consider how joyful I felt with such sweet words. For this reason, I desire to confess my truth to you...dearest in Jesus Christ.[81]

The spiritual solidity of the sister also appears in the correspondence that she had with Saint Alphonsus, who comforted her, declaring her mystical life to be authentic.

In April 1752, Gerard was already in the novitiate and in such a condition that, lest his recollection be disturbed, he was forbidden to talk to people outside the Institute. He himself tells us this in a letter of April 16, 1752. This letter is of interest because in it we see how God was leading Gerard through the dark night of the soul. There we read an expression very dense with meaning, which in part we have already read, but that now we place in the precise moment of his spiritual path.

Gerard writes: "Jesus, Mary. May the grace of divine love be eternally in the soul of Your Reverence. Amen. Oh God, what immense joy I have had today in my heart upon receiving your most esteemed [letter], which I so desired. But I speak to you with truth before God, that this desire is not mine, but the Most High's. He always makes me ask help from others, because I cannot, while the divine will wishes that I make my way beneath water and wind. Thus he wishes and I do too. For this reason, may his divine will always be done, if only God makes me worthy....Do not be surprised if I write you so affectionately, since the sole reason is that I esteem you as true spouses of Jesus Christ and so it enchants me to converse continually with you."[82]

Gerard the novice was in a painful aridity of spirit and had to walk toward God, conquering the storm of spiritual rain and wind, as if amid the desert, alone. Hence the splendor of the presence of God, which came to him through the longed for letter from his spiritual sister, whom he knew was full of God, inundated him with "immense joy." It was God who ignited in him this desire, while "his truth" was painful.

This fountain of light and heat also quickly came to an end, silenced for an entire year. The bishop prohibited the nuns from all correspondence with outsiders, even for spiritual reasons, and obliged them to follow the exclusive guidance of a Carmelite priest who came from Naples. When he learned of the ban, which affected him too, Gerard wrote the bishop the letter about absolute obedience that we have already meditated on.

Meanwhile, Saint Alphonsus had managed to write to Sister Mary and on December 12, 1752, he told her: "Let the Carmelites, Dominicans, and so on, as many as they want, come right in, without straying from what I have written to them. Let them write the doubts they have, but let them try to cut it short as much as possible. I have learned that the Carmelite father has taken daily communion away from you. I have not had any success with Monsignor (but keep that a secret), and I don't know what he will do."[83]

In fact, thanks to the intervention of Father Fiocchi and

Gerard, the bishop dropped the ban on writing and receiving letters, and by the beginning of 1753 Gerard was able to have a correspondence with them.

The first letter from this period introduces us to Gerard as he makes his way, borne on by pure faith. He writes: "One needs faith to love God; those who do not have faith miss God. I have already resolved with all this to live and die saturated with holy faith. Faith is my life, and my life is faith. Oh God, who wants to live without holy faith? I would like to exclaim always—and let it be heard by the entire universe—and to say always: long live our holy faith in our dear God."[84]

He made his way in pure faith, with no spiritual incentive to relive the long trial. But the trial worsened. In May 1753, he wrote to Maria of Jesus: "Pray a great deal to God for me, for I have a great spiritual need, and only God knows how afflicted and disconsolate I am now. If you wish, you can help me greatly before God. Do me this favor, for God knows well what I want to tell you." Even so he ended with this expression of profound mysticism: "Let us remain united and transformed into the being of God. Amen."[85]

"I am unwell," he writes on July 11 to the new superior. Ten days later he repeats: "I am afflicted, for this I beg you to pray to God a great deal for me." And he adds that his own prayers were "cold."[86]

The harsh interior trial went on, and a few months later the expressions in a letter he wrote reveal to us the nature of the spiritual night he was going through. He had entered into the solitude of the Redeemer on the cross: he felt the sins of the world as his own; his compassion through love reached the level of co-redemption in the pain and nausea that he felt upon contact with the sin of sinners—like Jesus on the cross on Holy Friday.

He wrote to his Maria of Jesus, who may have written him, congratulating him on his union with God: "Ah, my mother, how you mock me. Do you know why you write me in this way? To give me more sorrow for my sins....I have sunk in such a way that I think I shall not be able to rise up. I think that my sufferings will be eternal. I would not be worried if they were; *it would be enough if I loved God and gave him pleasure in all things.* This is my grief: that I believe I am suffering without God. My mother, if you do not help me, I will have a great problem. Because I see myself downcast and in a sea of confusion, almost on the edge of desperation. I believe that for me there is no God and that his divine mercy for me has come to an end. The only thing left me is his justice. See what a miserable state I find myself in. If you take seriously the faith [pact] with me, now is the moment to help me and to pray strongly to God *for my wretchedness, I beg you to take pity on my soul, for I do not have the nerve to appear before the creatures.*"[87]

"My sins," says Gerard; and he feels fallen, beneath the justice of God, without "mercy," near to "desperation." He ends: "See what a miserable state I find myself in." Gerard, the total innocent, without ever having committed a sin that separated him from the love of God, from his immensity, now finds himself oppressed by the "sins" that he calls "my sins," because that is how he experiences them.

In an earlier letter, of which a fragment has been preserved, he also speaks of "his sins": "I feel full of sins. Pray to God to pardon me. Everyone else is converted, and I continue to be obstinate. Have patience and suffer for me, so that the Divine Majesty may pardon me and receive me. I beg this of all your daughters. I am full of afflictions, and I cannot find anyone who believes me. That is what God wants for me. He wants me to die without compassion, abandoned by everyone. And that is the way I wish to live and die to give pleasure to my God."[88]

It was, then, a trial that lasted more than two years, from 1752 till the beginning of 1754. He felt crushed by sins that he experienced as his own, and meanwhile he went all over Lucania, Apulia, and Irpinia, snatching from sin individuals and towns and even a monastery here and there.

Immediately after Easter, April 14, 1754, an outer trial was added to the inner trial: the calumny. The jealousy of a girl who had left the Redemptoristine convent at Foggia made him appear to be a sinner in the eyes of other people. Saint Alphonsus did not believe the accusation, as Caione testifies; but he punished him anyway, as if he were an object of suspicion and therefore an object of control.[89] Perhaps God suspended his inner trial, since Gerard says that during this time he "entertained himself with the immensity of his dear God."[90] Once the calumny had passed, around the middle or the end of July 1754, he went to Naples with his spiritual director, Father Francesco Margotta; and the inner trial returned with greater intensity. This time God revealed what was Gerard's admirable truth beneath the weight of sins. Nevertheless, in Naples he did good to the just and to sinners. He performed prodigious feats, as when he walked over the sea to save some poor fishermen from shipwreck. He was a symbol of salvation from spiritual shipwreck, which had been taking place in him for more than two years.

On September 7, 1754, he wrote a letter to Sister Maria at Ripacandida. It is perhaps his most moving letter, the one that reveals "his truth," or his living and real, though mystical, transformation into Christ crucified who agonizes and dies on the cross for the sinners of the world. It was the truth of co-redemption.

"Dear, venerated sister, I write to you from the cross and because I do not have enough time I am obliged to write you in all haste. Have pity on my agony....My pains are so penetrating that they give me spasms of death. And when I believe I am dying, I find myself alive so as to be more afflicted and pained. I do not know what else to tell you; I am not capable of giving you my bile and poison so as to embitter you. I know that you are happy, and this joy is enough to encourage me [and] revitalize me in God."

This was a marvelous communion of charity, by which the serenity of Sister Maria, as a true spiritual sister, succeeded in encouraging Gerard and giving him strength in God. This thought appears to open a heavenly oasis for him, and Gerard thanks God. "May he always be blessed. He gives me so many graces and, instead [of] making me die beneath his holy blows, gives me more victory in life so as to give me even [his] torments and make me an imitator of my divine Redeemer. He is my master, and I am his disciple. I must learn from him and follow his divine steps."

Here is where we meet the truth about the state of agony in which Gerard found himself. "To be an imitator of the divine Redeemer," to make the same journey, to retrace his steps, to be co-redeemer not because there is anything lacking to the passion of Christ, but because by participating deeply in the sufferings of Christ, he communicates to others their actual efficacy through the ecclesial communion of the Mystical Body, by which one member influences another. It is always the redemptive action of Christ that redeems; but it passes, so to speak, through the charity of Gerard, who unites himself intimately to Christ on the cross. In this sense, the exegetes explain Saint Paul's affirmation: "Now I rejoice in my sufferings for your sake, and in my flesh I complete what is lacking to the passion of Christ" (Col 1:14). Gerard unites himself intimately to the Crucified; he is transformed into him, and the redemption of Christ, as passing through Gerard, is poured out on the sinners alienated from Christ. For this reason, Gerard follows the path of Christ and ascends the cross with him.

But he felt only the pain of this path and not its efficacy; he felt the sins as if they were his. He writes: "Now I do not travel, and I have no movement, finding myself crucified with Him, sad and (with) inexplicable sufferings. For me the lance to make me die does not exist. It is my gallows. There I obey…in order to obtain life in suffering."

The final phrase manifests anguish and pain. Gerard does not write his thoughts; he tries to express his state of mind in agony with Christ on the cross, and this state of mind is made of tears: "If it weren't for the effort I make, I would not have written it except by dint of tears." It's inappropriate to seek a logical succession of words, especially in this part of the letter. As a participant in the solitude of the Redeemer on the cross he writes: "Everyone has abandoned me….And I tell myself:

This is the will of my heavenly Redeemer, to be nailed to this bitter cross. I lower my head and say: this is the will of my dear God, I accept it and I find joy in doing whatever he orders and disposes."[91]

Any commentary would blur this sharp light that comes from the Crucified, who by dying transforms Gerard into himself so as to make him a minister of his love-pain that saves—"nailed to this bitter cross."

One month later, on October 4, 1754, he told the superior at Ripacandida: "I am very ill and I am moving to Caposele within a few days. Pray to God for me, poor wretch."[92] This was not an empty expression; it showed how he really felt. He himself makes us understand it, since he wrote on the same day to Sister Maria of Jesus: "My dearest sister, I reply to your venerated [letter] and I tell you and I thank you ever so much for the novena that you made to the Most Holy Trinity for me. My sister, I greatly sympathize with you, because you are alone, afflicted, and disconsolate, since you have no one with whom to vent your feelings and find consolation. I know with supreme certainty the troubles you have gone through and are going through. I tell you that I feel them more intensely in my heart than Your Reverence. You cannot imagine with what precision and clarity I perceive them. If I say that I feel them more than you, I am not lying. I don't explain things to you anymore, because I know that while Your Reverence is reading this letter, the Holy Spirit is making you understand all my affairs, better than I could explain them."[93]

Here we plainly see one of the aspects of Gerard's spirituality: the intimate communion with persons who are God's friends. He had always gone in search of these souls, in order to encourage them not to lessen their striving for charity and holiness. He had expressly resolved to do this.

Out of the same charity and love for the Crucified, Gerard took upon himself the sins of sinners whom he met, and that produced that state in him: "I am very ill." Why? A letter written the same day to Sister Maria of Jesus tells us: "I am so afflicted and disconsolate as to be under torture from divine justice. May his divine will always be blessed. What makes me tremble and causes me the greatest horror [is that] I fear I will not persevere. God forbid, because that would be the same as destroying me. I want you to say all your prayers with this intention." And he boldly underlined those key words.

The trial continued not so much for his personal purification, but above all because he had been chosen as a missionary of Christ on the cross—for the just and, much more, for the sinners.

We do not have other letters or documents about Gerard's inner state after October 1754. But his truth of co-redemption would eminently shine forth from September 1, 1755, until his death, as he was laid waste by tuberculosis and in the solitude of the Crucified. That is what remains for us to consider.

To Die in Christ

On August 23, 1755, after a long journey begging alms in Senerchia, Oliveto, Auletta, Vietri di Potenza, San Gregorio, and Buccino, through valleys and over mountains, beneath the torrid sun of July and August, with his lungs ruined, Gerard returned to Oliveto. He had been sent by other doctors to Dr. Giuseppe Salvadore, after suffering pulmonary hemorrhages caused by tuberculosis in San Gregorio and Buccino. He was welcomed by Arcangelo Salvadore, a priest and the doctor's brother. On the next morning, he wrote the following letter to the superior of Materdomini, Father Gaspare Caione: "Your Reverence should know that while I was kneeling in the church of San Gregorio, I had a hemorrhage, I went secretly to a doctor and I told him what had happened. He assured me that it wasn't from the chest but from the throat. He saw that I didn't have a fever; for this reason he repeated many times and with many different expressions that it wasn't anything. He bled the vein of my head; during this I did not feel discomfort.

"Yesterday afternoon, when I arrived in Buccino, as I was going to bed my usual cough returned, and I spat up blood as I had the other times. They brought two doctors, who gave me some remedies and bled me in the foot. The blood that I threw up, I also threw up without pain in the chest and without any trouble. They told me that it didn't come from the chest, and they ordered me immediately to go the next morning, which is today, to Oliveto, where the air is better and also to consult with the family physician Signore Giuseppe Salvadore. I have not yet met him, but the lord archpriest, his brother, tells me that he will come this afternoon. I inform Your Reverence of this, in order to know what I should do. If you wish me to leave immediately, I will go. If you wish me to continue collecting alms, I will continue without any problems, because now I feel better in my chest than when I was in the house. I have not had any more cough. Courage, send me a strong order, whatever it may be. I greatly regret causing Your Reverence worries. Joyfully, my dear father, it is nothing. Commend me to God, that he may make me always do his holy will, and I remain at...Oliveto, August 23, 1755."[94]

Deathly sick, Gerard went like a lamb from doctor to doctor, always serene and always disposed to go out on the road again, walking from town to town. His delicacy of feeling is striking, since he realizes that Father Caione will be worried, and so he encourages him: "It's nothing," he tells him. And on top of everything, the supreme issue: perfect conformity to the will of God. This is Gerard's moral stature.

Father Caione, perhaps by the same post that had brought the letter from Oliveto, replied that he could stay in the archpriest's house until he got better and, in the latter's judgment, was able to return to the house of Materdomini. Gerard remained in Oliveto until the morning of August 31; passing through Caposele for the last time, he went up the hill and arrived at the house when the midday sun was beating down strongly.

"His return to the house was on the last day of August. He returned pale and emaciated, but at the same time with a serene and amiable air. Upon seeing him, Father Caione had to make a great effort to hold back the tears that came to his eyes in abundance. [Caione always speaks about himself in the third person.] It was noon. Upon noticing that Gerard had a fever, he told him to go to bed at once. He obeyed joyfully and without losing his customary and unalterable tranquility. The pulmonary hemorrhages continued and increased day by day, causing him to lose a great deal of blood. All of this naturally made everyone fear for his health. He went on with an enviable serenity, a peace befitting paradise, and a heroic conformity to God's will. When the superior asked him, at the point of his most intense sufferings, if he was keeping up his conformity with God's will, he answered: 'Yes, Father. I imagine that this bed is the will of God, and I am nailed to it as if were nailed to the will of God. Still more, I imagine that I and the will of God are only one thing.' This made a great impression."[95]

In a letter written the year before, he had said: "This is the will of my heavenly Redeemer, to be nailed to this bitter cross." The bitter cross of the dark night of the soul, crushed beneath the sins of the world, now came to be a cross for the fragile body as well. "He had placed in his room, on the wall in front of the bed, a large crucifix of plaster and paper, with a shattered and bloody Jesus, to encourage him to suffer more joyfully the pains and troubles of his illness. During the day, he rose up from the bed as best he could, settled himself on a sort of couch that they placed for him beneath the crucifix, and stayed there for one or two hours, beside himself, with the look of a person in agony, joining his sufferings with those of his Redeemer."

Above the door of the room "he had put a sign in which could be read in capital letters: "Here God's will is being done, as God wishes and for as long as he wishes."[96]

I Have Done It All for God

Here one has to read calmly, as one meditates on it, a moving page from the passion and death of Gerard Majella. Some days before September 8, Caione reports: "As he was getting worse from day to day, it was decided to give him holy viaticum. The local superior designated Father Francesco Buonamano to bring it to him. When he came to his room, Brother Gerard was sitting up in bed, in an attitude so humble and reverent that it caused emotion and sadness to everyone who saw him. Father took the sacred host, showed it to Gerard, and said: 'Here is the Lord who will soon be your judge. Revive your faith and do some good deed.' Then Gerard, with a great feeling of both confidence and humility, answered: 'Lord, you know that whatever I have done and said, I have done it all for your honor and glory. I die happy because I believe I have not sought in everything any other thing but your glory and will.' Having said that, he took communion and was alone with Jesus for a while, to vent his heart's affection."[97]

The words of Father Buonamano may have exhorted Gerard to make acts of contrition. And the Holy Spirit placed on Gerard's lips the truth, which was the praise of God: he had always belonged to God; he had lived on the divine will and the Eucharist. Such was God's judgment, pronounced by the lips of Gerard himself.

A few days later, his spiritual director Father Francesco Margotta, sent him an order from Naples to get up and recover. He did get up and seemed to be reborn, "leaning on a simple staff," Caione says, "he walked around, not just in the house but through the garden as well."[98] But this apparent improvement did not last long. Before mid September he fell back in his bed, never to rise again. We know, however, that he remembered the two great loves of his apostolate: the persons who pleased God and the sinners.

Harmony With Persons Close to God

Caione says that "Despite all his indispositions, and the fact that he was within an inch of giving up the ghost at this time, he wrote various letters to different persons whom he knew, letters by which he helped their spiritual needs, never losing a moment of time."[99]

On September 14, he went to the brother who was assisting him and said: "Today in Foggia Mother Maria Celeste has passed on to enjoy God." Some days later the news arrived that just when Gerard had seen her fly up to heaven, she had died in Foggia.[100]

In Oliveto, he had met Isabella Salvadore, on whom God had fixed his glance, as if waiting for Gerard to direct her path to a life of holiness. Gerard did it with his customary drive, full of the Holy Spirit. During his sickness he thought about her, as she had suggested to him, and he wrote to her:

Blessed be our Most Holy Trinity and our dear and divine mother Mary.

My dearest sister in Jesus Christ, God knows how I am. Nevertheless, my Lord allows me to write you in my own hand; from which you can consider how much God loves you. But how much more he will love you, if you do everything I begged you to.

My dear daughter, you cannot imagine how much I love you in God and how much I desire your eternal salvation, because our blessed God wills that I keep a particular eye on your person. But know, blessed daughter, that my affection is purified of any worldly ardor. It is an affection divinized in God. I reply to you that I love you in God, not outside of God; and if my affection went ever so slightly outside of God, I would be a blackguard from hell.

And as I love you, so I love all the creatures who love God. And if I knew that a person loved me outside of God, on the part of my Lord I would curse her, because our affection must be purified in loving every thing in God and not outside of God.

The letter is from start to finish a hymn to love, so long as it is love in God. With this love, Gerard had always loved everyone without distinction, men and women, the just and sinners. He was not afraid of telling Isabella: I love you. Why all this? Because he knew well that true love is only the kind that shares in the love with which God loves humanity. Immersed in the infinitude and immensity of God, Gerard had discovered love in its origin. He lived from this love; and he sought to draw toward it all the persons whom he met.

This is a good place to understand why Gerard did so much to make young women consecrate themselves to God. Some critics might disapprove of Gerard's action, as if it were against the women's freedom, and, in addition, contrary to the joy of life to embrace a state of renunciation, limitation, and spiritual sacrifices. But that wasn't how Gerard saw it. It did not close but opened a person up to her highest potential in the divine dimension. Only those who do not know God and the profundities of the spiritual life could say that coming to be a "heart of God," that is, a person in whom God is not merely loved, but who loves and pours out his love on others, means being converted into a sacrificed and unhappy person.

Gerard wished to introduce into this immensity of the love of God the persons in whom he discovered a heart capable of opening up to the torrents of God's love. He encountered hearts with such a capacity especially among young women; and he wanted them to become happy by consecrating themselves to the love that burns in God's immensity. He speaks of this love in the first part of the letter to Signorina Isabella Salvadore. He had spoken to her about it in the week of August 23 to 31, 1755, when he was in her house and where one time, Caione informs us, "after dinner, he became transformed, speaking about the immensity of God, explaining with the most vivid and expressive comparisons, how we lived in God; listening to him brought enthusiasm and enchantment."[101]

In the second part of the letter he exhorts her to open up to God, to be God's alone: "Forward, nothing else is needed. Your heart, from this day forward, has to belong completely to God, and no one except God must dwell in it….The bride has to be jealous of her divine spouse….She must guard her heart, which must be called a temple of God, a house of God, the place of God, the dwelling of God. Those are the names for hearts consecrated to our dear God. Your very unworthy servant and brother in Christ, Gerard Majella of the Most Holy Redeemer."[102]

Intercession for Sinners

Let us now see the other object of Gerard's apostolic love, that is, the poor sinners. They, too, ought to have been a house for God's love. Instead they are victims of sin, which is rebellion against Christ and against the Father's love for us. What most afflicted Gerard was the fact that sinners loved their sin and did not beg God's pardon. What to do to move those hearts to beg forgiveness and thus open themselves up to the torrents of the love of God the father in Christ?

Three years before this, he had placed the sinners in his heart; he had taken on the burden of their sins the way Jesus did on the cross. He experienced the ugliness of sin to the point of nausea, of feeling himself to be a sinner, unworthy of God. But meanwhile the sinners became obstinate; he begged pardon for them and implored love through repentance. This was surely his final participation in the state of Jesus' agony. Caione reports: "Upon realizing that his death was near, with inexpressible fervor and feelings of humility he began preparing himself to appear before the divine Judge. He had a most pure conscience and perhaps had never lost his baptismal innocence. But seven or eight hours before he died he started to recite the psalm *Miserere,* with so much devotion and feelings of humility, which touched the brother assistant. He pronounced slowly, with great emphasis, and afterwards made an act of contrition, shedding abundant tears. But above all he stopped and repeated the verse, 'Against you, against you alone I have sinned, I committed the evil that you abhor.' And again this other: 'Wash me from my sin.' He spoke these words with a sad voice, sighing deeply and weeping. He said them with penetration and such an elevated idea of God and his infinite immensity that he filled Brother Andrew, who was assisting him, with a holy fear." [103]

A year and a half before this, when he had been calumniated, the thought of the immensity of God had brought him great joy. Now the immensity of God appeared to him in all its holiness, as if it had been offended by the sin that he felt was his, personally his. And he repeated: "Against you only have I sinned. I must respond to God."[104]

And one month before, when Father Buonamano had reminded him that he would soon be meeting with Christ the Judge, he found nothing in his conscience except love for the glory of God. Now he exclaimed: I have sinned against you, I have done what is evil in your eyes; wash me from my sin. He begged pardon for those who persist in their sins. Afterwards, looking at Jesus on the large crucifix that he had on the wall, he caught fire with love: "For two hours his eyes never ceased to look upon Jesus crucified and a beautiful image of the Virgin placed at the feet of the crucifix. And every time he looked, he exhaled burning sighs from his heart. With this he accompanied the intense acts of contrition, which he repeated many times." Thus love and pain come to be a single prolonged act, even as his life slipped away.

To Die With Christ

"When he was close to giving up his spirit to the Lord, no longer being able to make these acts with the accustomed intensity and vehemence, he said time after time in a low voice: 'My God, I repent. I wish to die to give you pleasure. I wish to die to do your most holy will.'[105] As if Jesus were repeating in Gerard his last words on the cross: 'Father, forgive them, for they know not what they do' (Lk 23:34); 'It is finished' (Jn 19.30); 'Father, into thy hands I commit my spirit' (Lk 23:36); and immediately afterwards, Jesus died.

"Around half an hour before he died, Gerard turned to Brother Saverio, who was assisting him, and let him know that he wanted a little water. The brother went to get it, and as he was gone too long, because he couldn't find the keys to the refectory, upon returning he found Gerard turned toward the wall. At first glance, he appeared to be sleeping. But after a few minutes he saw the patient turn around and heave a sigh, which made him realize that Gerard was expiring. He ran immediately to call another brother and Father Buonamano, who was the minister and superior of the house at the time (Father

Caione was temporarily in Pagani). But when the father arrived at the room he found him at death's door, and shortly afterwards he peacefully surrendered his soul to the Lord, at dawn on October 16, 1755."[106]

After telling Gerard's story, Caione ends with this prayer, with which we too will conclude this survey: "My dear brother, pray to God, whom you loved with such great ardor. Pray for me, unhappy sinner. Make my heart burn in the love of Christ God, so that I can be your companion."[107]

The Church adds: "Oh God, who has wished to draw Saint Gerard to you from his youth and made him conform to the image of your crucified Son, grant that we, too, by following his example, may be transformed into this same image." That is the image that the Holy Spirit modeled in Gerard and that the piety of the faithful sense and live in the prayer of the Church.

CHAPTER SEVEN

Gerard's Spirituality

Sabatino Majorano

LIFE AND SPIRITUALITY

R econstituting the spirituality of a saint is the attempt to penetrate into the intimate "secret," in the sphere of the purely human and of grace, of his or her life. It is never a simple task. First of all, we have to have a sense of sincere respect, capable of placing us safely beyond the temptations to force or manipulate the material, even those inspired by the legitimate concerns arising from the context in which he or she lived. The historical distance that separates us from the saint has to be bridged by a careful effort at reconstructing and interpreting the facts, in a way that also makes it possible to capture the continuity that unites his or her Christian adventure with ours. In addition, we have to control our enthusiasm for one or another aspect that might seem particularly significant and to patiently link the diverse aspects, so that the basic vision can emerge with clarity. In order to avoid remaining prisoners of a priori syntheses, it is necessary, above all, to let the saint himself or herself do as much of the talking as possible.

In dealing with Gerard Majella, the difficulties are still greater. The historical documentation about him is not abundant, even though the early Redemptorist community, prompted by Saint Alphonsus himself, made an effort to collect and preserve the most significant testimonies and comments.[1] In addition, Gerard was not a professional or a writer on spirituality, preoccupied with spelling out and transmitting a thoroughly balanced proposal. The few letters of his that we possess were written on an occasional basis. The *Rules* offer a very interesting description of his life, but they are no more than a disorganized collection of resolutions and spiritual memories.[2]

Nor should it be forgotten that Gerard was not a front-page personality. He spent the twenty-nine years of his life among the most humble people, busy in the many cares of daily life, with no thirst to play a leading role. He was news for a town in search of hope, but not for those who made the selection of facts and personalities for posterity. And for the early Redemptorist community, he was nothing but a lay brother occupied in the thousand tasks of concrete life, although he *was* esteemed, loved, and held up at a very early stage for imitation by the youngest as a "model of virtue and observance."[3]

These sorts of difficulties are made worse by the fact that popular memory very quickly took over Gerard. The people lovingly wrote his biography, choosing and amplifying the characteristics that brought him closer to the simple folk, and made him more sensitive to the harshness of the challenges that the poor have to confront every day. It accentuated his ready and generous solidarity for the needy, his closeness to and familiarity with God, which made the path of miracles "normal" for him, and his unusual passion for penance.

The reading of Saint Gerard that the liturgy proposes for us stresses the relationship of assimilation to Christ crucified. We are invited to pray: "Oh God, who drew Saint Gerard to you from his youth and made him conform to the image of your crucified Son...." At issue here is a dimension confirmed by all the sources on Gerard, but enriched by nuances and perspectives that confer on him a profound style of serenity and life, which has to be appreciated much more than it has been in the past.

In the final analysis, the biographers don't seem to pay any special attention to the problem of critically reconstructing Gerard's spirituality. It's not that this focus has been missing, but it has not gotten the specific treatment that it would be right to expect.[4]

The modality of my reflections emerges from awareness of all this. I have no intention of offering a comparative study of the diverse interpretations given so far to Gerardian spirituality in order to stress the points of convergence. Nor is it my central concern to dwell on the specifically historical aspects in order to get a better grasp of the roots of Gerard's spirituality. These are certainly very important topics, but they would require a more extensive treatment.

Instead, I intend to propose a synthetic rereading of the characteristics that spell out more clearly Gerard's spiritual path as they emerge from his spiritual writings, integrating the *Notes* of Caione with some witnesses contained in the *Summarium*. I would like to invite readers not so much to a theoretical discussion as to a simple listening to Gerard; I am convinced that this is the only way to penetrate his "secret" and to get hold of this living word that the Spirit, through the figure of Gerard, continues to send our way, even now, in ecclesial and social contexts that are profoundly different from his.

ALWAYS UNITED TO HIS "DEAR GOD"

Anyone who opens Gerard's correspondence will be immediately struck by the depth and spontaneity of his communion with God. He never appears drawn in upon himself, even at the times of greatest difficulty and misunderstanding. He always lived in intense and loving communion with his "dear Redeemer," with his "dear God," as he used to say.[5]

Writing to Sister Maria of Jesus, he repeated insistently: "Let us love our God, who alone deserves to be loved. And how could we live if we didn't love our dear God from the heart?" And he confided in her: "I remain in Naples, accompanied by Father Margotta, and now more than ever I am going to busy myself unreservedly with my dear God." But he was that way all his life: an "unreserved surrender to his dear God."[6]

During the beatification trial, the Redemptorist Francesco Alfani recalled, speaking of Gerard's confreres who had lived with him: "They said that there was not a single instant when his mind wasn't focused on God, in whose contemplation he was so immersed that, like a profound theologian...he spoke of the highest mysteries of our faith and particularly of the august Most Holy Trinity and of the Incarnation of the Word....He was seen continually possessed by such a force of divine love that he broke into frequent exclamations of faith that shook all those who were present."[7]

This loving communion with God did not make Gerard forget about the needs of daily life and, above all, the many needs of his brothers. It was the result of a look of faith that perceived in events, even the harshest, the salvific presence of the Redeemer. There was a great deal of significance in his habitual remark, related by Caione, that "if God took this mask away from our eyes, we would see paradise everywhere. Beneath these stones, beneath those rocks, too, is God"[8]

Such was the intensity of this communion that at times it was enough for him to gaze at an image to make him overflow with ecstasy. There was the time, for example, when he was preparing the refectory for the community dinner, and "he looked at the painting of the 'Ecce Homo,' and such was the ardor with which he contemplated it that he remained on his knees, beside himself, contemplating the picture."[9] The same thing happened on another occasion before an image of Mary, in the Capucci house. He was seen "suspended in the air... shouting, in the presence of many people: Look how beautiful she is! He kissed and continued to kiss the image with immense and extraordinary ardor."[10]

He never ceased exhorting the addressees of his letters to have this look of faith that was transformed into trusting communion. He wrote, for example, in the first months of 1753, to Sister Maria of Jesus: "Anyone who does not have faith is missing God. I have taken the decision to live and die kneaded in the holy faith. Faith is life for me, and my life is faith. Oh God, who wants to love without holy faith? I would like to exclaim forever, and to be listened to all throughout the world, and to be always saying: long live our holy faith in our dear God. Only God deserves to be loved. How can I live if I am missing my God."[11]

For Gerard, the deepest suffering came when this look of

communion seemed to be clouded over. In the first months of 1754, he confided to Sister Maria: "That is how things go today: one goes up and the other goes down. I believe that my troubles have to be eternal. But I wouldn't be bothered if they were [eternal]. It would be enough that I loved God and pleased him in everything. This is my trouble: to believe that I am suffering, abandoned by God."[12]

LOVE OF NEIGHBOR

For the believer it is not possible to separate the love for God from love for others. If we have a clear awareness of the intensity of Gerard's communion with his "dear" God, we won't be at all surprised by the depth and naturalness of his relations with his neighbors. The fragment of the letter sent in early 1753 to Sister Maria of Jesus, which I have quoted earlier, is important in this respect: the faith that Gerard talked about didn't simply mean a relationship with God, but also the special brotherly relationship that united him with the nun.

"Our loving Jesus is always with you, my dear mother, and may 'Mamma' Mary Most Holy keep you always in the loving being of our dear God." Then he added, with a touch of joyful irony, to this opening wish: "Here is the answer to your very respectful letter. I tell you it is necessary to write to all the universe and make it understand...that it counts as one of the wonders of God that Your Reverence remembered me, your servant, after so long a time....I rejoice infinitely over this and I praise the supreme Maker. Enough for now. Be it as it may, I place everything in the hands of my dear God, and I pardon you. If afterwards Your Reverence complains about me, I tell you that I am not Sister Maria of Jesus, who promises much and doesn't deliver. I cannot forget what I promised....That is how I am: the more I see myself separated from Your Reverence, the more I hasten to make my way along with you in order to meet my dear God once more."[13]

Earlier, on April 6, 1752, he had written: "Oh God, what

great joy I have felt today in my heart upon receiving your very precious letter, which I was waiting for so ardently. But, given that I am speaking to you with truth in the presence of God, this aspiration does not proceed from my will, but from the Most High, who moves me to beg for help from others, because I cannot.... Meanwhile, I find consolation in the fact that your daughters are decidedly committed in my favor at the feet of his Divine Majesty. And from him I certainly hope and wish, for my part, that he may repay you copiously."[14]

His communion was of a kind that gave a privileged place to prayer. Gerard never tired of asking for prayers for himself and others, and of promising prayers to those who wrote to him. On October 4, 1754, he reminded Sister Michela, the superior of Ripacandida: "Only I beg you, from time to time, command by obedience all my dear sisters to always remember me in their holy prayers, since I, unworthy as I am, will always do the same thing for all of them."[15] The horizon, nevertheless, was always that of the salvation that opened up to eternity. "Let them always pray to God for me," he wrote days later, to another nun, "and tell him to make me a saint, please, because I am wasting time. Oh my God, what bad luck I have, for I let so many moments and hours and days pass uselessly, that is, without knowing how to use them. Oh, how much I waste."[16]

But this didn't cause him to forget the many problems and needs of daily life. He wrote many beautiful letters aimed at collecting the dowry that poor girls required to enter a convent. He didn't blush at asking help from anyone who could give him a hand.[17] But he insistently reminded Sister Michela:

> As for the difficulties that Sister Maria Giuseppa is having, you tell me to conform to the will of God. Yes, Lord, take away from me that [will] and what is left to me? And about the money that is in my power, which I received from friends, you tell me that you wish to deposit it, and that if she doesn't get to become a nun, it will serve to get her married. Mother of mine, what are you saying? That is something neither I nor any-

one else can do, because that would amount to dishonoring our congregation, since I sought and begged for help with the purpose of making her a nun and not marrying her. And if that can't be done, we have to return the money to its owners.[18]

Gerard's sensitivity for others also led him to take an interest in the needs of the simplest people. One's attention is caught by the letter he wrote on August 28, 1754, to Sister Maria Celeste of the Holy Spirit: "Dear Sister, I recalled that since last year Your Reverence has been wanting a book of songs. I haven't sent it because I did not return [to the capital]. I waited for the opportunity. Now that I find myself in Naples again, I remembered. Here you have it; I send it to you. Sing in your cell, in order to come to be a great saint, and always pray to God for me."[19]

This charity was also transformed into miracles when it was a question of going out to meet the poor. Popular memory has especially emphasized how much he did during the harsh winter of 1755. Here, too, Caione's testimony is essential: owing, he says, to the "extreme shortages" caused by the intense cold, "more than 120 poor people flocked to our caretaker's office every morning. It is impossible to express the great charity with which Gerard took pity on them and ran off to get help for their miseries. He became all things to all men. He consoled them with his usual heavenly words; he instructed them in matters of the faith; he delivered devout sermons to them, and finally he gave them alms and sent them off doubly comforted."[20]

WITH SINCERE AND SERENE FREEDOM

Gerard lived all this with a spirit of freedom and of sincerity that attracted and surprised those who met him. He radiated a total availability to the Spirit, the fruit of that look of faith with which he saw and evaluated every event. There was a significant remark made by the rector of Materdomini after the episode of a barrel that had remained open without the wine being spilled: "God is amusing himself with him in a singular manner. One has to let him act according to the Spirit who is leading him. It is not possible to explain in any other way this stupendous prodigy."[21]

The same "vow to do what is most perfect, that is, what seems to me to be the most perfect before God" was inscribed in this climate of freedom and made it manifest. Gerard, in fact, was concerned about adding certain "reservations...to avoid all confusion or scruple, which could prevent me from acting."[22]

The horizon always had to remain wide and open. At the end of the *Rules*, he listed among the "Affections": "My God, would that I could convert as many sinners as there are grains of sand in the sea and on earth, leaves on the trees, blades of grass in the fields, atoms in the air, stars in the sky, rays of the sun and moon, and all the creatures of the earth."[23]

This sort of freedom was reconciled with ready and generous obedience. The testimonies on this point from the beatification trial keep echoing one another. Don Tommaso Cozzarelli, for example, affirms: "A rather strong motivation in favor of the observance by God's servant came from the fact that he believed the voice of the superior...was the voice of mandate of God himself. He considered disobeying it a most grave sin and wickedness. There was born in him, therefore, the heroic exercise of obedience. A gesture, a voice, a word from the superior was enough to make him carry out the most difficult things, sometimes joining to admirable and stupendous obedience...the greatest simplicity, along with a desire to be despised for [the love of] Jesus Christ."[24]

This powerful feeling of the value of obedience did not prevent him from noting in the "Memories" that, "I will call everyone's attention, even the Father Rector's, when he speaks ill of his neighbor."[25]

With his strong sense that God's "cause" was his own cause, Gerard was also sure that obedience made his own cause God's cause. Hence the inner freedom and confident serenity that never slackened, not even when he was calumniated by Nerea Caggiano. He was "summoned to this college of Pagani by the holy founder," says the Redemptorist Claudio Ripoli, "and while he was harshly castigated, he did not waste a single word in justifying himself; and, in constant serenity, not the slightest complaint issued from his lips. But when he was with some persons in private he confessed with complete security: If our rule prohibits us from justifying ourselves, my cause is [the] cause of God."[26]

An episode related by Caione is extremely significant on this score. It is worthwhile transcribing it completely: "He had received a special grace from God: the freedom from temptations against purity; he did not even know what they meant— so much so that he let his eyes roam freely. Noticing this, I called him and said: Why are you immodest with your eyes instead of keeping them lowered? He answered: Why do I have to hold them that way? Knowing his simplicity, so as not to awaken evil thoughts in him, I said: Because that is how I want it. From then on he never raised his eyes, not, to be sure, out of fear of temptations, which he never had, but out of obedience."[27]

Gerard's freedom was not superficiality, much less simple-mindedness. More than once, in his letters, he takes precautions to avoid negative interpretations. "Don't be surprised by such an affectionate way of writing to you," he reminded Sister Michela, "because I am moved by three motives to do so: first, because you are the spouse of Jesus Christ, and I esteem and venerate you as such; second, because you are a daughter of my dear [Saint] Teresa, whom I treasure so much that I would give my blood and my life to defend always and extol the glory of my dear God; third, because we are brother and sister in my Lord; precisely for these reasons we most love each other always in a pure manner in God."[28]

Still more significant are the lines he sent to the young Isabella Salvadore, lines that express suffering because they were written during his last illness: "God knows how I am. And nevertheless my Lord lets me write you in my own hand.

This will allow you to realize how much God loves you....My dear daughter, you cannot imagine how much I love you in God and how much I desire your eternal salvation, because the blessed God has wished me to pay special attention to you. But you must know, blessed daughter, that my affection is free from all worldly concupiscence. It is an affection divinized in God. I repeat, therefore, that I love you in God, not at the margin of him. If my affection departed from God in the least, I would be a blackguard from hell. And so, as I love you, in the same way I love all the creatures that love God; and if I knew that any one of them loved me on the margin of God, I would curse her on the part of my Lord, because our affection must be purified, loving all things in God and not on the margin of God.[29]

Thanks to this profound freedom, Gerard could remain faithful to the expressions of popular piety without reducing himself to them. Faithful to love for the sacred images, which he not only guarded and zealously spread, but also learned to sculpt in paper and plaster. Faithful to the prayers that he promised to others and that he asked for himself.[30] Faithful to the numerous acts of penance.[31] All this, however, was integrated into the depth of communion and encounter with God that transformed the image into a sign of presence that absorbed him to the point of ecstasy.

THE EUCHARIST

Love for the Eucharist was immense in Gerard. Already in his youth, Caione recalls, "One especially had to admire the modesty with which he walked about the city and spoke with people, and the external attitude and reverence with which he remained for hours at a time in the church, before the Most Blessed Sacrament, which he often visited. He also had a great concern that others too should visit Jesus in the sacrament; and many, encouraged by his fervent example, felt moved to visit him frequently, which caused him a great and inexpressible joy."[32]

This was a love that grew upon his entering the Redemptorists. In popular memory, he appears completely rapt in front of the sanctuary, heedless of the passage of time. One day his thanksgiving after communion went on almost till noon. When his confreres reminded him of his obligations to the community, he simply replied: "Oh, you have little faith: what job do the angels have? And speaking in this way, he made his way back to the kitchen along with his brothers; and they saw to their surprise that everything had been prepared for breakfast."[33]

In front of the tabernacle it was hard to control the intensity of the dialogue with his dear Redeemer. Antonio de Cosmio testified that "when he assisted during the day at the exposition of the Blessed Sacrament, despite the permanent effort to hide himself from the view of others, Gerard's countenance became luminous. He was seen to be anxious and agitated; he was totally concentrated, and as if beside himself; he seemed to be a seraph in the moment of adoration."[34]

But the Eucharist was never an excuse for neglecting the tasks that had been assigned to him. With his characteristic spontaneity, Gerard also reminded the eucharistic Christ of his subjection to obedience. "From what was publicly said, I know and depose," affirmed Gaetano Terrotola, "that Brother Gerard punctually obeyed his superior when he forbade him from continuing in prayer before Jesus in the Blessed Sacrament. One time, passing nearby, Gerard was heard to say: 'Let me go, I have things to do!' The superior, when informed of this, wished to know the reason. Gerard modestly revealed what had happened. The superior was stunned with admiration for the holiness of the servant of God, with his profound familiarity with Jesus Christ in the Blessed Sacrament."[35]

Above all, the Eucharist taught him the depth and generosity of self-surrender: the "madness" of love, according to his own words. At times when he was praying before the Eucharist, he was seen laughing; when asked by his superior to explain, he ingenuously recounted that he had often heard a voice coming from the tabernacle and telling him, 'Madman, madman! A day will come when you will get over this madness of yours.' And he said that he used to reply to this voice, 'Lord, aren't you the one I learn the madness from? Why, being an infinite God, have you locked yourself up in a narrow monstrance out of love for me?'"[36]

It was a madness that had to take concrete form in availability and openness toward the brothers. Caione observes: "He had an extraordinary love of work, such that he never wasted time. When he didn't have anything to do, he strove to help the others in their tasks....When it was necessary to bake bread for the community, he worked as much as four men; he kept telling the other brothers: 'Let me do the work. You stay quiet and rest.' And thus he worked alone. While performing his material tasks, however, he remained in constant recollection and union with God. He was always seen with his eyes raised to heaven, as if beside himself.'"[37]

THE WILL OF GOD

Conforming to the will of God was Gerard's permanent aspiration, even on his deathbed. He confessed this to Father Caione, his superior: "I imagine that this bed is the will of God, and I am nailed to this bed as if I were nailed to the will of God. Even more, I imagine that the will of God and I have become one and the same thing." Caione adds: "This is what gave him a great sensitivity [before God]. On the door of the room he had had a sign posted on which, in capital letters, these words could be seen: Here the will of God is being done, as God wishes and for as long as God wishes.[38] At this point Gerard was in perfect harmony with the vision of Saint Alphonsus.[39]

All his biographers are agreed in stressing his conformity with the will of God as the nucleus of Gerard's spirituality. Nevertheless, not all of them adequately emphasize the fact that his "yes" was a joyful, convinced, confident "yes"; it was a "yes" that "grew."[40] He trusted in his "dear God," because he knew well that his will for humanity and for every human being is a program of life, fullness, and happiness.

We should not be surprised if, while begging Sister Maria of Jesus for prayers for the health of a nun who was gravely ill, he added: "I don't want her to die. Tell my dear God that I want her to become more holy and to die very old, so that she may rejoice in spending many years in the service of God. Courage, deal with the divine power. And this time may God let things happen as we wish. In the name of God, I give you the order not to let her die."[41] For Gerard this too meant coming to be one single thing with the will of God.

On April 24, 1752, he had written to the same nun "a letter worthy of being remembered forever."[42] Gerard says: "I cannot imagine how a spiritual person, consecrated to his God, can encounter any bitterness on this earth, disgusted with the always beautiful will of God, which is the sole substance of our souls....What else does God want from us except that his divine will always be done perfectly, as he wishes, where he wishes, and when he wishes, with us always ready to [welcome] his slightest indication."[43]

Even when faced with the cross, the "yes" to the will of God had to keep all its confidence and all its generosity. Gerard knew perfectly well that only in this way could he prolong in favor of his neighbor the salvific mystery of Christ's paschal cross. It is enough to reread the words that he wrote to Sister Maria of Jesus around the end of 1754: "I know that you are happy. And this joy is enough to encourage me and give me strength in God. Blessed be he, who grants me so many graces and who, instead of making me die beneath his holy blows, gives me a victory of life so that I can suffer still more and thus imitate my divine Redeemer."[44]

This is the aspect of Gerard's spirituality that receives the primary emphasis in the liturgy. And the memory of the people also gives it a particular stress. The witnesses at the beatification trial recalled that "Gerard was seen almost always joyful, even in his most painful illnesses; and he seemed saddened and downcast only on the days of the Passion of Jesus Christ, as he meditated on the sorrows of the Redeemer."[45] In order to participate even more in the cross of Christ, he redoubled the rigor of his usual penances: fasts, hair shirts, flagellations, in such a way that he appeared pale, stirring up at the same time feelings of tenderness, without being able to resist the power of the affections.[46]

The same witnesses, nevertheless, agree in stressing that all this took place every time that Gerard confronted sin: "He was always joyful and affable even with the humblest person, and he was observed to be melancholy only when he saw sins and sinners, whom he sweetly admonished; and as much as he could invited them to return to God.[47] Because of this he intensified his penances and his generous "yes" to the cross.

There are, no doubt, various keys to reading the penitential content of Gerard's spirituality, beginning with the popular roots of his homeland. I believe, however, that the ultimate reason is to be found in his resolute and joyful "yes" to the mystery of the death and resurrection of Christ: he had to prolong the mystery of the cross in favor of his brothers. He was burning with the same anxiousness and the same joy experienced by the apostle Paul: "I rejoice in my sufferings for your sake, and in my flesh I complete what is lacking in Christ's afflictions for the sake of is body, that is, the Church" (Col 1:24).

CONCLUSION

At the beginning of these reflections, I said that my principle objective was to invite readers to a moment of "listening" to Gerard. That is why I made abundant use of his writings, above all, his letters. It seems to me that a spirituality emerges from them that calls upon us to widen our heart and broaden our horizons, but without ever losing sight of the fact that everything has in the cross its obligatory passage and sure path.

In conclusion, it is good to let him have the floor one more time. On January 22, 1752, he wrote to Sister Maria of Jesus: "God knows well the affection that you awaken in me to see you so afflicted. It is not a natural attachment, but a kind of envy. Blessed be the Lord always, who keeps you in this state to make you into a saint. Courage, be joyful! And fearless! Be strong and valiant when facing the battles, in order to obtain a greater victory in our kingdom of heaven. Let us not be frightened of anything except what the Evil One sows in our hearts, because that is his office. And our task is not to let him conquer....It is true that at times we find ourselves confused and weak. But there is no confusion in God; there is no weakness with God's power. Because it is certain that in the battles God himself helps us with his divine arm. For this reason, we can be joyful and extend ourselves further to [accepting] the divine will. And we bless his works for all eternity.[48]

NOTES

CHAPTER 1

1. Caione, Gaspare, *Notizie della vita del F. laico Gerardo Maiella,* ed. Majorano, S., *Gerardo Maiella, Appunti biografici,* Naples, 1988 (*Contributi gerardini* 4), (hereinafter Caione), p 24. Tannoia, *Vita del Servo di Dio Fr. Gerardo Majella* (hereinafter Tannoia, *Gerardo*), 1811, 7th ed.; Naples, 1838, *cap.* III, English trans. *Lives of Companions of St. Alphonso Liguori*; anon. Cong. Orat, London, 1849, (hereinafter *Companions*), pp 246f. *Gerardo, Companions,* p 245. Caione, p 23, speaks of a lightness of heart that set Gerard laughing with his whole body.

2. Tannoia, *Gerardo,* pp 366, 373, 411, and 262. The flautist was playing the great Metastasian verse "I wish for Thee, my God, alone," and Gerard sang the chorus-line as he danced, "Thy will, O God, and not mine own." Gerard always had a better taste in musical matters than most Fathers and Brothers, and more modern taste than Alphonsus. The Rector Major did not care for any dancing: "If you wish to sing, sing spiritual songs, but take care never on any account to dance; the very fact of taking your companion by the hand may cause bad thoughts and temptations"; *Vera Sposa,* XXIV.vi; *True Spouse,* p 708. *Cf.* Alphonsus's *obiter dictum:* "Our life must be far from that of seculars, no enterprise, no game, among us, no writing even, like that of the world"; Gregorio, O.,"*Sentimenti di Monsignore,*" S.H., IX, 1961, pp 439–475, No. 29 on p 453.

3. Tannoia, *Gerardo; Companions,* p 372.

4. Caione, p 79.

5. Gerard to Maria of Jesus, May 1753, *Lettere di S. Gerardo,* ed. Capone, D., and Majorano, S., 1980, No. 11.

6. Gerard to Maria of Jesus, August 28, 1754, *Lettere di S. Gerardo,* No. 30.

7. Gerard to Maria of Jesus, August 23, 1755, *Lettere di S. Gerardo,* No 43.

8. Tannoia, *Gerardo; Companions,* p 331.

9. Ibid., p 357. Tannoia records, *Companions*, p 245, another story of Gerard's being "ravished into an ecstasy" when serving his apprenticeship in the Muro tailor's shop and how, ecstatic still, he hid under the cutting table, whence he was drawn by the angry foreman. "Gerard was so far from losing patience that he only replied with a sweet smile" which the foreman naturally took for an impertinence, and hit him again.

10. Tannoia, *Gerardo; Companions*, p 246. There were three friaries in the Muro area, the Conventuals at San Antonio, the Capuchins at San Francesco, and Eustachio's community at Santomenna, where fourteen friars lived under the Guardianship of Father Bonaventura.

11. *Ibid.*, p 250 and Caione, p 24. Luca Malpiede, the San Fele schoolmaster, seems to have been no more able than Gerard to control the boys. He returned to Muro after enduring their raggings for a month, convinced, wrongly, that teaching was not for him. Ferrante, N., *Storia Meravigliosa di San Gerardo Maiella*, Rome, 1955, (hereinafter Ferrante), pp 54f.

12. Tannoia, *Gerardo; Companions*, p 242.

13. *Companions*, p 248 and Caione, p 23.

14. *Companions*, p 243 and Caione, p 20.

15. Caione, p 20. Birgitta was not more understanding of this incident than Tannoia, *vid. Gerardo, cap.* I.

16. *Companions*, p 251 and Caione, p 21. There was another demon dog waiting for Gerard in the kitchen at d'Iliceto, Caione, p 42.

17. Caione, pp 24f. Claudio Albini had been Vicar General of Caserta, of Salerno, and of Urbino, and, having been handed on by these bishops, had been sent to serve Bishop Manfredi at Muro. They had soon come to fisticuffs. So, as a way out of this difficulty in curial relations, on May 25, 1736, Pope Clement XII had made Albini bishop of Lacedonia. More rows followed, with the cathedral Canons, the university Regents at Rochetta, the Orsini feudal landlords. Albini died suddenly, June 25, 1744, while visiting archbishop Giuseppe Nicolai at San Andrea di Conza and was buried in the church of the Reformed Franciscans.

18. Caione, p 30.

19. *Ibid.*, p 29.

20. Tannoia, *Gerardo; Companions*, p 241.

21. *Ibid.*, p 249.

22. *Ibid.*, p 258. Gerard never surrendered that family sense of the relation of play to reality, of what a play could mean for one's appreciation of reality. He was quickly affected by any performance. Some years later, watching a similar Passion Play arranged by Canon Giove for Abbess Capano and her Benedictine nuns, *Companions,*

p 312, he was so affected that "he was raised to a considerable height from the floor."

23. *Companions*, p 258.
24. *Ibid.*
25. Caione, pp 30f.
26. Ferrante, N. *Storia meravigliosa di S. Gerardo Maiella*, Rome, 1965, (hereinafter "Ferrante"), p 128, with the suggestion that the assistant was a "desperado" whom Gerard had met on the road.
27. Tannoia, *Gerardo; Companions*, p 266.
28. *Ibid.* Tannoia alleges eyewitness testimony of both Andrea Longarello and Francesco Giovenale, 1719–1782.
29. Alphonsus to Caione, May 19, 1755 in *Lettere di S. Alphonso Mari a de' Liguori*, Rome, 3 vols., 1887, English trans. *Letters of St. Alphonsus de Liguori*, ed. Eugene Grimm, 5 vols., New York, 1891. For the tradition of the useless Gerard, *vid.* Ferrante, p 10.
30. Caione, p 147: "*Un soggetto inutile alla Congregazione.*"
31. Caione, p 34.
32. Stories of obedience to unuttered command occur at *Companions*, pp 292, 315, and 415. Stories of his leading parties of Students and of reprobates, Caione, pp 10 and 15.
33. Gerard's birth and baptism are discussed by Ferrante, "*Il nome e cognome di S. Gerardo,*" S.H., II, 1954, pp 461 and 462, and "*Quando e nato S. Gerardo?*" S.H., III, 1955, pp 456f.
34. Caione, pp 43ff.
35. *Ibid.*, p 41.
36. Tannoia, *Gerardo; Companions*, pp 360f.
37. *Companions*, p 311.
38. *Ibid.*, p 402.
39. *Ibid.*, p 322.
40. *Ibid.*, pp 329f.
41. *Ibid.*, p 381.
42. *Ibid.*, p 361.
43. Caione, p 71.
44. The grand Sicilian nun's life and work had been made more widely known by Girolamo Turano's two recent publications, *Vita e virtu della V. S. Maria Crocifissa*, Agrigento, 1704, Venice, 1711, and *Scelta di Lettere Spirituali* Agrigento, 1704. *Vid.* Bernardo Apice, 1728–1769, to Maria Arcangela Lipp, May 26, 1762, in Giammusso, *Lettere dalla Sicilia*, No. 28, and Alphonsus's remarks, Gregorio, O., *Sentimenti*, S.H., IX, p 464.
45. Tannoia, *Gerardo; Companions*, p 382.
46. Caione, pp 99f. A less confident priest came asking Gerard to help him understand *Il Pastore della buona notte* by Juan de Palafox y

Mendoza, 1600–1659, the prolific bishop of Los Angeles, and being signed "in the name of the Trinity," found he could very well get the sense of what he had before thought quite impenetrable.

47. Caione, p 101. Perhaps they were all seeing for the first time the work method of an honest tailor who had not, at the end of the cutting, a length of cloth which he could devote to his own purposes. *Cf.* Alphonsus, *Theologia Moralis, Lib. IV, cap.* iii, on the state and duties of seculars, *dub.* X, the obligations of merchants, iv.2, Gaude, 292.

48. Tannoia, *Gerardo; Companions,* pp 302 and 303.

49. *Ibid., Companions,* pp 304, 312, and 316.

50. *Ibid.,* p 361.

51. Caione, p 54.

52. Tannoia, *Gerardo; Companions,* pp 330 and 396.

53. *Companions,* p 421.

54. *Ibid.,* p 431.

55. *Ibid.,* p 299.

56. *Posizioni e Articoli Per i Processi Ordinarii,* for beatification of Domenico Blasucci, Rome, 1893, p 50; Blasucci was born at Muro, March 3, 1732.

57. Tannoia, *Gerardo; Companions,* pp 294 and 382; *Murana seu Compsana Beatificationis Ven. S. di D. Fr. Gerardi Majella, Summarium,* Rome, 1871, p 284. The song was well known:

> *Fiori felici voi, che notte e giorno*
> *vicino al mio Gesu sempre ne state*
> *ne vi partite mai, finche d'intorno*
> *tutta la vita alfin no vi lasciate*

58. Cafaro to Alphonsus, July 9, 1747, *Epistolae Ven. Servi Dei Pauli Cafaro, CSSR,* Rome, 1934, No. 9, and Cafaro "*ad Fratrem laicum ignotum,*" June 30 (1753?), *ibid.,* No. 62.

59. Tannoia, *Gerardo; Companions,* p 385 and Alphonsus's *Brevi notizie della vita del R. P. Paolo Cafaro* in *Via della Salute,* 1766, English trans. Grimm, *Miscellany,* 1890, pp 226f., with reference to 2 Corinthians 12:7.

60. *Vid. Posizioni* for Blasucci beatification, 55, with Tannoia's *Vita* of Blasucci, *Companions,* p 212, where the Brother Infirmarian says that Gerard's heart was "so dried up within him that he felt driven almost to despair," with the parenthetical comment, "these are his very words." This is the experience which informs his letter to prioress Maria Michele di Francesco, late summer 1753. He knew what it was to live "in a house where the Superior does not show affection for those who are tempted," and what it is for them

to feel "neglected, despised, driven to despair," *Lettere*, No. 18, *cf.* Nos. 5 and 24 to Maria of Jesus, April 16, 1752 and 1753.

61. Gerard's personal Rule of Life, *Regolamento di vita, Scritti Spirituali*, ed. Majorano, S., *Contributi Gerardini* 8, Materdomini, 1992, pp 144–156, *Ricordi*, No. 33. There are four transcriptions of this Rule, Caione, I and II, Tannoia, *Gerardo*, cap. XI, and *Summarium*, pp 311–318.

62. Tannoia, *Gerardo; Companions*, p 415.

63. *Ibid.*, p 299.

64. Caione, pp 73f.

65. Tannoia, *Gerardo; Companions*, p 333.

66. *Ibid.*

67. Caione, p 74.

68. Tannoia, *Gerardo; Companions*, pp 417f; The "Constitution on the Missions," 1747, had insisted on the missioners' being self-protective in this matter: "They shall never go alone" even if they have to be accompanied "by some priest or cleric when there are few of their own Brothers," *vid. Analecta CSSR*, I, 1922, pp 172ff, and *Founding Texts of Redemptorists: Early Rules and Allied Documents*, Rome, 1986, (hereinafter *Founding Texts*), p 348; Alphonsus to Fathers, 1744, where the first sentence of "Rules to be observed during the Missions" declares, "They shall never go alone," regulating for "at least two Fathers, or one Father with a lay Brother, or in case of necessity some secular priest."

69. Tannoia, *Gerardo; Companions*, p 317.

70. *Ibid.*

71. *Ibid.*, pp 328f.

72. *Ibid.*, p 348. Caione, p 91, refers to Nerea's involving the Capucci girl. He thought that Nerea had left the Foggia convent as much because she was "homesick" as for love of her confessor." There is a review of these complexities in Felipe, Dionisio, *San Gerardo Mayela*, Madrid, 1954, *cap.* XXXI, pp 373–387.

73. Ferrante, p 502.

74. Tannoia, A. M., *Della Vita ed Instituto del Ven. S. di Dio Alphonsus M. Liguori*, Naples, 1798, *Lib.* II, *cap.* ix, p 115 (hereinafter all references are to the Italian reprint, Materdomini, 1982, of the 1798–1802 edition. For a prefiguring of Gerard's imitation of Christ, *ibid.*, I, xvi, p 61: "Alphonsus did not open his mouth in his own defense and did not make any excuse; on the contrary it cheered him to see himself so abused and humiliated."

75. Constitution on Missions; *Founding Texts*, pp 348f.

76. Tannoia, *Gerardo; Companions*, p 405.

77. *Ibid.*, p 349.

78. *Vera Sposa*, XI.4, citing a Torres letter from Sabbatini's *Vita* of the famous Jesuit, vol. II, *cap.* ix.

79. Caione, p 79.

80. *Ibid.*

81. Tannoia, *Gerardo; Companions*, p 351.

82. Caione, p 81.

83. Tannoia, *Gerardo; Companions*, p 354.

84. *Founding Texts*, p 168.

85. *Ibid.*, pp 202f.

86. *Ibid*, p 305. *Cf.* Alphonsus's instructions issued after the Canonical Visitation of the Student House, Ciorani, in 1761. Declaring that his instructions are "taken for the most part from our Rules and from the Constitutions," he applies what is said of Fathers to "our young men" who are going to be Fathers. The first instruction is concerned with times when they are in hot water: "They shall show all possible respect, veneration, and obedience, as well to the Prefect as to be Lecturer; they shall neither defend nor excuse themselves in their presence."

87. Gerard's *Rule of Life*, "Maxims dearest to my heart," Nos. 5, 2, 3, and 6.

88. Tannoia, *Gerardo; Companions*, p 354.

89. *Ibid.*, p 274.

90. *Ibid.*, p 358.

91. *Ibid.*, p 329.

92. *Ibid.*

93. *Ibid.*, p 358.

94. For Melfi as a "theater," Tannoia, *Gerardo*, XVIII, p 68.

95. Tannoia, *Gerardo; Companions*, pp 363f.

96. *Ibid.*, p 360; *vid.* Gerard to Celeste Crostarosa, March 8, 1755, *Lettere di S. Gerardo*, No. 37. For the Jesuits' convent foundation, *vid.* Tannoia, *Gerardo; Companions*, p 339.

97. Tannoia, *Gerardo; Companions*, p 405.

98. Alphonsus to Caione, September 21 and 28, 1754, and during October 1754, with justified forebodings that Manfredonia was about to cause trouble; he ran away on November 21, returned May 30, 1755, and was dismissed as incorrigible, 1756.

99. Angelo Latessa died, October 5, the Student, Pietr'Angelo Picone, b. 1733, died on November 9, 1754.

100. Tannoia, *Gerardo; Companions*, p 378. When Margotta was sad and silent at recreation, Alphonsus sang him a song:

> *How grand and sweet, my Mother dear,*
> *Is your name, O Mary*

Margotta did not cheer up.

101. Tannoia, *Gerardo; Companions*, p 425.
102. *Ibid.*, p 424.
103. Gerard to Celeste Crostarosa, March 8, 1755, *Lettere di San Gerardo*, No. 37.
104. *Ibid.*
105. Caione, pp 117–120.
106. Gerard to Caione, August 23, 1755, *Lettere*, No. 43.
107. Tannoia, *Gerardo; Companions*, p 434; *vid.* Swanston, H. F. G., *Singing a New Song*, Liguori, 1997, p 171 with note 161.
108. Tannoia, *Gerardo; Companions*, p 439; *vid.* for Carminiello's ringing a cheerful bell at Gerard's death, *Caione*, p 153. Tannoia says, *ibid.*, p 440, that there was another Brother looking after Gerard with Carminiello; Caione, pp 147–153 mentions Brothers Andrea, Saverio, Stefano, and Gennaro.
109. Caione, pp 153f.
110. Tannoia, *Gerardo; Companions*, p 441.
111. Caione, p 153.
112. *Ibid.*, p 154, Tannoia, *Gerardo;* Companions, pp 442f, and *Vita*, IV, xxxvi, p 193; Alphonsus sent a death-card to Ripacandida, *vid.* Alphonsus to Maria of Jesus, July 22, 1757.
113. The engagement of the missioners with the Buono Murante family, especially with "Mamma Vittoria" is evident at Gerard to Maria Michela, *Lettere di San Gerardo*, No. 16; *vid* also Ferrante, pp 176ff. Mauro, whom Alphonsus called, affectionately, "Mauriccio," proved an inconstant member of the Congregation, coming, going, coming, and at last returning to mamma to die. In January 1756, he was still the white-headed boy, "I am expecting you, my dear," Alphonsus wrote on January 7, 1756, "and hours appear to me ages."
114. Alphonsus to Murante, January 7, 1756.
115. Alphonsus to Caione, January 11, 1756.
116. For the "journey-structure," *vid.* Caione, pp 117–135 and Angelomichele de Spirito, "*La presenza redentorista in Irpina,*" *Richerche di Storia Sociale e Religiosa*, XXVI, 1951, pp 169–197. For miracles, *vid.* Tannoia, *Gerardo; Companions*, pp 420ff, and the testimony of Dr. Gaetano Federici at the beatification process, pp 69f.
117. Tannoia, *Gerardo; Companions*, p 255.
118. Caione, p 137.
119. *Ibid.*, p 144.
120. Gerard to Maria of Jesus, January 7, 1754, *Lettere di San Gerardo*, No. 31. *Cf.* Caione's record of Gerard's confiding to Brother Gennaro his wish to die of tuberculosis on account of the Community's leaving such patients so much alone, Caione, p 142.

121. Caione, p 144.
122. *Ibid.*, p 151. *Cf.* Gerard to Maria of Jesus, January 7, 1754, where he himself seems to be making a pun between "*aceto*," vinegar, and "*accetto*," "I accept"; *Lettere di San Gerardo*, No. 31.
123. *Lettere di San Gerardo*, No. 31.
124. Caione, p 136.
125. Caione, post-word, p 151.
126. Tannoia, *Gerardo; Companions,* pp 361 and 381.
127. Gerard to Santorelli, *Lettere di San Gerardo*, No. 27.
128. *Lettere di San Gerardo*, p. 330. The exclamation is not in the *Summarium* text, nor Caione II nor Tannoia, *Gerardo, cap.* IX. The editors of *Lettere* comment, note 17, that "the omission from these other sources derives perhaps from a difficulty in comprehending."
129. Gerard was very aware of the sorts of wrong-headed questions that fascinate a dull theologian. The Jesuit, Paolo Giunta, had plagued Maria Crocifissa about "the freedom of God in creating the world," and she had had to answer distinguishingly in terms of "act of divine Production," "effusion of divine essence," and transfusion *ab extra," vid.* Cabbibo, S., and Marilena, M., *La Santa dei Tomasi,* Turin, 1989, pp 162f and 174, note 24, all while protesting that the Lord had assured her that "from the Chair of my Cross, I do not propose scholastic treatises but things mysterious and divine," Ms 4920 f 267 v, cited by Locatelli, S., *La Ven. Maria Crocifissa Tomasi e il Seicento mistico Italiano,* p 71, in *Regnum Dei,* XIII, 1957.
130. *Lettere di San Gerardo*, No. 41.
131. Gerard to Celeste Crostarosa, March 8, 1755; *Lettere,* No. 37.
132. He began to sign himself not only with "*G. M. G. T"* (Jesus, Mary, Joseph, Teresa) but also with "*Pazza mia dei Pazzi"* ("My madwoman among the mad" or "my madwoman [Maddalena] dei Pazzi").
133. Gerard, *Rule of Life; Lettere di San Gerardo,* p 332.
134. *Lettere di San Gerardo*, No. 44.
135. *Ibid.*, Nos. 35 and 44; *cf.* also "My most Holy Trinity" and My and your Most Holy Trinity," *ibid.*, Nos. 32 and 27.

CHAPTER 3

1. This biographical quotation and those that follow are taken from Gaspare Caione, *Notizie della vita del fratello laico Gerardo Maiella del SS.mo Redentore,* two manuscripts edited by N. Ferrante and A. Sampers in *Spicilegium Historicum CSSR* 8 (1960), 187–209, 217–297.

2. For these and other texts by Saint Gerard quoted here, see Gerardo Maiella, *Scritti Spirituali,* ed. Sabatino Majorano, Materdomini, 1992. They are published in Chapter Five of the book.

3. N. Ferrante, *Storia mervagliosa di S. Gerardo Maiella* (Rome, 1965), p 53.

4. A. Di Coste, *Un giglio olezzante della famiglia redentorista, ossia il ven. Domenico Blasucci* (Rome, 1932), pp 34ff., 142–143.

5. G. De Lucca, *Sant'Alfonso. Il mio maestro di vita cristiana* (Alba, 1963), pp 59–60.

6. Girolamo Turani, *Vita e virtù della serva di Dio suor Maria Crocifissa della Concezione* (Girgenti, 1704). The first book, Antonio da Olivadi's *L'Anno Doloroso* (Naples, 1690) was given to him, possibly by Fra Bonaventura de Muro, his uncle. Gerard wanted to become a Capuchin like him.

7. *Cf.* G. Orlandi, *Missioni parrocchiali e drammatica popolare,* AA VV, *Atti del convegno di studi sul folklore padovano* (1974), (Modena 1976), pp 305–333; Orlandi, "La missione popolare redentorista in Italia. Dal Settecento ai giorni nostri," in *Spicilegium Historicum,* 33 (1985), pp 51–141.

8. C. Levi, *Cristo si è fermato a Eboli* (Milan, 1984), pp 104ff. The work was published in 1940.

9. *Cf.* E. Pani Rossi, *La Basilicata* (Verona, 1868), p 305.

10. Conferenza Episcopale Italiana, Chiesa Italiana e Mezzogiorno. *Sviluppo nella solidarietà* (October, 1989), n. 26. Saint Gerard had some 36 saints as special "advocates and protectors."

11. Ferrante, *Storia meravigliosa,* p 232.

12. *Cf.* E. De Martino, *Sud e magia* (Milan, 1959); G. De Rosa, *Vescovi, popolo e magia nel Sud* (Naples, 1971); A. De Spirito, *Il paese delle streghe. Una ricerca sulla magia nel Sannio campano* (Rome, 1976).

13. Gerard never went outside the Kingdom of Naples; but, because of his lifestyle and his special protection, he won the "trust" of many emigrants. His beatification and canonization coincided with the phenomenon of the migration by Italians in the last decades of the nineteenth and the first decades of the twentieth century.

CHAPTER 4

1. We know that there are signs of eastern asceticism in the "sacred troglodytism" of Matera, which echoes the phenomenon of the country churches of Cappadocia. In addition, we are not far from the monastic Eparchy of the Latins, which was continually traveled over during the Middle Ages by Italian-Greek saints and ascetics, who transformed the region into a "hotbed of Hellenism."

At a given moment, after the fall of the barrier separating the Byzantine empire from the rest of Italy, the south was turned into a crucible of various kinds of asceticism, including Arab; and it would be almost impossible today to distinguish the different original elements. *Cf.* B. Capelli, *Il monachesimo basiliano ai confini calabrolucani* (Naples, 1963).

2. See letter n. 31 in Chapter Five of this book.

3. The trial, which began in 1834, was held in Muro Lucano, where Gerard was born, and in Conza, the diocese to which Materdomini, where he died, belonged. The curial notaries transcribed 164 sworn testimonies, which were later collected in large volumes whose originals are kept in the archives of the Redemptorist Postulator General in Rome. An authenticated copy is in the Vatican Secret Archives: *S. Gerardo Maiella. Processus in Compsana Curia seu Transumptum.* Hereafter cited as *Processus Maiella.*

4. There is a connection between Saint Gerard and the mule, the most important beast for the peasants of his region. The mule lives next to the house; it accompanies people in their work and on long trips. The name of the saint is invoked to save the animal and even to bring it back to life. See *Processus Maiella,* vol. II, pp 1246–1247.

5. G. Caione, *Notizie del nostro fratello Gerardo Maiella,* in *Spicilegium Historicum,* 8 (1960), pp 187–209. A more recent addition is *Gerardo Maiella. Appunti biografici di un suo contemporaneo* (Caposele, 1988). It should be noted that while Caione says a "lad" (*fanciullo,* over seven years of age), in the canonization trial the term used is *Gesù Bambino* (less than six years of age).

6. As when the blind man played "*Il tuo gusto e non il mio*" ("Your taste and not mine," cf. *Processus Maiella,* vol. I, pp 257–258). [As shown in the painting used during the ceremony of beatification. This image, which was venerated for many years in Wellington, New Zealand, is now kept in the shrine of Saint Gerard in Materdomini.]

7. *Processus Maiella,* vol. I, p 284. On another occasion, when two poor girls arrived after Gerard had already distributed the bread, he gave them "two white and smoking loaves," *Ibid.,* vol. I, p 478.

8. *Ibid.,* vol. I, p 424.

9. *Ibid.,* vol. II, p 882. *Cf.* vol. I, pp 424–425, and vol. III, pp 1618–1619.

10. *Cf.* P. Macry, *Mercato e società nel Regno di Napoli* (Naples, 1974), p 284.

11. *Processus Maiella,* vol I., p 305. *Cf.* vol. II, pp 1298–1299.

12. P. Macry, *Mercato e società,* p 205.

13. *Cf. Processus Maiella,* vol. I, p 705.
14. *Ibid.,* vol. III, pp 1560–1561, 1571, 1634; vol. I, p 511.
15. *Ibid.,* vol. I, p 464.
16. Fra Antonio de Tricario relates that four bandits fired at him, wounding his mule. He managed to escape, but the animal arrived back in town almost dead, so far gone that the veterinarian could no nothing for her. He then recalled that he had a relic of the saint (a small bone) and he exclaimed, "Brother Gerard, make my mule better or I'll throw you away." He tossed the relic at the head of the animal, which got up immediately. Upon seeing this, the veterinarian said, "What you've got there is a lightning bolt, not a saint," *ibid.,* vol. I, p 727.
17. *Ibid.,* vol. I, p 306.
18. *Ibid.,* vol. II, p 1227.
19. *Ibid.,* vol. I, p 250; cf. *ibid.,* vol. II, p 1308.
20. *Ibid.,* vol. I, pp 731–732.
21. *Ibid.,* vol. I, p 45, and vol. III, p 1729. Albini was bishop of Lacedonia from 1736 to 1744, when he died at the age of sixty-five years. Recent investigations have corrected this image of an inhuman bishop, Gerard was subject to him between 1742 and 1744.
22. *Ibid.,* vol. I, pp 318–320.
23. *Ibid.,* vol. II, p 43.
24. *Ibid.,* vol. I, p 699.
25. *Ibid.,* vol. I, p 705.
26. *Ibid.,* vol. III, pp 1714–1720.
27. *Ibid.*
28. *Ibid.,* vol. I, p 307.
29. *Ibid.,* vol. I, p 477. *Cf.* vol. II, p 846.
30. *Ibid.,* vol. I, pp 714–715; vol. II, p 1327.
31. Here we enter an extremely dangerous minefield. Romana Guarnieri was well aware of this. She is a scholar who has established her reputation for expertise in exploring the many currents, some clear, some muddy, swirling through the history of European mysticism. R. Guarnieri. *Il movimento del Libero Spirito* (Rome, 1965), 351–708. Much as the Church tried to contain, reduce, or eliminate the eastern influences in southern Italy, they survived to some extent in the mid-eighteenth century, even influencing the behavior of some priests and religious. From the struggle against the Iconoclasts to the incursions of the barbarians, from the rock temples to the spread of Basilian monasteries, there was a continual coming and going of spiritual movements all over the region. Nor may we forget that Arab mysticism, which was not alien to the monastic religious trends

in the south, was full of the "divine madness" that Gerard openly professed.

32. *Processus Maiella,* vol. I, p 306.

33. Secret Vatican Archive, Congregation of Rites, Trial 6402, p 6.

34. *Ibid.,* p 54.

35. *Ibid.,* p 60.

36. *Cf.* A. De Spirito, "Il santo nella storia del Mezzogiorno," in *Sociologia* 2 (1976), pp 99–118.

37. "Christ stopped at Eboli, where the highway and the train leave the sea coast of Salerno and enter the desolate lands of Lucania. Christ has never gotten this far, nor has time arrived, nor the individual soul, nor hope, nor the relation between cause and effect or between reason and history." Carlo Levi, *Cristo si è fermato a Eboli* (Turin, 1975), p 3.

CHAPTER 5

1. Gaspare Caione (1722–1809) was very close to Gerard. He was the superior of the community of Materdomini. His biographical notes on Gerard, which were collected immediately after his death by Saint Alphonsus, have been handed down to us in two versions: the first, more synthetic and immediate; the second, more ample and elaborate. Both were published by N. Ferrante, A. Sampers, and J. Löw in *Spicilegium Historicum CSSR* 8 (1960), 187–209; 217–297. A more recent edition may be found in G. Caione, *Gerardo Maiella, appunti biografici di un contemporaneo,* ed. S. Majorano (Naples, 1988). Hereafter referred to as "Caione."

2. *Cf. Murana seu Compsana Beatificationis et Canonizationis Ven. Servi Dei Fr. Gerardi Majella laici professi Congregationis SS Redemptoris. Summarium* (Rome, 1871). Cited as *Summarium.*

3. The writings of Gerard have been amply utilized by all his biographers. A first edition of them was put together by O. Gregorio, *Lettere e scritti di S. Gerardo Maiella* (Materdomini, 1949). A more careful and complete edition is the one by D. Capone and S. Majorano, *Le lettere di S. Gerardo Majella* (Naples, 1980). The most recent one is Gerardo Maiella, *Scritti spirituali,* ed. S. Majorano (Materdomini, 1992), 160 pp. This last edition has been used for the Spanish version.

4. We always follow the original text. When this is not possible, we have recourse, in descending order, to the *Summarium* and then to Caione, with the preference given to the first edition of the latter. Finally, the text of Tannoia is used when no other sources exist. So that the reader can keep exact track of all this, the notes for each

letter indicate not only the source used, but the possible presence of others.

5. Caione, p 73.

6. A. Tannoia, *Vita del servo di Dio Fr. Gerardo Majella laico della Congregazione del SS. Redentore* (Naples, 1824).

7. For this reason the present edition also puts forward those letters that have come down to us only through the transcriptions mentioned, indicating each time that this has been done. Nevertheless, we omit the letter to the spiritual director that O. Gregorio includes in his edition, claiming to have found it in the Redemptorist archives in Pagani. The style and content are too remote from Gerard's authentic letters. In any case, Gregorio himself made the attribution to Gerard only as a hypothesis. See. Gregorio, *Lettere e scritti*, p 78.

8. Caione, pp 63–74.

9. A. Tannoia, *Della vita ed istituto del Ven. Servo di Dio Alfonso de Liguori* (Naples, 1798), vol. I, p 222.

10. Caione, pp 76–77.

11. Domenico Caione, in his ample introduction-guide to Gerard's correspondence, reconstructs the events step by step. *Cf.* Capone and Majorano, *Le Lettere*, pp 30–93.

12. Caione, p 77.

13. Tannoia, *Vita*, p 90.

14. *Ibid.*, p 91.

15. "A la Madre Suor Maria di Gesù Cristo Salvatore," Materdomini, Archives of the Sanctuary; *Summarium*, pp 297–299.

16. Tannoia, *Vita*, p 90.

17. Materdomini, Archives of the Sanctuary; *Summarium*, pp 299–300.

18. Tannoia, *Vita*, pp 90–91.

19. Capone and Majorano, *Le Letere*, pp 41–49.

20. Materdomini, Archives of the Sanctuary; *Summarium*, pp 300–301.

21. *Summarium*, p 70.

22. "A la Madre Suor Maria di Gesù Cristo Salvatore," Materdomini, Archive of the Sanctuary, *Summarium*, pp 301–303.

23. Caione, pp 74–76; Tannoia, *Vita*, pp 100–103.

24. Caione, p 74.

25. Tannoia, *Vita*, p 93.

26. "Al Nostro Rev. P. Consilitore P. D. Giovanni Mazziri del SS Salvatore," *Summarium*, pp 310–311.

27. Capone and Majorano, *Le Lettere*, p 80.

28. "Al Nostro M. Rev. P. Rettore Maggiore Il P. D. Alfonzo di Leuore del SS. Salvatore," Materdomini, Archives of the Sanctuary.

29. *Summarium*, pp 295–296; *Spicilegium Historicum*, 8 (1960), p 202 (fragment).
30. Capone and Majorano, *Le Lettere*, p 45.
31. *Summarium*, pp 289–290.
32. Materdomini, Archives of the Sanctuary; *Summarium*, pp 290–291.
33. "Per la Madre Maria Michela di S. Francesco S[a]v[eri]o Priora," Rome, Archives of the Postulator General CSSR; *Summarium*, pp 307–308.
34. Caione, pp 77–78.
35. *Cf.* Letter n. 5.
36. Tannoia, *Vita*, p 94.
37. "Per la Madre Maria Michela di S. Francesco S[a]v[eri]o Priora," Materdomini, Archives of the Sanctuary; *Summarium*, pp 291–292.
38. Materdomini, Archives of the Sanctuary; *Summarium*, pp 293–294; *Spicilegium Historicum*, 98 (1960), 204 (fragment).
39. Tannoia, *Vita*, pp 94–95.
40. *Ibid.*, pp 96–100.
41. *Ibid.*, p 100.
42. Materdomini, Archives of the Sanctuary.
43. *Summarium*, pp 306–307.
44. *Summarium*, pp 296–297; *Spicilegium Historicum*, 8 (1960), p 204 (fragment).
45. Tannoia, *Vita*, p 92.
46. *Ibid.*, pp 139–142.
47. Capone and Majorano, *Le Lettere*, p 121; *cf.* N. Ferrante, *Storia meravigliosa di S. Gerardo Maiella* (Rome, 1959), p 258.
48. "A Maria di Gesù." *Summarium*, p 309.
49. Capone and Majorano, *Le Lettere*, pp 125–126.
50. *Summarium*, p 69.
51. Tannoia, *Vita*, p 91.
52. [F. Kuntz, F. Pitocchi], *Lettere di S. Alfonso Maria de' Liguori*, vol. I (Rome, 1887), p 284; *cf.* Capone and Majorano, *Le Lettere*, p 137.
53. Tannoia, *Vita*, p 142.
54. Materdomini, Archives of the Sanctuary, *Summarium*, pp 294–295.
55. Tannoia, *Vita*, p 143.
56. *Summarium*, pp 319–320.
57. *Cf.* Capone and Majorano, *Le Lettere*, pp 153–155.
58. *Summarium*, p 310.
59. Capone, p 85.

60. Materdomini, Archives of the Sanctuary; *Summarium,* pp 304–305; *Spicilegium Historicum,* 8 (1960), p 204 (fragment).
61. Materdomini, Archives of the Sanctuary.
62. "Alla Madre Suor Maria di Gesù Cristo Salvatore," Materdomini, Archives of the Sanctuary; *Summarium,* pp 305–306.
63. Materdomini, Archives of the Sanctuary, *Summarium,* pp 304–305.
64. Tannoia, *Vita,* p 92.
65. Capone and Majorano, *Le Lettere,* p 187.
66. *Summarium,* p 320.
67. Capone and Majorano. *Le Lettere,* pp 188–189.
68. "Alla M. Reverenda Madre. La Reverenda Madre suor Maria Celeste del SS. Salvatore. Priora del Monistero del SS. Salvatore di Foggia." Materdomini, Archives of the Sanctuary; *Summarium,* pp 288–289.
69. Tannoia, *Vita,* p 177.
70. "Al Nostro R. Padre Il P.D. Celestino Derubertis del SS. Redentore, Pagani," Gars am Inn, Redemptorist Archives.
71. Caione, p 33.
72. "Al Rev. Padre D. Celestino de Robertis del SS. Redentore, Pagani," Materdomini, Archives of the Sanctuary; *Summarium,* p 297.
73. Capone and Majorano, *Le Lettere,* p 198.
74. Materdomini, Archives of the Sanctuary; *Summarium,* pp 292–293; Tannoia, *Vita,* pp 137–138.
75. Ferrante, *Storia meravigliosa,* p 336.
76. Tannoia, *Vita,* p 138.
77. *Ibid.,* p 139.
78. *Spicilegium Historicum,* 8 (1960), p 197; Caione, pp 122–123; Tannoia, *Vita,* p 170 (fragment).
79. Caione, pp 138–139.
80. *Ibid.,* p 135.
81. *Ibid.,* p 138.
82. "A suor Michela di S. Francesco Saverio," in *Spicilegium Historicum,* 8 (1960), p 204.
83. "A suor Maria di Gesù," in Tannoia, *Vita,* p 91.
84. To the same, in *Spicilegium Historicum,* 8 (1960), p 201.
85. To the same, in *Spicilegium Historicum,* 8 (1960), p 201; Caione, p 85; Tannoia, *Vita,* p 110.
86. Rome, Archives of the Redemptorist Postulator General; *Summarium,* pp 321–322.
87. Capone and Majorano, *Le Lettere,* p 207.
88. Caione, p 82.
89. Caione and Majorano, *Le Lettere,* pp 224–225.

90. Caione, pp 155–163, and *Spicilegium Historicum*, 8 (1960), pp 202–205; Tannoia, *Vita*, pp 46–54; *Summarium*, pp 311–318.

91. The text in Tannoia shows obvious signs of being touched up, not just in the style, but also in the content (for example in the *Memories*, which are distributed in a way different from the sources: they are synthesized and shortened). The version in the *Summarium* is, on the level of language and style, the least elaborate. It generally agrees with the fragments in Caione, but without the latter's omissions (for example, those relating to the whippings, which also recorded by Tannoia). *Cf.* Capone and Majorano, *Le Lettere*, p 321, n. 14.

92. *Summarium*, p 308. At the end it is noted: "Transcribed on Saturday, the 8th of October, 1768, the second day of the ten of spiritual exercises that every member of the Congregation has to make every year according to the rules, in Materdomini of Caposele by Father Celestino de Robertis of the Most Holy Redeemer."

93. The title that appears in the first biography of Saint Gerard is, "Regolamento di vita scritto e composto e da esso praticato" (Life rules written and composed and practiced by him); *cf.* Caione, p 155. Here we follow the text of the *Summarium*, pp 311–318.

CHAPTER 6

1. G. Caione, "Notizie del nostro fratello Gerardo Majella," in *Spicilegium Historicum*, 8 (1960), pp 187–209, here 201–102. This is the first version of Caione's biography. Henceforth referred to as "C."

2. Rome, Redemptorist General Archives, *Copia publica Processus Ordinaria auctoritate Murana constructi, etc.*, p 1306. Hereafter *Pr. Ord. Muro.*

3. G. Caione, "Notizie della vita del fratello laico Gerardo Majella del SS. Redentore," second version of Caione's text, in *Spicilegium Historicum*, 8 (1960), pp 217–297. Quoted from the edition of S. Majorano, *Gerardo Majella: appunti biografici di un suo contemporaneo* (Materdomini, 1988), p 80. Henceforth "M."

4. A. Tannoia, *Vita del servo di Dio fr. Gerardo Majella, laico della Congregazione del SS. Redentore* (Naples, 1816), Part I, p 110.

5. M., p 165.

6. M., pp 100–101.

7. Rome, Redemptorist General Archives, *Copia public Processus Ordinaria aucttoriate compsana….*, pp 1478–1479. Hereafter *Pr. Ord. Conza.*

8. Letter n. 24 in Chapter 5 of this book.

9. Letter n. 5.

10. This was the testimony of the priest Antonio d'Errico on July 17, 1844, in the canonical trial at Conza. *Pr. Ord. Conza,* pp 1296–97. But let us listen to a witness who spoke directly with the mother of the three young ladies and who also made a deposition in this trial. This was Signore Felipe Vital, an official of the episcopal curia of Lacedonia, who said: "In the family of the Capuccis and from the mouth of Signora Manuela Capucci, when I was between fifteen and eighteen years of age, with all her relatives present, I heard her tell that one time Brother Gerard spoke familiarly with the lady's daughters, and she thought to herself, that this was inappropriate; still more, she rejected it internally; but while she was thinking, Brother Gerard, who could even read thoughts, told her: "Madam, you are unfair with me, thinking ill of my dealings with the girls, whom I wish to see consecrated to God. But, on the other hand, I praise your prudence, and I would wish that all mothers of families were so cautious about their daughters' dealings with persons who are not members of the household, because in that way God is not offended," *ibid.*, pp 1277–1278.

11. Letter n. 18.

12. M., pp 78–79.

13. Letter n. 21.

14. Letter n. 6. It is not uncalled for to say that the expression, "Paradise in heaven and paradise on earth," and "to be transformed into a single thing with the will of God and to remain that way for all eternity," may already be found in the great theologian and poet, Dante, when he has the blessed souls in paradise say: "It is part of this happiness to be within the divine will, because our wills are united....In his will is our peace; it is like the sea, toward which everything moves," *Paradiso* III, 78–86.

15. "Rules," *Memory* n. 29, in Chapter 4 of this book.

16. M., pp 115–116.

17. C., p 203.

18. M., pp 115–116.

19. C., p 202.

20. M., p 74.

21. Letter n. 6.

22. M. p 79.

23. *Pr. Ord. Conz.,* p 526.

24. M., p 39.

25. *Summarium super virtutibus....Animadversiones, Cf.* III, *de obstaculis* (Rome, 1871), p 17.

26. M., pp 161–162.

27. Letter. n. 7.

28. "Rules," *Feelings.*
29. *Lumen Gentium*, n. 39.
30. C., p 125; T., I, 34.
31. A. Rodríguez, *Exercise of Perfection and the Christian Virtues,* Part II, tr. 7, ch. 8, Venice, 1686, pp 503–506.
32. *Ibid.*, Part II, tr. ch. 11, pp 548–549.
33. *Ibid.*, ch. 14, p 569.
34. A. de Liguori, *Theologia Moralis, liber* VI, n. 305.
35. Rodríguez, *Exercise* ..., Part II, tr. 8., ch. 15. p 579.
36. M., p 164.
37. M., p 20.
38. *Ibid.*
39. T., I, pp 12—13; *Pr. Ord. Muro,* p 34.
40. *Pr. Ord. Muro,* pp 178, 215, 393, 1249.
41. *Ibid.*, p 30.
42. M., pp 20–21.
43. M., p 21. Cf. *Pr. Ord. Muro,* p 34.
44. *Pr. Ord. Muro,* pp 178, 215, 256, 300, 1271.
45. *Pr. Ord. Muro,* p 33.
46. M. p 19.
47. Letters n. 30 and n. 36.
48. M., p 22.
49. T., I, 20.
50. Mautone in *Pr. Ord. Muro,* p 38. For C. Dilkgskron, see *Leben des Ehrwürdigen Dieners Gottes Gerard Maria Majella* (Dülmen, 1899), p 37; ____, *Chronologische Zusammenstellung der Wichtigsten Ereignisse aus dem Leben des seligen Gerard Majella,* p 407.
51. Dilgskron, *Leben...,* p 41.
52. T. I, p 26.
53. *Ibid.*
54. M., pp 165–166.
55. C., p 192.
56. M., p 33.
57. *Ibid.*
58. *Epistolae ven. servi Dei Pauli Cafaro* (Rome, 1934), p 44.
59. M., p 67.
60. *Pr. Ord. Conza,* pp 96–97.
61. M., pp 33–34.
62. M., pp 41–42.
63. M., p 38.
64. M., p 35.
65. M., p 42.

66. T., I, p 28.
67. M., pp 50–51.
68. T., I, p 31. In Neapolitan dialect: "se il cannarone è ripieno."
69. M., pp 40–41.
70. M., p 38.
71. Saint Alphonsus, *Vita del rev. padre D. Paolo Cafaro,* in *Opere di S. Alfonso M. de' Liguori* (Turin, 1867), vol. IV, p 660.
72. T., II, p 128.
73. We have seen that the word "substance" is a typical word for Gerard's letters.
74. It can be deduced from the fact that he was the one who gave Gerard the order to remain without fever until he returned from the mission, and this circumstance could not have taken place except between November 1751 and February 1752, when Father Carmelo Fiocchi arrived as superior. Or perhaps it was before then, because for a brief time Father Salvador Gallo was superior. *Cf.* M., pp 164–165.
75. A. Tannoia, *Della vita ed istituto del Ven. Servo di Dio Alfonso M. Liguori* (Naples, 1728), I, p 222.
76. Letter n. 1.
77. M., p 77.
78. *Pr. Ord. Muro,* p 1317.
79. M., pp 44–45.
80. M., pp 58–59.
81. Letter n. 2.
82. Letter n. 5.
83. *Lettere di sant' Alfonso,* vol. I, p 208.
84. Letter n. 10.
85. Letter n. 11.
86. Letters n. 13 and 15.
87. Letter n. 24. The emphasis is Gerard's.
88. Letter n. 3.
89. M., p 78.
90. M., p 80.
91. Letter n. 31.
92. Letter n. 32.
93. Letter n. 33.
94. M., p 122; Letter n. 43.
95. M., pp 135–136.
96. M., p 136.
97. M., pp 139–40.
98. M., p 142.
99. M., p 138.

100. T., II, p 182.
101. C., p 201.
102. Letter n. 44; *cf.* M., pp 138–139.
103. M., p 148.
104. C., p 199.
105. M., pp 150–151.
106. M., p 151. Caione writes: "verso le ore sei e mezza, poco più o meno, alli 13 ottobre 1775." At that time the day began to be reckoned from sundown; the date of the thirteenth is surely a mistake.
107. M., p 151

CHAPTER 7

1. Saint Alphonsus wrote to Gaspare Caione in January 1756: "I am sending you this *information* from Father Giovenale about Brother Gerard. Keep it and record it as best you can, as I asked you insofar as you have the time....I am also sending you his writing. You may keep it to remind yourself" [*Lettere* (Rome, 1887)] vol. I, p 409. The work of Caione constitutes a privileged source. We use the edition, *Gerardo Maiella. Appunti biografici di un suo contemporaneo* (Caposele, 1988). Hereafter *Appunti*. The popular tradition is amply collected in *Murana seu Compsana Beatificationis et Canonizationis Ven. Servi Dei Father Gerardi Majella laici professi Congregationis SS. Redemptoris. Summarium* (Rome, 1871). Hereafter *Summarium*.
2. The letters and the Rules in chapter five of this book.
3. They never ceased to consider him a mirror of regular observance and a model of the virtues....For that reason they proposed him to the lay brothers as a model of holiness and heroic virtues" (*Summarium*, pp 148–149); such was the testimony of the Redemptorist rector, Camillo Ripoli, at the beatification trial.
4. Beginning with A. Tannoia's *Vita del servo di Dio Fr. Gerardo Majella laico della Congregazione del Redentore* (Naples, 1824), which does not have a chapter specifically dedicated to spirituality. Exceptions, however, are not lacking, such as Dionisio De Felipe, *San Gerardo Mayela coadjutor de la Congregación del Santíssimo Redentor* (Madrid, 1954), which devotes two chapters to it: one to asceticism (pp 511–530) and another to mysticism (pp 531–555).
5. He also uses it in some final salutations in his letters: see letters n. 10, 15, and 36 in Chapter 5 of this book.
6. Letter n. 45.
7. *Summarium*, p 32.

8. *Cf. Spicilegium Historicum*, 8 (1960), p 201.
9. *Appunti*, p 35.
10. *Summarium*, p 47.
11. Letter n. 10.
12. Letter n. 24.
13. Letter n. 10. In the summer/autumn of 1753 he would write bitterly to the same nun: "I have received your much appreciated letter, about which I have a great deal to complain. In the first place, because you write me coldly; besides, because you are always repeating that I do not pray to his Divine Majesty for Your Reverence. My sister, God knows and sees my heart. For now you do not see the result because [God] does not hear my prayers, because of my great unworthiness. Tell me, therefore, how I ought to behave on this point; but do not tell me anymore that I forget to pray to God for Your Reverence, because you would be saying something against the faith." Letter n. 20.
14. Letter n. 5.
15. Letter n. 32
16. Letter n. 34.
17. *Cf.* Letters 13–17.
18. Letter n. 16.
19. Letter n. 30.
20. *Appunti*, pp 94–95.
21. *Summarium*, p 155.
22. *Cf.* in Chapter 5, "Rules for Life," the explanation of the vow and reservations....
23. *Ibid.*, Affections.
24. *Summarium*, p 157.
25. Chapter 5, Rules; Memories.
26. *Summarium*, p 151.
27. *Appunti*, pp 165–166.
28. Letter n. 32. He has similar things to say to the "very dear sister in Christ," Sister Maria of Jesus: "Do not be surprised if I write you with so much affection, because I love you [all] for only one reason: because you are the truest spouses loved by Jesus Christ; and hence I feel moved to converse continually with you, But the only reason that touches me in the innermost part of my heart is that all of you are spouses who represent and remind me of the Mother of God." Letter n. 5.
29. Letter n. 44.
30. In the first days of April 1752, he wrote to Sister Maria of Jesus, then the superior at Ripacandida: "I beg you, therefore, to order with maternal solicitude all your most obedient daughters to visit

just once your Divine Spouse on my behalf. And during this visit
let them recite for me a "Glory be to the Father." That is all. And
finally let each one of them often say for me: Mercy, Lord. Never
let them forget in the future to commend me to this divine One
wounded for love; for I, unworthy as I am, will never forget to
remember them in holy communion. And I say the Hail Mary for
all of you with great punctuality.... I beg you, please, for the love
of Jesus Christ and Mary Most Holy, to send me a copy of the little
statue of Saint Teresa, because I no longer have the one they gave
me. It was taken away from me in a monastery where I wanted to
keep it. And so as not to make them lose their devotion, I had to
give it to them." Letter n. 4.

31. The Rules are very detailed, both in the resolutions and in the
penances and devotions. The extensive list of saintly protectors is
preceded by these emphatic affirmations: "I choose for myself the
Holy Spirit as my only consoler and protector. May He be my
defender and the conqueror in all my struggles. Amen. And you,
my only joy, Immaculate Virgin Mary, may you also be my unique,
second protectress and consolatrix in all that may happen to me."

32. *Appunti,* p 26.

33. *Summarium,* pp 34–35.

34. *Ibid.,* p 70.

35. *Ibid.,* p 146.

36. *Ibid.,* p 70.

37. *Appunti,* pp 33–34.

38. *Ibid.,* p 136.

39. Saint Alphonsus writes: "All our perfection consists in loving our
most lovable God. Charity is the bond of perfection (Col 3:14). But
all the perfection of love for God consists in uniting our will to the
most holy will of God. This is the principal effect of love: to unite
the desires of the lovers, so that they have the same will." "If we
wish to please the heart of God completely, let us try to conform
ourselves to his holy will in all things; and not only to conform
ourselves, but to unite ourselves in what God disposes. Conformity with the will of God indicates that we unite our will to his.
But uniformity presupposes much more: that we make of our will
and God's will one will alone, so that we wish only what God
wishes and the will of God is always ours." *Uniformità alla volontà
di Dio,* in *Opere ascetiche* (Rome, 1933), vol. I, p 283 and p 286.

40. As he wrote to Sister Maria of Jesus: even in difficulties "we can
remain in joy and grow greater [by accepting] the divine will."
Letter n. 2.

41. Letter n. 7.

42. *Appunti,* p 74.
43. Letter n. 6.
44. Letter n. 31.
45. *Summarium,* p 69.
46. *Ibid.,* p 67.
47. *Ibid.,* p 44.
48. Letter n. 2.